CW01650800

WHEN ROCK WENT TO COLLEGE

LEGENDS LIVE at LANCASTER UNIVERSITY 1969–1985

Barry Lucas & Paul Tomlinson

Featuring posters by John Angus
and photos by Geoff Campbell

Paul dedicates this book to his two roadies … Cheryl and Jess.

Barry dedicates this book to his wife Mary, children Moya, Simon and Sergio, and grandchildren Caleb, Santino, Alys and Cara –
see, grandad wasn't always old and grey!

First published in 2017
by Palatine Books,
Carnegie House,
Chatsworth Road
Lancaster LA1 4SL
www.palatinebooks.com

Copyright © Barry Lucas and Paul Tomlinson

All rights reserved
Unauthorised duplication contravenes existing laws

The right of Barry Lucas and Paul Tomlinson to be identified as the authors of this work has been asserted in accordance with the Copyright, Designs and Patents act 1988

British Library Cataloguing-in-Publication data
A catalogue record for this book is available from the British Library

Paperback ISBN 13: 978-1-910837-11-5

Designed and typeset by Carnegie Book Production
www.carnegiebookproduction.com

Printed and bound by Multiprint Ltd

The views in this book are those of the authors, and the story is told from their perspective, based on their memories of the events at the time and subsequent research. The publisher cannot be held responsible for the accuracy of the information provided nor give a guarantee that the details are complete and accurate.

Contents

	Introduction by Alan Murray	4
	Foreword by Andy Kershaw	6
ONE	A Moment in Time	8
TWO	Talkin' 'bout my generation	12
THREE	The A–Z	19
FOUR	The Pink Custard Lightshow	319
FIVE	Pushing the Boundaries	324
SIX	Regrets, I've had a few but …	334
SEVEN	The Off Campus Social Centre AKA The Sugar House	342
EIGHT	Lancaster? Where's Lancaster?	350
	Facts 'n' Stats	357

Introduction by Alan Murray

Lancaster University alumnus.
Former Chief Finance Officer of The Burton Group and Chloride Group.
Former CEO Hanson Group PLC 2002–2007.

Lancaster University opened in 1964 in the middle of a decade that many people regarded as one of the most significant of the twentieth century. In 1961 President Kennedy set the goal of putting a man on the Moon by the end of the decade. The Berlin Wall was constructed in 1961, accelerating tensions in the Cold War. The Vietnam War began in the same year, was to continue through the decade into the 1970s and inspire a younger generation to challenge the reasons for the conflict on a widespread basis. In the field of technology, Concorde made its maiden flight in 1969, and the compact cassette was introduced in 1964. Christian Barnard performed the first heart transplant in 1969, while the contraceptive pill was available from 1960 onwards.

The world of music, and in particular pop music, was not immune to these changes. Going into the 1960s the music scene was a mixture of jazz, skiffle, solo artists and the relatively new rock 'n' roll. The 1960 NME poll winners were Cliff Richard and the Shadows, Elvis Presley, Connie Francis and Gene Vincent. Best single was 'Apache' by the Shadows. There was no mention of LPs, 45s were the medium of choice driven mainly by the demands of radio stations who wanted a three-minute song and no more. By 1970, the NME poll winners had a different look – the Beatles won best LP for 'Let It Be', best single was Mungo Jerry's 'In the Summertime' on the back of their success at the Hollywood (Staffordshire!) Festival, which saw the first UK performance by The Grateful Dead. Richard Branson's Virgin made its appearance that year as a mail order album business. Sales of LPs rocketed in 1970, marking a change in the way artists and the public looked at music. Obviously, LPs allowed bands much more scope to develop their music. Some radio stations and DJ s were key in promoting these changes. In particular, John Peel at Radio 1 was a major influence, ensuring that British and American bands were given the exposure on the airwaves.

With this change in the way artists were recording music came the need to change the way live music was presented. The days of a concert of eight to ten artists on the bill, with no more than twenty minutes for each set, were becoming less common – this was the format of the *NME* poll winners concerts at the Empire Pool, Wembley. Artistes wanted to play music from their albums and it was these same tracks that the fans wanted to hear too. The format of the concert changed to one of two acts (headline and support) with the headline playing for an hour or two. Individual songs could last for the equivalent of the whole side of an album and required much more equipment than in previous years (better PA/instrument amplification and better mixing capabilities). Lighting also became a bigger part of the presentation of the music. A concert became a theatre experience.

In line with the feeling of the time, the 1960s saw more festivals and free concerts. In 1968, the first Isle of Wight festival was held, with T Rex and Fairport Convention headlining. In 1970 the same event saw The Doors, Joan Baez and Jimi Hendrix attract more people than Glastonbury and Live Aid combined. Woodstock was staged in 1969 in New York State and attracted 400,000 people to see the likes of Crosby, Stills, Nash and Young, The Who and Jimi Hendrix. In Hyde Park a series of free concerts were staged: in 1969 Blind Faith played, followed by The Stones; 1970 saw Pink Floyd in the Park playing tracks from *Atom Heart Mother* after their earlier concert there in 1968. The music of the early 1960s had moved on from a three-minute song to longer, more complex music by the end of the decade.

You may ask what all these developments in the music business in the 1960s have got to do with this book and the series of music events that were promoted on the Lancaster campus. Music had become a great part of people's lives, particularly through the second half of the decade. New albums by major artists were eagerly anticipated by the fans. In a pre-internet world, the best way to promote artists and their music was through exposure to a live audience. Record companies almost demanded that bands went on tour and usually with a support band that was on the same label. The number of bands touring in the early 1970s meant that venues had a choice of who to book. Some promoters would handle the whole tour and apart from the municipal venues like the Free Trade Hall in Manchester, Victoria Hall in Stoke-on-Trent and the Empire in Liverpool, they would look to universities and colleges. On the college circuit, Lancaster and Leeds seemed to get the very best bands. Most colleges and universities required that you were signed in by a student if you were to see these bands. By offering open access to students and the public alike, bands knew that they were reaching the most diverse audience with no discrimination. The University itself built a reputation with local people for being open and part of the community which was important at a time when such a small number of people went to university. In the case of Lancaster, being able to see the very best bands on your doorstep was important. If you lived between Preston and Carlisle your choice of music venue was limited without travelling to a major city. In addition, many of the bands liked and requested to play Lancaster which was borne out with multiple appearances by the likes of Eric Clapton and Van Morrison.

This book is a celebration and recollection of the artists and performers at Lancaster between 1969 and 1985, in a period when music seemed to be a much more major part of many people's lives. We hope you enjoy recalling your great nights in the Great Hall at Lancaster University.

A Moment in Time

ONE

"The past is a foreign country: they do things differently there."

L. P. Hartley, *The Go-Between*

It was Saturday 25 February 1984 and I was driving down to Manchester Airport to pick up Barry Marshall, one of the top music promoters in the UK. He was flying up to see one of the venues on his tour of Tina Turner – Lancaster University. Barry Marshall was one of the few promoters I hadn't dealt with before, yet here he was, placing one of the hottest acts in the world on a small, north of England college stage. How on earth did that happen? How did a small university of 4,500 students, in a small city of 60,000, nowhere near a major conurbation, become one of the most famous venues in the country? How had the mighty Leeds University been displaced as the major college venue in the UK? Why were artists from all over the world willing to play in a place they had never heard of?

Well it's a story worth telling because, for a moment in time, Lancaster was at the forefront of popular music – it was the stuff of legends.

We need, first, to go back to 1968 when, to much amazement – certainly that of my teachers in Leeds Modern and Cheltenham Grammar schools – I gained a place at the University of Lancaster. "Why choose Lancaster?" I hear you ask. Well, I had been forcibly transported, two years earlier, by my parents, to the savage, uncivilised world known as 'The South'. In the summer of 1966 – notable for many great events such as Henry Cooper versus Cassius Clay, England versus the mighty West Indies (Sobers et al), Sir Donald Campbell's tragic death, and the little matter of an English football team actually winning something – I was exiled against my will from my beloved Yorkshire to the barren wastes of Cheltenham. From Leeds, where I was to have been emancipated from school uniform in the sixth form (you would actually be allowed to wear your own, fashionable clothes), to Cheltenham, where I found out, to my howls of disbelief, that I was expected, nay ordered, to wear a mortar board and gown in the sixth form. And that from ten yards outside your front door, through the centre of town, two buses, to ten yards from the school gates! The S.S., cunningly disguised as school prefects, ensured this with the ultimate deterrent of Saturday morning detention. This was 1966 and the height of the Swinging Sixties, for goodness' sake!

Anyway, I ended up there, and my parents, unbelievably selfishly, would not let a fifteen year old live on his own in Leeds and visit them in the school holidays. Would you believe it? So here was I, applying through UCCA, more in hope than expectation, for a university place. My English teacher said that I should get an 'A' level. My History teacher said, "Lucas, your low animal cunning might get you a pass." But that was it. So I had a go, for a laugh; three years at uni was better than working and a grant (remember them?) was enough to live on, and with a beer-top-up job in the vacations that would give me a three year sabbatical to work out what I wanted to do with the rest of my life. So, six choices of uni to fill in: well, no problem with five northern ones straight away. All had to be 'second class' as I couldn't read English at the old, established universities because I had dropped Latin at thirteen (bored stupid) and you had to have 'O' level Latin to read English at those, but which was to be the sixth? "Anyone know a northern university?" I asked in the sixth form common room. "Lancaster," some joker yelled, to great amusement. So Lancaster it was, sixth and last desperate choice; not Yorkshire but at least it was in the North. The Deputy Headmaster, and Careers Advisor, didn't even know that Lancaster had a university. He thought I was going to St Martin's: "a good teacher training college there," he announced knowingly, although I could see in his eyes the terror that I might be contemplating joining the ranks of his noble profession.

And surprise, surprise (thanks, Cilla), Lancaster was the only one to offer me a place. I like to think it was their foresight. After all it was before the results were out, but, more probably, it was a reflection of their own desperation to fill places, bordering on gratitude. Although to be fair to them I did get two 'A's and a 'B' (yah boo sucks to you Cheltenham Grammar School!).

So there I was, eighteen years old, suitcase, rucksack, falling out onto Lancaster's desolate railway station. It was raining, of course. In Intro Week it always did. Lancaster weather has been nothing if not predictable over forty odd years. "Welcome to Lancaster" – rain! (But "exams are here" – eighty degrees Costa Cauldron.) Well here I was, skinny but suntanned. I had just returned early from our first family holiday abroad. Dad had booked a fortnight in Lloret de Mar as obviously he didn't think I would pass those exams either. But were they going to give up the second week? No! I had to return early and alone – Sir Charles Carter would not agree to postponing Freshers' for a week. I actually asked him, honest – I rang the University admissions to see if I could arrive a week later, but no chance. So one day Spanish sun, chilled sangria, paella, the next Lancashire rain, warm Mitchell's beer and hotpot.

Lancaster station resembled a scene from one of those WW2 evacuation movies. It seemed like hundreds of lost teenagers, suitcases, carrier bags and bewildered faces (all it needed was name tags and gas mask boxes around our necks).

"Lonsdale College – anybody in Lonsdale?" called out two worldly looking second years.

"Yes."

"Off campus?"

"Yes."

"Where?"

"South Road."

"Never heard of it. Bus for campus!"

Never heard of it, where on earth had those unfeeling monsters in University House stuck me? South Road – I could picture it, some desolate track leading to a Cold Comfort Farm, miles towards Preston. "University – what University?" I had no choice but to get a cab, thank heavens he'd heard of it. It was a ten shilling ride via Morecambe, Carnforth, Scafell Pike and Galgate but finally I arrived at South Road (I was later to discover it was a ten-minute walk from the railway station).

The newly opened Central Hall

One of my early experiences seemed to confirm the worries that I had about 'Cold Comfort Farm', or the University of Lancaster as it was known to the outside world. Students were designated a 'moral tutor' to look after their welfare and sort out their personal problems. To show you how ridiculous it was, I became one in the late '70s and had six or seven very nervous first years to give guidance to. Anyway, in 1968, as a rather 'nervous' fresher myself, I was instructed to go and meet my moral tutor, who turned out to be a rather large, African mathematician called Dr O'Doom. I knocked reluctantly on his door and waited for some African Christopher Lee to call, ominously, "Enter". But Freshers' Week was only half way through, the best was yet to come.

My first experience of the pulsating Lancaster University social scene followed and what an unforgettable experience that was! It probably, subconsciously, determined my future career. That first evening was the Lonsdale College Freshers' Disco in the refectory. A bit of bread and cheese, a sausage roll and as many pieces of pork pie as you could eat, or smuggle in your pockets for later. Oh and a glass of revolting, sweet, warm, white wine and – would you believe it – from Spain, where I'd been thirty-six hours before. Now, it was just about drinkable in the balmy, evening heat of the Med., but in the rain-swept wilds of Lancashire? The disco started and from nowhere came hordes of praying mantis disguised as third years. They descended to have the pick of the innocent young freshers. Unfortunately, not a 'cougar' to be seen, the girls were fair game; us boys were, unfortunately, safe. After an hour of peering over, or through, the ranks of enemy storm troopers, I left frustrated and went back to my digs in South Road. Within half an hour all twelve of us had returned from their various college socials with the same disillusioned tale. A last drink in the pub!

On what is now the Pointer roundabout once stood a terrace with the Boundary pub in it. In 1968 it was a typical northern drinking place, long, thin and spartan. After getting twelve pints we all went to sit in the nice front room, or lounge as the southerners amongst us called it. We settled down into armchairs and settees, thinking what a pleasant change it was from the spit and sawdust next door. Twenty minutes later an embarrassed, apologetic landlord stuck his head round the door: "Would you lads mind coming back into the pub now as my wife would like to watch our television?" Twelve rather meek freshers left his front room and returned to the bar. Couldn't wait 'til next year, bring on the freshers!

“Talkin’ ’bout my generation”

TWO

In 1968 Lancaster University was somewhat different to the metropolis it is today – they've even had the effrontery to move Lonsdale College to Galgate!

The University started its move from St Leonard's House in Lancaster city centre to the campus at Bailrigg in my first year, 1968. That year it became a split campus; Lonsdale, Bowland and Cartmel colleges were open, and Furness, Fylde and County became operational during the next eighteen months.

The Central Hall, as it was first known, was to open in October 1969 so until then the social events, discos/parties/dances/concerts etc. were mainly held in Bowland and Lonsdale refectories. It was in Bowland, in 1968, that I first became enthralled by live performance – a love which exists to this day. I think I've only occasionally heard a band live when I couldn't say something positive about the show: "The lead guitarist/bass/drummer/singer was good/not bad/promising" etc. Well, one night in Bowland refectory was my epiphany. I was sitting on the floor (most of the beans and chips had been cleared) with my three-quarter full pint of McEwans bitter (I know, I know, but it was the only beer sold on campus in those days) on the wooden stage in front of me. Music/show production was pretty primitive: a small wooden stage about twelve inches high, PA arriving with the band, all crammed into a Ford transit, and the lights were four lamps on a stick either side of the stage. But …

The band was Aynsley Dunbar Retaliation, an excellent British Blues band, with a terrific first album out, *Dr Dunbar's Prescription*, which I am playing now, as I write this. A four piece, there was Aynsley Dunbar on drums, Victor Brox on organ, Alex Dmochowski on bass and John Moorshead on lead guitar. Sitting at John's feet, listening to him, watching him bend the notes, hearing and feeling the music, I understood what a total experience of sight, sound and feel a live rock show was. And to cap it all, when I reached out to have a slurp, my three quarters of a pint had metamorphosed into a quarter of a pint – the vibrations of the music through the stage had reduced a pint of McEwans bitter to an ice cream cone of froth! I was hooked.

The Great Hall opened in my second year. Fairport Convention played the first concert, and with all those uncomfortable, crested, wooden seats assembled it was very rock 'n' roll – I don't think. This was to provide a foretaste of the University's lack of understanding of popular culture which was to play such an important role in the years to come. Lancaster was, and obviously still is, constructed on a college system. A copy of the Oxbridge college system set, not around a city, but on a hill outside of town – a college campus. In those days the economic, social and political strength of the student body was exercised through the colleges, more specifically the JCRs (Junior Common Room – what

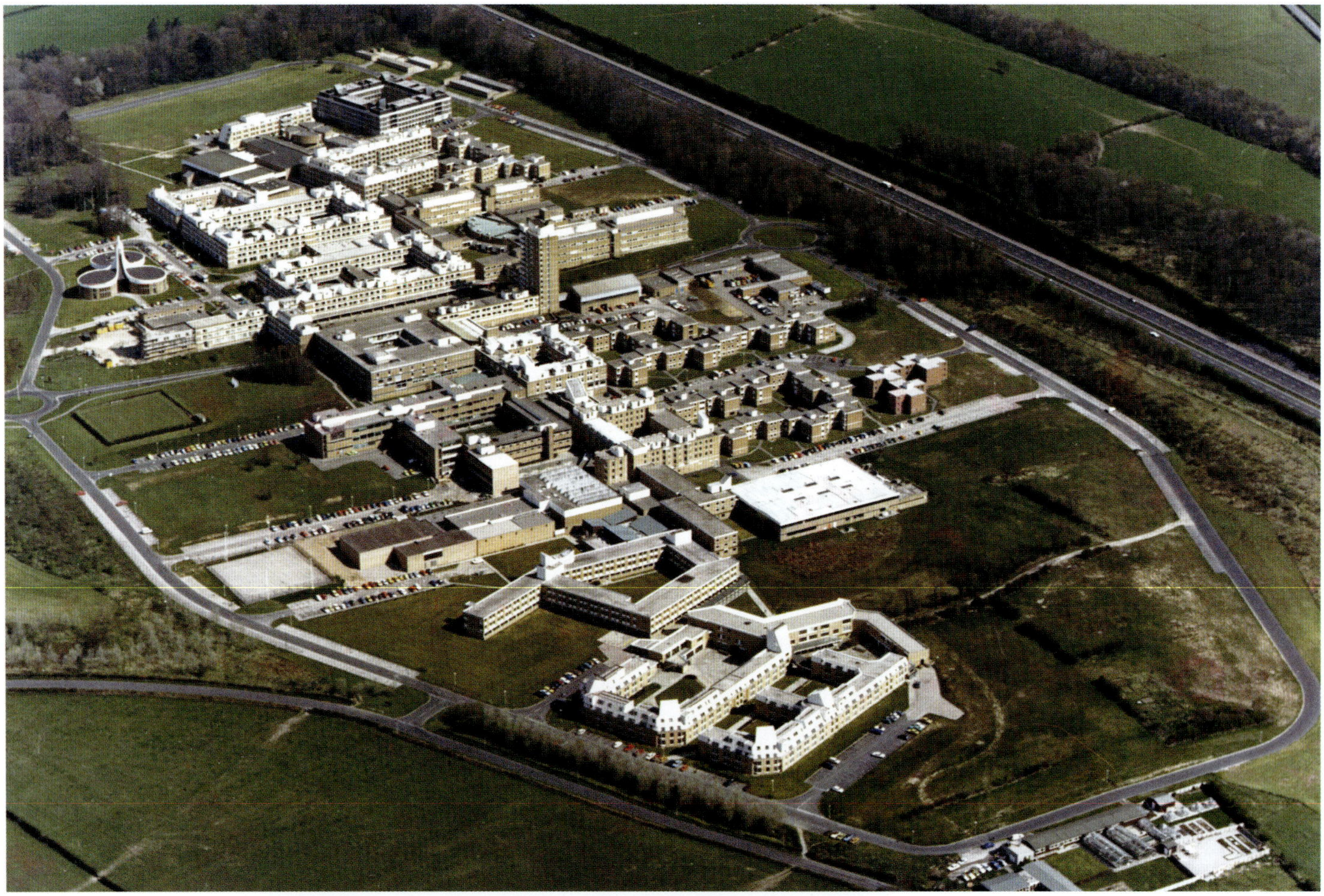

Aynsley Dunbar

a quaint, dated expression). A Students' Union didn't really exist but there was a body, The Student Representative Council, which was really only a meeting place for the JCR Presidents and Treasurers. A strong, successful JCR President was a far more powerful and influential figure than the SRC Chairman. However that was all to change and to some extent it was the Great Hall concerts which led to that evolution.

Each JCR had a social secretary, elected by its college's students – as is no doubt the role today. But then each JCR took it in turns to promote a night in the newly opened Central Hall. A small budget was provided to the social committee but remember – in January 1970 Deep Purple played Lancaster for £350 – those were the days! Well, just after Christmas it leaked out that Bowland College had a budget of £600 to spend on an act, a great deal of money then. Rumours ran wild, who would it be? The 'underground' music scene of those days centred on *New Musical Express* and *Melody Maker*, with little or no coverage on the radio, TV, or in national daily newspapers. The early '60s serious rock artists had now forsaken the Singles Chart for album sales and all the new, 'student' bands followed suit.

Top Of The Pops was ridiculed, except when an act like The Doors appeared to take the piss. Mums and dads had never heard of the acts you would spend your pocket money, grant cheques etc. on. It was almost a secret society passed by word of mouth, "Have you heard the new LP by …?"

Well, Bowland's Social Secretary spent his money – sorry, his students' money – on The Equals – a top singles band and staple of *TOTPs*, and your mum probably loved them as they played happy disco music! Now The Equals, Eddie Grant et al, probably have more kudos today amongst music fans than they had then. But the booking set in motion a chain of events which was to have a profound effect on Lancaster University and the social lives of several generations within a sixty mile radius …

"Hope I Die Before I Get Old."

So it was that, in a rage of frustration and indignation, Gaz Taylor, a rather eccentric friend of mine, stood against the incumbent Bowland social secretary in the annual election. Gaz, he of the copious hair, wispy beard and outrageous, black, floppy hat, persuaded me to stand in the Lonsdale election. We both won and immediately set our plans in motion. Two budgets are bigger than one. Then we worked our persuasive cunning to get Furness College's social committee to be our 'sleeping partner' – three budgets are even better than two. Suddenly we had over £1,000 to spend on a Great Hall event, but who? Yes, that's right, Who indeed! Gaz knew a small provincial booker just starting out in a traditional entertainment agency in Ferriby, near Hull, coincidently both mine and Gaz' birthplace. Robb Winn, later to join Island Records Agency in London, was told, "Get us The Who!" What an amazing concept today – "Who do you want to book?" "The Who." "OK." Phone call returned an hour later, "It'll cost you £1,000 plus £50 booking fee for me – that's £1,050."

"Done."

Hey, that's a novel idea, I wonder if it'll catch on – want a band, ring their manager, agree a fee, book 'em – couldn't happen today though, could it?

Well, now all hell broke out. £1,000 on a band, it couldn't be done. The Four Horsemen of The Apocalypse would be let loose! The JCRs would be bankrupt – civilisation as we knew it would cease to exist. Lonsdale and Bowland College presidents got together to stop their out-of-control, irresponsible, newly elected lunatics. We signed the contract and just got it in the post box in Alexandra Square as Maurice Hubbard, Lonsdale's President, came racing down the Spine.

But we'd shown 'em – a grand ha! – we laugh in the face of danger and disaster. The politicians were highly critical. So we booked Quintessence for £250 and added a third band, Hammer, for £50; that'll show the politicos! We were convinced – well, after eight bottles of Newcastle Brown in Lonsdale bar we were convinced – that it would be a storming success!

The day arrived, 15 May 1970, a sell-out, proper, professional touts selling tickets (where do they get them from?) along the Spine, queues around the Great Hall. The concert itself was amazing, but what an introduction to the 'business'. The tour manager was called John Wolff, and he was appropriately named; he was a nightmare, and a shaven-headed one at that. Pete Townshend, sensing my terror, said, "Oh, he's OK once you get to know him."

"Mind you," said Roger Daltrey, "He's been with us ten years and we still don't know him!"

The light show was amazing; eight white spots borrowed from the Nuffield Theatre. Eight students in the balcony on them, pull the plug out for off, stick it in for on. Watch the bald demon on the side of the stage for instructions, he'll point at you when he wants it off or on. And don't you dare get it wrong! Sophisticated or what? Several years later the Great Hall was to host one of the first computer-controlled light shows with the Thompson Twins; we were witness to rock growing up.

Daltrey was on stage in his fringed jacket, swinging his mic on a long lead around the stage, threatening to decapitate Moon and Townshend. Here he was, in the same clothes as he wore when he stole the show in Woodstock, but in Lancaster!

After the show the band and entourage retired to their hotel, The Royal Kings Arms – the only hotel in Lancaster at the time – and settled in the bar. 1970 was the height of the anti-Vietnam demonstrations worldwide (remember Kent State University, Ohio, the National Guards murdering student demonstrators?) and the American students had organised an all-night vigil in Market Square. This was a very good place to have an overnight demonstration as the square was also the location of a massive underground toilet. At around two o'clock in the morning, Roger Daltrey and Pete Townshend asked the night porter at the hotel to prepare several trays of sandwiches, teas and coffees. The porter was delighted because, although it was late, he was feeding one of the most famous groups in the world. But no, the two rock superstars loaded up a couple of trolleys and off they trundled to Market Square to feed the demonstrators and sit chatting with them, plotting the revolution until the, even later, early hours. Nice touch – I'd hope they would still do that today, maybe …

Courtesy of Marion McClintock. Photographer unknown

The Who

15 May 1970 Supports: Quintessence | The Hammer

In January 1970 The Who embarked on a tour in promotion of the rock opera album *Tommy,* released in May 1969. The band started the tour performing the rock opera in Paris, Denmark, Germany and The Netherlands before returning to the UK.

The first UK date on 14 February 1970 was in Leeds University's refectory, where the album *Live At Leeds* was recorded.

Three months later in May, The Who were Barry Lucas' first Great Hall concert booking. They visited Lancaster on one of only twelve university dates on their sixty-eight-date US, European and UK tour schedule.

Band members:
Roger Daltrey – lead vocals, tambourine, harmonica
Pete Townshend – lead guitar, vocals
John Entwistle – bass guitar, vocals
Keith Moon – drums

Unfortunately no definitive setlist for the Lancaster concert exists, but it would probably have included much material from the album *Tommy*, maybe opening the show with the 1965 single 'I Can't Explain'. The set may have ended with either 'Magic Bus' or 'My Generation', with the track 'The Seeker' being sometimes included in the setlist.

Quintessence were a jazz/psychedelic prog. rock band formed in April 1969 in London. The band had an Indian flavour to their sound. The original lineup included Sambhu Babaji (bass guitar), Maha Dev (rhythm guitar), Shiva Shankar Jones (vocals, keyboards, percussion), Jake Milton (drums, percussion), Allan Mostert (lead guitar) and Raja Ram (flute, percussion). They performed at the first two Glastonbury Festivals and released a total of five studio albums. Quintessence played on into the 1980s before breaking up.

First on stage was a Hull band called **The Hammer** who existed for a couple of years in the early seventies. The band had minimal success but were most notable for their keyboard player from Cleethorpes, Rod Temperton. Rod went on in later years to become a renowned songwriter in the USA, penning hits for George Benson and Michael Jackson, including Jackson's massive singles 'Thriller' and 'Rock With You'. Temperton won a Grammy Award in 1991 for his work on 'Birdland', from Quincy Jones's album *Back on the Block.* He passed away at the age of sixty-six in October 2016.

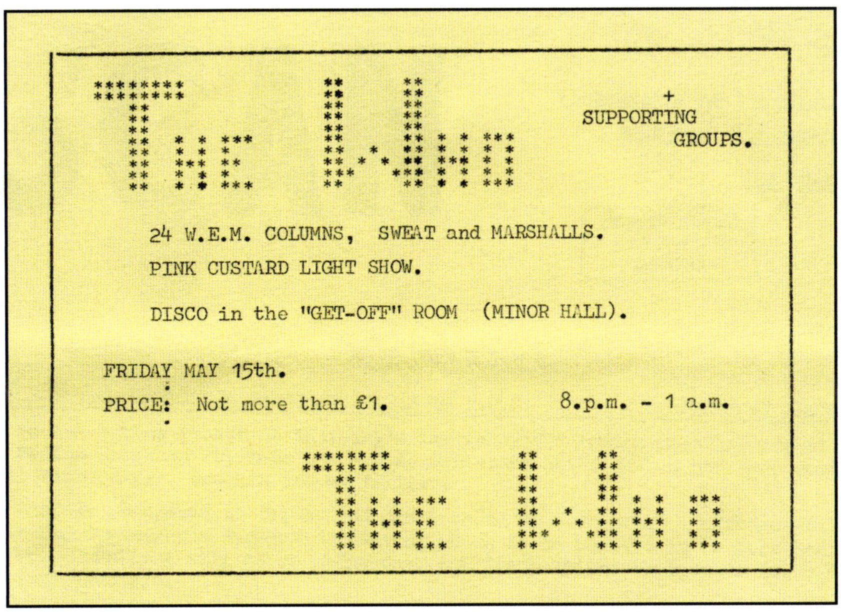

The A–Z

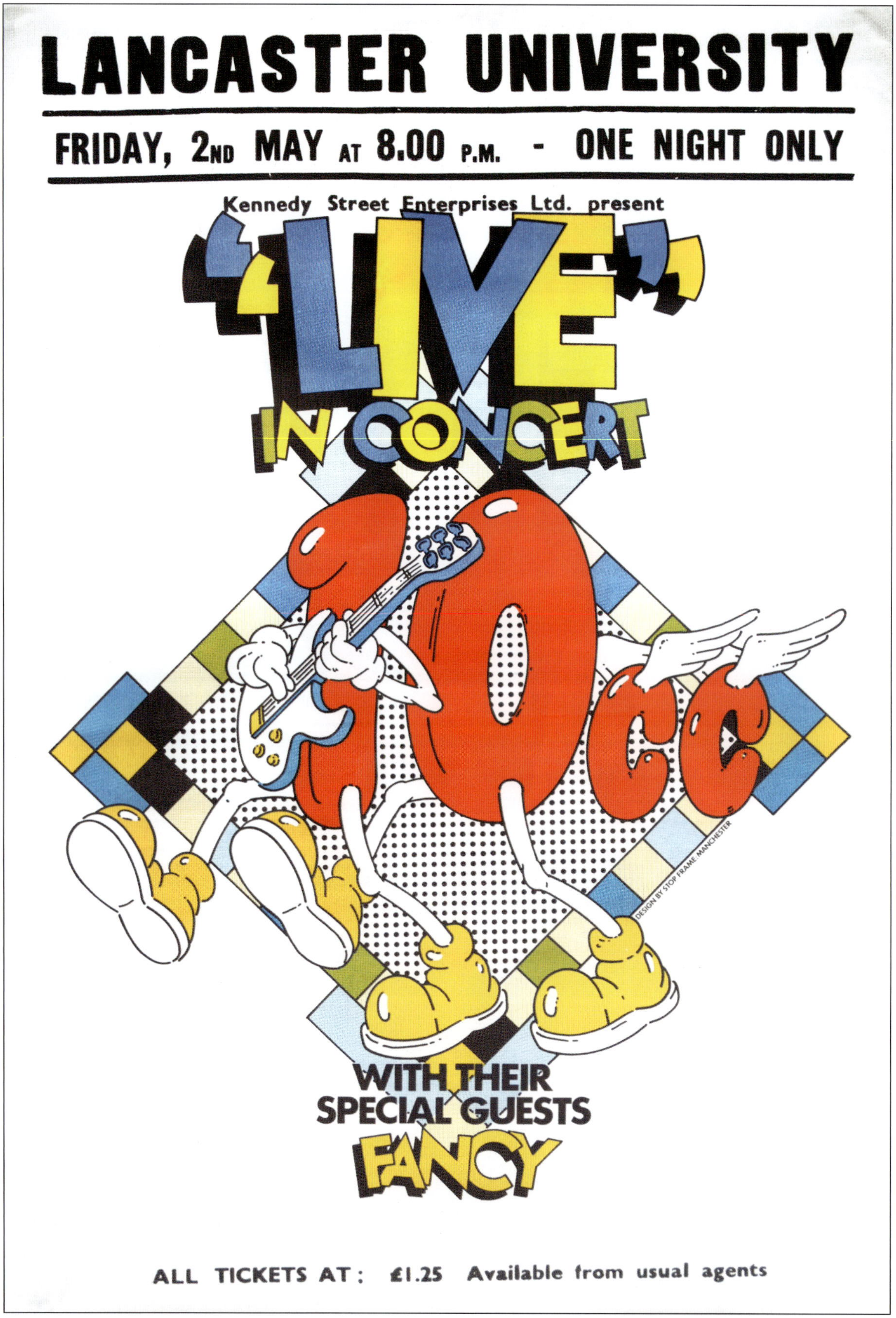

Courtesy of Sir William Taylor

THREE

10cc

2 May 1975 Support: Fancy

The classic 10cc lineup of Lol Crème, Kevin Godley, Eric Stewart and Graham Gouldman visited Lancaster University three years after their formation. They played the Great Hall in promotion of the release, in March 1975, of their third studio album *The Original Soundtrack*.

The single 'I'm Not In Love' from the album reached the No. 1 slot in the UK Singles Chart of June 1975.

10cc celebrated their fortieth anniversary in 2012 and continue to tour, with Graham Gouldman the only original member.

Band members were seen earlier that evening, before the concert, dining in an Italian restaurant on Church Street in Lancaster.

Support band **Fancy** were the creation of Ray Fenwick and were put together with session musicians he worked with following his short stint with The Spencer Davies Group. The band existed for only a couple of years but during that time had a couple of US hits, one being a cover version of The Troggs 'Wild Thing'.

©David Bradbury

A Flock of Seagulls

2 April 1983 Support unknown

A Flock of Seagulls were formed in Liverpool in 1979 by lead singer Mike Score and his brother, Ali.

In 1982 the group's third single, 'I Ran (So Far Away)', became a worldwide hit, most notably reaching No. 1 in Australia, then reaching the Top 10 in the US and New Zealand, but only No. 43 on the UK Singles Chart. The parent album *A Flock of Seagulls* and another single, 'Space Age Love Song', was also successful for the band in 1982.

They ultimately went on to be best known for their hit 'Wishing (If I Had a Photograph of You)' which reached No. 10 in the UK Singles Chart in late 1982. The song was taken from the album *Listen,* released in May 1983 shortly after their visit to Lancaster.

Band lineup:
Mike Score – vocals
Ali Score – drums
Paul Reynolds – guitars
Frank Maudsley – bass

AC/DC

30 October 1976 **Dirty Deeds Done Dirt Cheap Tour** Support: Tyla Gang
21 October 1977 **Let There Be Rock Tour** Support: Suburban Studs

AC/DC came to test the structural integrity of the Great Hall twice in successive years. With Bon Scott up front and the legendary Angus Young belting out the riffs, these were two classic concerts for the lucky few who were there. Their first visit to the university promoted the album *Dirty Deeds Done Dirt Cheap,* released in September 1976.

1976 band lineup:
Angus Young – guitars
Malcolm Young – rhythm guitars
Bon Scott – vocals
Mark Evans – bass guitar
Phil Rudd – drums

Lancaster setlist: 'Live Wire', 'Rock And Roll Singer', 'Jailbreak', 'She's Got Balls', 'The Jack'; 'School Days', 'Rocker', 'TNT', 'It's a Long Way to the Top (If You Wanna Rock 'n' Roll)', 'High Voltage', 'Baby Please Don't Go'.

Almost exactly one year later and AC/DC was back in town, five months after the release of their classic album *Let There Be Rock.*

1977 band lineup:
Angus Young – guitar
Malcolm Young – rhythm guitar
Bon Scott – vocals
Cliff Williams – bass guitar
Phil Rudd – drums

Lancaster setlist: 'Let There Be Rock', 'Problem Child', 'Hell Ain't A Bad Place To Be', 'Whole Lotta Rosie', 'High Voltage', 'The Jack', 'Bad Boy Boogie Rocker', 'TNT'.

Following the sudden death of Bon Scott in February 1980, the remaining members of the band briefly considered quitting. They eventually concluded, however, that Scott would have wanted AC/DC to continue. Auditions were held and AC/DC chose Brian Johnson as Scott's replacement. Johnson was one of the founding members of the rock band Geordie formed in Newcastle in 1971.

More recently Brian Johnson announced his departure from the band due to hearing problems, his replacement being Guns N' Roses frontman Axl Rose, who stepped in to perform as lead singer for the remainder of the band's 2016 Rock or Bust World Tour.

Tyla Gang are a British pub-rock/new wave band formed by Sean Tyla, following his departure and the break-up of the band Ducks Deluxe in 1975. Sean Tyla is an English rock guitarist, keyboardist, vocalist and songwriter, sometimes known as the "Godfather of Boogie," who has also worked with Joan Jett. They released two albums before Tyla dissolved the band in 1979. In 2010 the Tyla Gang re-formed in their original lineup and have since released two albums. Sean Tyla recently celebrated his seventieth birthday.

Suburban Studs were a Birmingham punk band formed in 1976. Their only album, *Slam*, was released in 1977. Maybe an unusual choice of support for AC/DC, as Suburban Studs were more used to backing the Sex Pistols and The Clash for gigs at the 100 Club in London.

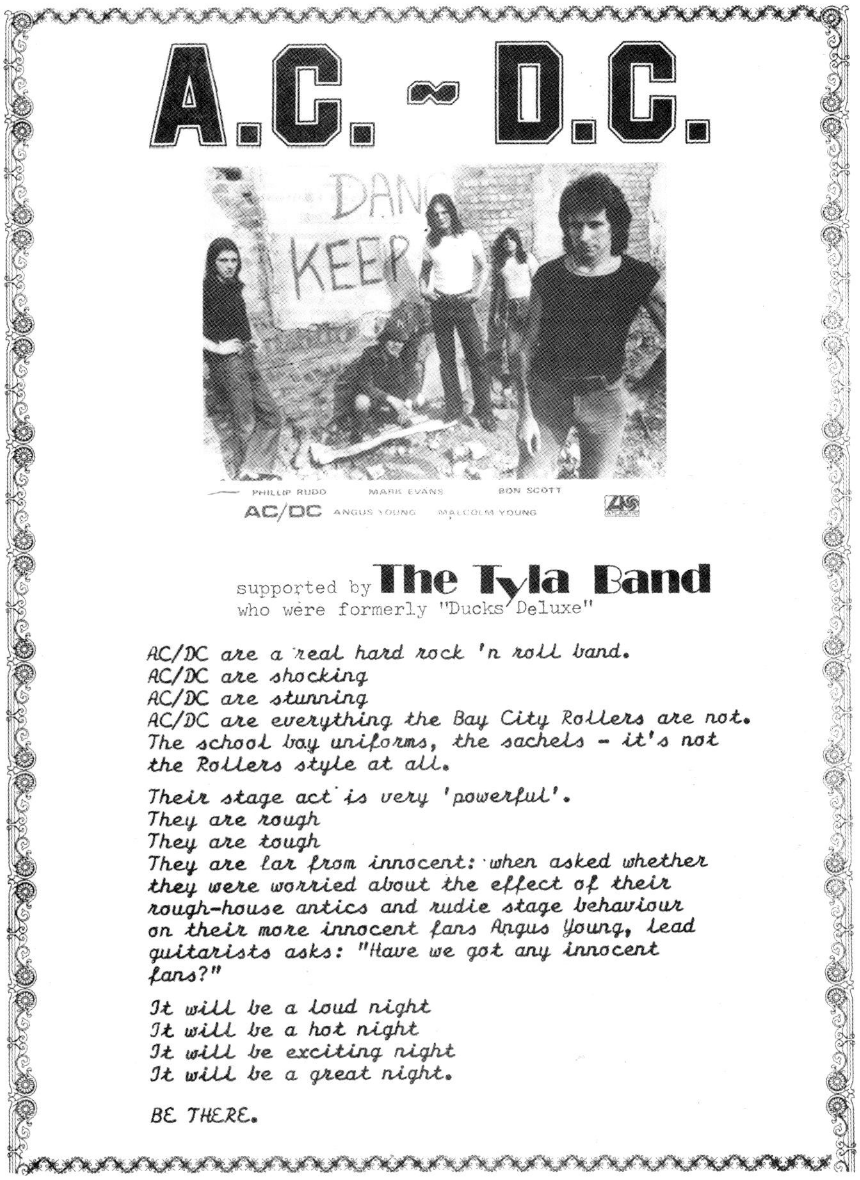

A.C. ~ D.C.

PHILLIP RUDO MARK EVANS BON SCOTT
AC/DC ANGUS YOUNG MALCOLM YOUNG

supported by **The Tyla Band**
who were formerly "Ducks Deluxe"

AC/DC are a real hard rock 'n roll band.
AC/DC are shocking
AC/DC are stunning
AC/DC are everything the Bay City Rollers are not.
The school boy uniforms, the sachels - it's not the Rollers style at all.

Their stage act is very 'powerful'.
They are rough
They are tough
They are far from innocent: when asked whether they were worried about the effect of their rough-house antics and rudie stage behaviour on their more innocent fans Angus Young, lead guitarists asks: "Have we got any innocent fans?"

It will be a loud night
It will be a hot night
It will be exciting night
It will be a great night.

BE THERE.

AC/DC
+ SUBURBAN STUDS
UNIVERSITY OF LANCASTER
7.30PM FRIDAY
21ST OCT.
£1.50

John Angus

AC/DC

I was introduced to AC/DC at an early age! They are still one of my favourite bands and I go to see them in arenas to this day. I saw them recently in Manchester with Axl Rose fronting the band. Many years ago now, I was in London at an NUS social secretaries conference and I was meant to be going for a meal that evening with John Glover, one of the directors of Island Artists. However, he phoned me to say that he wasn't feeling well, but he had arranged for me to meet up with Richard Griffiths, a young booker who was a good guy and desperate to meet up with me! OK, free meal, drinks etc. and he worked for a small agency with acts I wouldn't be interested in so there would be no sales pressure to spoil the evening. Why not?

We met up and, after the meal, he said that he was managing a little Aussie band (you know where this is going don't you?) and would I mind going to see them and give him my opinion. They were playing at The Marquee that night. OK, I replied, nothing else going on; if I went back to the conference I would only spend all night in the bar getting berated by drunken social secretaries moaning that they never got the bands Lancaster put on and how unfair it was. So I went to Wardour Street into the legendary Marquee Club. It was my first time and what an amazing disappointment. Here, in this venue, almost every legend of rock music had appeared. But it seemed to be not much bigger than Lonsdale refectory – it looked like a three hundred capacity pub venue! It was just unbelievable.

Then AC/DC hit the stage – running – and about a hundred people in the Marquee were almost literally gob- and ear- smacked. Angus Young was dressed as an eleven year old school boy and Bon Scott was belting out the vocals with Angus on his shoulders, cracking out those unmistakable riffs. I looked around a room full of "The Business" – top agents, managers and promoters (I bet they didn't pay for their tickets either). Richard looked at me, "They're bloody brilliant aren't they?"

"Oh yes, I love 'em!" I enthused.

"I'll never keep hold of them, will I?" The young agent, eyeing a room full of the who's who of the music business royalty, wistfully asked.

"Nope," I agreed sadly.

Now fast forward a couple of years. I had the chance to book AC/DC for the Great Hall. I had already worn their *High Voltage* album virtually smooth and we had been pushing it like crazy at 'Ear 'Ere Records as Nigel (my business partner) was a great rock guitar fanatic. But could I get an audience? NO! About 500 hardy rock souls turned up. We lost money. But WHAT A SHOW! Bon Scott charged round the hall like the maniac he was, with Angus on his shoulders, a radio guitar and microphone used for the first time in the Great Hall. It was truly amazing, although some of my stewards complained to me after the show that it was all taped because there were no microphone or guitar leads trailing around the hall after them!

I have always believed that a promoter promotes music that his punters want to hear. I never believed, as some did, in preaching to, or trying to educate, an audience. Only a couple of times have I tried to convince the Lancaster crowd it was wrong, and that if they trusted me they would be converted to see the light. This was one of those times when, exactly a year later, I booked them again. Surely the word had got around and more people would have heard about the last show and about the rave press the band were receiving. Surely Lancaster will have woken up by now? At least the band thought they were major stars now with their rider containing a few new "silly bollocks" clauses: 200 Marlboro cigarettes, twenty tubes of Smarties with the brown ones taken out – well it gave somebody gainful employment I suppose. But yes, it worked! This time 600 turned up – lost money again! Some people never learn, me included.

Barry Lucas

The Adverts

17 February 1978 Support: Dick Envy

The Adverts were an English punk band who formed in 1976 and broke up in late 1979. The band's lineup included one of the first female punk artists, Gaye Advert, on bass guitar.

They are best remembered for their single 'Gary Gilmore's Eyes' which reached No. 18 in the UK Singles Chart of September 1977.

This was the second appearance in the Great Hall for The Adverts. June of 1977 saw them provide support for their Stiff label mates, The Damned.

Later in their career they went on to support Iggy Pop on tour.

Back up for the evening was supplied by the London-based punk outfit **Dick Envy**, fronted by American punkette Vermillion Sands.

The band were very active on the London punk circuit, mainly as a support to some of the bigger names of the time.

The Alarm

8 February 1984 Support: Orson Family

The Alarm, from Rhyl in North Wales, originally started out in 1977 as a local punk band with the catchy name of The Toilets, before a name change to Seventeen in 1978 and subsequently The Alarm around 1981.

Originally consisting of Mike Peters (vocals, guitar), Dave Sharp (guitar), Eddie Macdonald (bass) and Nigel Twist (drums) 1983 saw The Alarm's best known hit 'Sixty Eight Guns' reach No. 17 in the UK singles chart, with the album *Declaration* which contained the single, climbing to No. 6 in the UK album charts.

Around the same time the band were offered the support slot on U2's War tour in America.

Although The Alarm officially disbanded in 1991 Mike Peters still tours and records with his current version of the band today.

The Orson Family were a short-lived four piece English psychobilly/goth rock band formed around 1982. The band includes Gene Vincent, Eddie Cochran, Lou Reed, The Jam and The Cramps as their influences.

They released two albums, including one live, and a single called 'The Sweetest Embrace'. The Orson Family disbanded in late 1984.

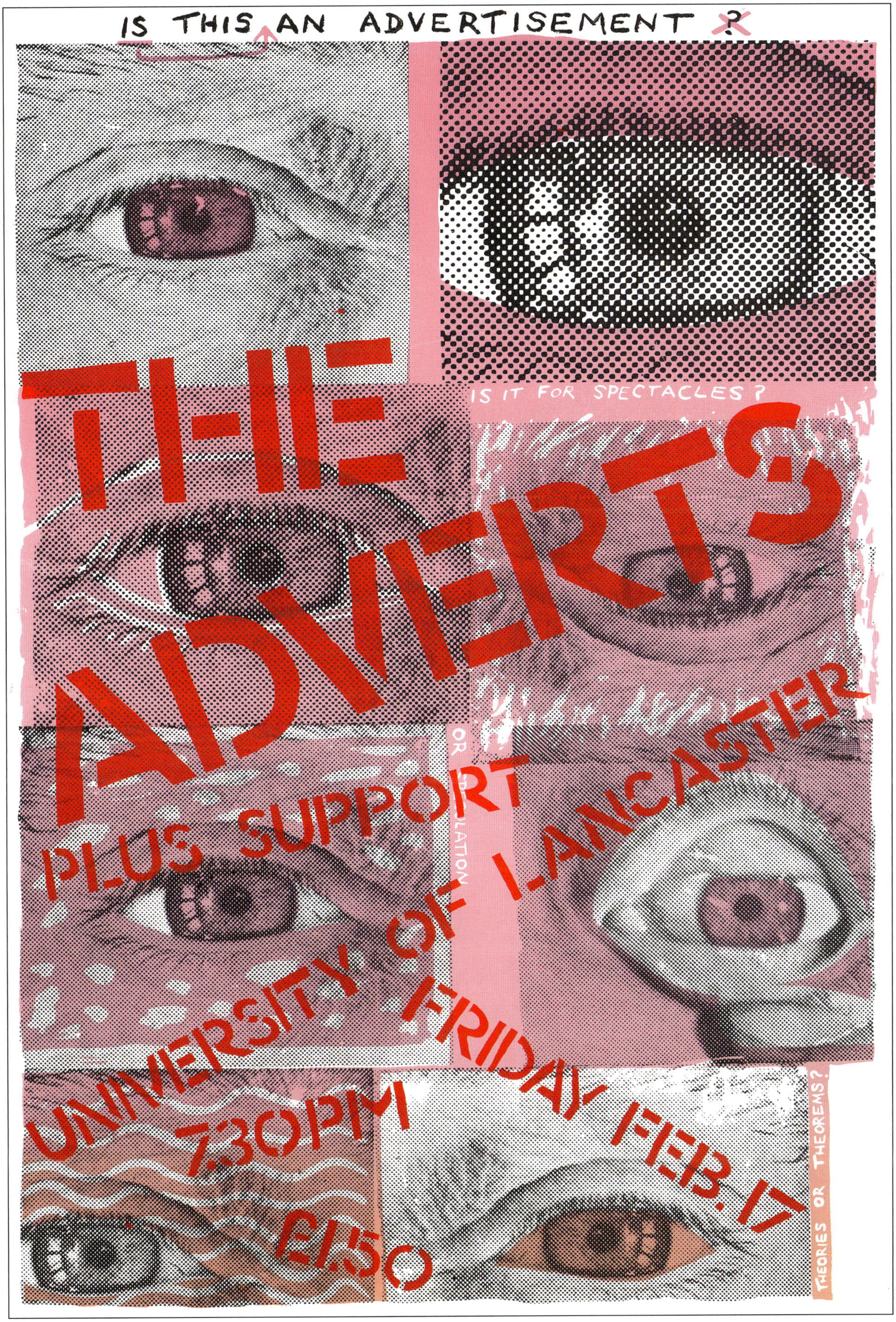
IS THIS AN ADVERTISEMENT ?
THE ADVERTS
IS IT FOR SPECTACLES?
PLUS SUPPORT
UNIVERSITY OF LANCASTER
FRIDAY FEB. 17
7.30PM
£1.50
THEORIES OR THEOREMS?

John Angus

Altered Images

11 May 1982 Support: Subway Sect

Altered Images were a Scottish new wave band fronted by Clairc Grogan that had six UK Top 40 singles, including 'Happy Birthday' which reached No. 2 in the Singles Chart of October 1981.

A reviewer of the concert in *SCAN* newspaper stated that:

> "Altered Images are, Siouxsie and The Banshees for those who can only eat two shredded wheat. They were very average"

Altered Images disbanded in 1983, with Claire Grogan going on to become a film and television actress, appearing in the film *Gregory's Girl*.

Formed in 1976, **Subway Sect** are a very early punk band led by Vic Goddard. According to *SCAN* newspaper's concert reviewer on the night: "They were tremendous and the crowd demanded an encore"

Vic Goddard and Subway Sect are still active, over forty years after their formation.

Altered Images and Claire Grogan ©Geoff Campbell

Alison Moyet

3 November 1984 Support unknown

Prior to finding success as a solo artist, Alison Moyet, from Billericay in Essex, was one half of the British synthpop duo Yazoo, alongside former Depeche Mode member Vince Clarke on keyboards.

In total she achieved nine Top 30 singles and five Top 10 single hits in the UK charts including, 'Is This Love?' reaching No. 3 in 1986 and 'All Cried Out' which peaked at No. 8 in September 1984 shortly prior to this university appearance.

Alison Moyet was a winner of the British Phonographic Industry Award (Brit Awards), for British Female Solo Artist in 1985 and 1988.

Now in her fifties, she continues to perform and in June 2017 released her ninth studio album *Other.*

There is not really a lot I want to say about this concert except that I like Alison and was a fan from the moment I heard her first recording. She had caused a lot of interest and enthusiastic comments when she broke onto the scene and this was a major tour. However it was also my record loss on a show. In fourteen years and several hundred bands, I had never lost this amount of money. She was paid £4000 and I lost just over £4000. Obviously there are promotion costs on every show but as a reflection of tickets sold that is pretty spectacular. I could not understand it. I still can't …

Barry Lucas

Amazing Blondel

12 November 1971	Supports: Bronco I John Martyn
10 November 1972	Support: Stefan Grossman
25 January 1974	Support: Gasworks

Veterans of five Great Hall appearances, Amazing Blondel are an English acoustic progressive folk band. The band were formed around 1969 by Eddie Baird, John Gladwin and Terry Wincott.

Their music has been compared with that of Gryphon, Pentangle and Jethro Tull. They released a number of LPs for Island Records in the early 1970s and much of the material performed in their two early support appearances would have come from the albums *Fantasia Lindum* and *Evensong*.

Amazing Blondel's first Great Hall concert was providing support for Pentangle in November 1970.

Amazing Blondel returned in January 1971 when they were back again as the support band for Traffic in the 'Elton John no show' concert. Less than a year later, the band returned for the first of these three Lancaster concerts as headliners in their own right.

Amazing Blondel are still active today.

Bronco were an English country-rock band signed to Island & Polydor Records from 1969–1973, previously appearing in the Great Hall as headliners in February 1971.

This was the very first appearance in the Great Hall of **John Martyn.**

Born in Brooklyn, New York, **Stefan Grossman** is an American acoustic fingerstyle guitarist and singer, still performing today.

Gasworks were a folk duo formed in the late 1960s by John Brown and Mike Draper. John and Mike performed an esoteric mix of romantic songs influenced by music hall, played on a multitude of instruments including a phono-fiddle.

This band were friends of/known to Gaz Taylor, my co-promoter in the early days. Originally from the Scunthorpe area, Amazing Blondel were indeed a truly amazing act, performing medieval folk music – an obvious must for rock fans I hear you say. I know, I know, but it worked!

Don't ask me why, but they always went down a storm – and don't get me wrong, I loved 'em, they were brilliant, but to young rock fans?

However, we persevered over the next few years. Supporting, or being supported by, a variety of acts, including John Martyn, Bronco, Stefan Grossman and Roger McGough, among others. Like several good acts I believed in, I stuck with them and eventually they were able to headline nights in the Great Hall and pull a 1000-plus crowd to their shows. Good lads, great music, they really deserved their moments of fame.

Barry Lucas

Argent

20 November 1970 — Supports: Barclay James Harvest | Farm | Sam Apple Pie
1972 — Support: Hackensack

Argent were an English rock band founded in 1969 by keyboardist Rod Argent, formerly of The Zombies.

Argent's biggest hit was the Rod Argent and Chris White composition 'Hold Your Head Up' which reached No. 5 in the UK single chart of 1972. Their other major chart success was the single 'God Gave Rock and Roll to You', making No. 18 in 1973.

Rod Argent, after many years of writing hits for an array of other artists, is about to set out on his own 2016 tour, playing live for the first time in years.

Prior to headlining twice at Lancaster, in 1971 and 1975, a great second act on the bill was Manchester prog. rock band **Barclay James Harvest**.

The third of three Great Hall support appearances for Aylesbury band **Farm** in 1970. The Great Hall had seen Farm as guests of Deep Purple in January, followed by a concert backing Procol Harum in April 1970.

Sam Apple Pie was a British blues-rock band, of the late 1960s and 1970s, noted for having played at the first Glastonbury Festival in 1970.

UK Heavy Metal band **Hackensack** were formed in 1969 by Nicky Moore and existed until 1974. The band released one album on the Polydor label, entitled *Up The Hard Way*.

Band lineup:
Nicky Moore – guitars, keyboards, vocals
Simon Fox – drums
Stu Mills – bass
Ray Majors – vocals, guitars

In 1981 Nicky Moore and his band featured as guests of Wishbone Ash on their *Number The Brave* Tour.

Following the breakup of Hackensack in 1974, drummer Simon Fox joined Bill Nelson's Be-Bop Deluxe.

LANCASTER UNIVERSITY
SOCIAL COMMITTEE PRESENTS
ARGENT
PLUS
BARCLAY JAMES HARVEST
PLUS
FARM
LATE EDITION
SAM APPLE PIE
FRIDAY 20th NOVEMBER
in The Central Hall
7-30 p.m. to 1 a.m. Late Bar and Buses
10/- ADMISSION
COME EARLY TO ENSURE ADMISSION

The Crazy World of Arthur Brown

9 May 1970 Supports: The Henry Lowther Band | The John Dummer Band

The Crazy World of Arthur Brown are an English psychedelic rock band formed by singer Arthur "The God of Hellfire" Brown in 1967. Arthur is originally from Whitby in North Yorkshire. With an alarming stage act and a debut single, 'Devil's Grip', this paved the way for the band's success with their No. 1 hit 'Fire'.

Released in 1968, 'Fire' was one of the one-hit wonders in the United Kingdom and United States in the 1960s. But what a one hit to have! 'Fire' sold over one million copies and was awarded a gold disc.

In later years, Brown released several solo albums and in 1975 appeared in The Who's rock opera movie *Tommy* as the priest. Arthur Brown presently continues to tour and record.

Henry Lowther is a jazz trumpeter from Leicester who went on to work with numerous notable musicians, including Elton John and Van Morrison. He was also part of the lineup of The Keef Hartley Band, who provided support for Edgar Broughton's 1970 Great Hall concert.

The John Dummer Band, also known as John Dummer's Blues Band, were notable for the inclusion of Tony McPhee in their lineup, who moved on to form The Groundhogs and is rightly regarded as one of the finest blues guitarists to come from this country. The band also played as a support act for Howlin' Wolf and John Lee Hooker on their UK tours. In 1977 Dummer joined the band Darts as their drummer and featured in their 1979 Great Hall concert.

Atomic Rooster

30 October 1970 Supports: Terry Reids Band | Innocent Child

Atomic Rooster are an English rock band, originally formed by two former members of The Crazy World of Arthur Brown, Vincent Crane, the master of the swirling Hammond organ, and drummer Carl Palmer, who went on to form Emerson, Lake and Palmer. The band initially existed from 1969 to 1975. Throughout their history, Vincent Crane was the only constant member and wrote the majority of their material.

Atomic Rooster are best known for the hard progressive rock sound of their hit singles 'Tomorrow Night', a UK No. 11 hit, and 'The Devil's Answer', which did better, going to No. 4, both in 1971. Vincent Crane passed away in 1989 at the young age of forty-five.

Lancaster band lineup:
Vincent Crane – organ, piano, bass pedals
John Du Cann – guitar, vocals, bass
Paul Hammond – drums, percussion

In 2016, Atomic Rooster re-formed with permission from Crane's widow, with a new lineup featuring two members from the various 1970s incarnations of the band.

Terry Reid is famous for his powerful soulful voice and notable for turning down offers to join Led Zeppelin and Deep Purple. He is still active at present.

Little is known about the second support act **Innocent Child**

Average White Band

2 March 1979 Support: Inner Circle

Formed in 1972 by Alan Gorrie and Malcolm "Molly" Duncan, Average White Band are a Scottish funk and R&B band that had a series of soul and disco hits between 1974 and 1980.

They appeared at the university supporting the release of their seventh album, *Feel No Fret,* with a band lineup of:
Alan Gorrie – bass, vocals
Hamish Stuart – guitars, vocals
Roger Ball – keyboards, alto saxophone
Malcolm Duncan – tenor saxophone
Steve Ferrone – drums
Onnie McIntyre – guitars, vocals

AWB are best known for their 1975 hit single 'Pick up The Pieces' which reached No. 6 in the UK Singles Chart and was a No. 1 hit in the US.

The track was taken from the album *AWB,* also known as *The White Album*, and brought the band major success in America, reaching No. 1 in the US Albums Chart.

'Let's Go Round Again' was another popular disco number for the band in 1980.

Two members of Average White Band, Malcolm Duncan and saxophonist Roger Ball, were previously members of the band Mogul Thrash, who appeared as support band for Johnny Winter's Great Hall gig of 1971, while Onnie McIntyre and founder member the late Robbie McIntosh, were session musicians on Chuck Berry's hit single 'My Ding-a-Ling'.

As of 2017, over forty years after their formation, Average White Band continue to tour and record.

Support came from Jamaican reggae outfit **Inner Circle** who are still active today. The band was formed in 1968 by the brothers Ian and Roger Lewis and are known for their blending of pop and rock with reggae.

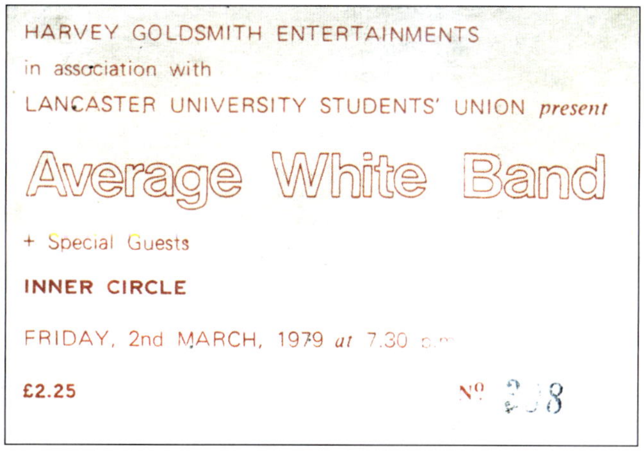
HARVEY GOLDSMITH ENTERTAINMENTS
in association with
LANCASTER UNIVERSITY STUDENTS' UNION *present*
Average White Band
+ Special Guests
INNER CIRCLE
FRIDAY, 2nd MARCH, 1979 *at* 7.30 p.m.
£2.25
Nº

In the mid '70s the soul legend James Brown was so disgusted that a funk band from Scotland was having such acclaim that he created his own version called The Above Average Black Band. It wasn't long though before he acknowledged how good AWB were and disbanded his creation.

Steve Middlesbrough, local DJ legend, went to this gig. Let him tell the story:

> "I had been to several live shows that year, mainly featuring great soul/funk bands. The shows had been breathtaking in their presentation but here was something different. It was the first of many gigs that I attended in the Great Hall and was memorable for the most amazing entrance by a band that I have ever seen. Standing at the back of the hall with some friends, we were eagerly awaiting the band. What would the next few moments hold, explosions, pyro, lights …? Then a few guys wandered onto the stage, one walked up to the mic. 'We were just playing footie out back and thought we ought to come in here and play you a few tunes,' said a broad Scottish voice. It was the greatest opening to an act I've ever seen."

Barry Lucas

Bad Company

7 December 1974 — Support: Duster Bennett

20 March 1979 — **The Desolation Angels Tour** — No support

Bad Company were formed in Westminster, London, in 1973 by two former Free band members, singer Paul Rodgers and drummer Simon Kirke. Joining them to complete the lineup was ex-King Crimson bassist Boz Burrell, and Mott The Hoople guitarist Mick Ralphs.

1974 saw Bad Company appear in the Great Hall for the first time to promote the release of their debut album *Bad Company*. The album contained the hit single 'Can't Get Enough' and spent twenty-five weeks in the UK Albums Chart, entering at No. 10 and reaching its highest position of No. 3 in its second week.

Possible 1974 Lancaster setlist: 'Little Miss Fortune', 'Rock Steady', 'Ready For Love', 'Don't Let Me Down', 'Easy On My Soul', 'Bad Company', 'Deal with the Preacher', 'Movin' On', 'Can't Get Enough', 'The Stealer', 'Rock Me Baby'.

The band's fifth album, *Desolation Angels*, was released just three days before Bad Company arrived in Lancaster for their second visit in 1979.

Possible 1979 Lancaster setlist: 'Bad Company',' Good Lovin' Gone Bad', 'Gone, Gone, Gone', 'Burnin' Sky', 'Shooting Star', 'Rhythm Machine', 'Ready For Love', 'Simple Man', 'Oh, Atlanta', 'She Brings Me Love', 'Run With The Pack', 'Evil Wind', 'Honey Child', 'Rock 'n' Roll Fantasy', 'Movin' On', 'Live for the Music'.

Encore: 'Feel Like Makin' Love', 'Can't Get Enough'.

Paul Rodgers finally called it a day with the band shortly after the release of *Rough Diamonds*, Bad Company's sixth album, in 1982.

From 2004 to 2009, Paul Rodgers collaborated with Brian May and Roger Taylor of Queen for a number of tours as lead vocalist. It was made clear at the time that Rodgers would not be a replacement for Queen's former lead singer, Freddie Mercury, who died on 24 November 1991, but simply be 'featured with' former Queen members.

Happily, in 2008 Bad Company decided to reform and the band continues to record and tour with Paul Rodgers, Mick Ralphs, and Simon Kirke on drums.

A *SCAN* newspaper concert reviewer said of the March '79 concert:

> "Right from the start it had the ingredients of a classic gig. An enormous queue, the air full of expectancy, leather jackets and dirty denims, a stage crammed full of stacks and battery upon battery of lights. For the first time in four years Bad Company were returning to Lancaster. At 8.15 sharp, when the masses had finally pushed, shoved and squeezed their way in, the lights went out, a roar came up – and on they came!"

Anthony "Duster" Bennett was a British blues singer and harmonica player. He was backed on his 1968 debut album, *Smiling Like I'm Happy*, by members of Fleetwood Mac. In 1970 he was a session harmonica player and member of John Mayall & The Bluesbreakers during a US tour. Duster Bennett was tragically killed in a car accident in 1976 at the young age of twenty-nine.

Bad Company 1979, photographer unknown,
courtesy Colin Sumner

Bad Company

When my second favourite band of all time packed up (Free were ranked only behind the Doors in my pantheon of all time greats) I was totally devastated. A couple of years later the remnants were re-united as Bad Company – a true super-group of the '70s. They appeared twice, but it was the first date that was really exciting. It was announced that this super-group were only going to do a very, very select tour of six dates, with Mel Bush as their promoter. I got on well with the Mel Bush Organisation but even so I was amazed when he approached me to be one of those six dates. This was much to Leeds University's chagrin as they had desperately begged for a date.

Mel had always put shows, the more middle-of-the-road acts, into Preston Guildhall and so he rewarded them with a date as well. I think it was mainly to thank Alan Baker, who was an outstanding hall manager. It may be hard to imagine now, but Preston was a relatively new venue then without the problems that promoters were later to encounter. I knew that the size and the status of the show would prohibit me from watching any of it but they were my favourite band so I decided to go down to Preston, the night before, to watch. I got myself, Nigel Waller and Alan Murray on the guest list, booked rooms at The Tickled Trout (the band's hotel) and was as excited as any fan.

Unfortunately I was (and still am) of the old school – you can't watch rock 'n' roll sitting down, especially in comfortable, cinema-style seating. It's just not rock 'n' roll! We managed three numbers and retired to the bar, where we were joined by a lonely figure in a floor-length snakeskin coat. We recognised him immediately as the '60s star Dave Berry (with his band, The Cruisers, he had a fantastic hit with the 'The Crying Game') who felt exactly the same way and we spent a couple of hours bemoaning the death of rock 'n' roll. Five years later, Dave Berry was to appear in the Great Hall for a rag ball on the same bill as Darts. As I drank I assured everyone we'd create the atmosphere necessary to watch Bad Company in a proper rock venue, stand-up an' all – Lancaster, the next night.

But we had to get through the rest of that night. We got back to the hotel and continued drinking. Promoters, record company reps, journalists, band, and finally road crew, joined us. At about 1.00 am I found myself in the company of Paul Rodgers. I believe him to be the next best thing to Jim Morrison and therefore, as the latter was dead, in my eyes I was talking to the best rock singer on the planet. He had just started playing guitar on stage – I suppose he wouldn't have dared do it if Kossoff had still been around – and I was sufficiently alcohol-brave to ask him what he was thinking of as he wasn't a guitarist, he was THE SINGER! If I was his manager, I assured him, I would chop his hands off; his voice was his instrument. He didn't argue, just looked pityingly at the drunken, burbling specimen in front of him and left to find some sensible conversation. He was in such a hurry he left his drink – I finished it for him! I finally staggered out of the bar at 3.00 am after mine-sweeping all the unfinished drinks on the empty tables – not an edifying sight. In fact a true disgrace. Not quite as bad as Nigel who spent the rest of the night sat on his expensive hotel toilet, head in the wash basin, emptying his body from both ends at once! Nice!

Lancaster University's gig was, as I knew it would be, brilliant. Just what a rock 'n' roll concert should be: drivin' music, crazy, animated, dancing crowd. It's only rock 'n' roll but I like it.

However, it wasn't so memorable for one musician, the support act, Duster Bennett. The tour was rather hastily put together and it meant that the sound check was somewhat long and drawn out. So much so that, by the time Bad Company had finished, we were past the door opening time. I had things to put in place before we were ready to open, but the schedule was such that Duster was told to go on and begin his set well before I could open the doors. Consequently Duster had to go on stage, pretend there was an audience and play. It took several numbers into the set before I was in a position to open the doors and let the audience in. I can think of several support acts who deserved to play to an empty hall but Duster Bennett wasn't one of them.

The next time Bad Company appeared at Lancaster they were truly world superstars, with several hit singles and albums. When I had got the PA in, sorted the playing and door opening times out with the promoter, Harvey Goldsmith, and the bands had done the necessary sound checks, Alan Murray and I would nip down to Lancaster to grab something to eat, our tea. This was usually in The Blue Anchor but, for some reason that escapes me now, this particular night we chose The Albert. We were just settling down to our braised steak and chips when in walked Bad Company! The whole band had taken up my recommendation and come to The Albert for their tea. Up to the bar to order pints strolled Paul Rodgers, complete with full-length leather coat and scarf, topped off with a very impressive leather cowboy Stetson. Leaning on the bar was an old regular of about seventy or eighty years. He looked Mr Rodgers up and down and asked him what he was doing in his local. Paul replied that he was at the university.

"What ya studying?" he was asked.

"Music," Mr Rodgers replied. The old guy gave him a pitying look as if to say, "You're wasting your time, you won't make a living with that, son."

Barry Lucas

Baker Gurvitz Army

February 1975 — Support unknown, possibly Strife

Former The Gun and Three Man Army members Paul and Adrian Gurvitz joined forces with ex-Cream and Airforce drummer Ginger Baker in 1974 to form Baker Gurvitz Army. Also drafted into the band was former Sharks and Nothineverappens member Mr Snips (aka Steve Parsons) on vocals. This visit was in support of the January '75 release of their album *Elysian Encounter.*

The band released three albums before the death of their manager, which led to the eventual breakup of the band. In the aftermath, Baker briefly led a band called Energy and was also associated with Atomic Rooster and Hawkwind.

Ginger Baker was to return to the Great Hall stage with Hawkwind, drumming for them on their UK 1980 Christmas Tour.

The evening's support slot could possibly have been supplied by the power rock outfit **Strife**, who also appeared as a support band for Budgie in 1978.

Barclay James Harvest

16 April 1971 — Supports: Root and Jenny Jackson | Victor Brox | Gwenyway

31 October 1975 — **Time Honoured Ghosts Tour** — Support: Café Society

Oldham progressive rock band Barclay James Harvest were founded in 1966 by Les Holroyd (bass, guitars, keyboards, vocals), Stuart "Woolly" Wolstenholme (vocals, mellotron, keyboards, guitars), John Lees (vocals, guitars) and Mel Pritchard (drums).

They played a total of three concerts in the Great Hall, the first providing support for Argent in 1970. Their second visit to Lancaster saw the band as a headline act, performing tracks from their second album *Once Again*, released in early 1971 and containing probably their best known song 'Mocking Bird'.

Four years later, Barclay James Harvest returned for their third visit, promoting the October 1975 release of the album *Time Honoured Ghosts.*

Lancaster setlist: 'Song For You', 'Crazy City', 'In My Life', 'Sweet Jesus', 'Hymn For The Children', 'Paper Wings', 'Child Of The Universe', 'One Night', 'Moongirl', 'For No One', 'Titles', 'Jonathan', 'Mocking Bird'.

Two versions of the band continue to record and tour: John Lees' Barclay James Harvest, since 1988, and Barclay James Harvest featuring Les Holroyd, who have been touring since 2002.

Root and Jenny Jackson, born in Trinidad, were a brother and sister soul/RnB outfit based in Huddersfield, West Yorkshire. In a similar mould to Ike and Tina Turner the duo were backed by their six piece band, The High Timers.

Victor Brox, from Manchester, is an accomplished musician who has worked with Eric Clapton, Ritchie Blackmore and Ian Gillan of Deep Purple. He has been described by Jimi Hendrix and Tina Turner as their favourite white blues singer. He is still performing as Victor Brox Blues Train.

Café Society were a trio comprising Tom Robinson, Hereward Kaye and Raphael 'Ray' Doyle. They recorded one self-titled album on the Konk record label, produced by Ray Davies of the Kinks. Tom Robinson, who joined Café Society in 1973, went on to have chart success with his own Tom Robinson Band. The band's single '2-4-6-8 Motorway' reached No. 5 in the UK Singles Chart of 1977, and Robinson's solo hit 'War Baby' peaked at No. 6 in 1983.

Active in the early 70s, **Gwenyway** were an acoustic-rock outfit formed by musician Pete Marsh from Cumbria. During the post Beatles era and influenced by the likes of Crosby, Stills, Nash & Young, he assembled the band Gwenyway to perform acoustic covers. During his long career Pete Marsh has worked with the likes of Manfred Mann, 10cc and Vangelis and is still active recording, having released the album *Back To The Beginning* in 2017.

TO-NIGHT

LANCASTER UNIVERSITY
SOCIAL COMMITTEE

presents

a welcome return with

BARCLAY JAMES HARVEST

'ROOT and JENNY JACKSON'

with VICTOR BROX
plus 'GWENYWAY'

Lights - Disco - Bar - Buses

TICKETS 60p - Simmons - Wisemans
75p at the Door.

Barclay James Harvest 1975 ©David Bradbury

Tom Robinson and Café Society ©David Bradbury

Barclay James Harvest

I promoted Barclay James Harvest twice as headliners at Lancaster University, but it was the second date, 31 October 1975, that remains in my memory for a couple of reasons. But before I describe them, I must tell of one of the more bizarre clauses in the band's rider. This stated that the promoter on the night must wear a white suit! Totally ridiculous but it did get me a rather fetching new outfit that I later wore to an NUS conference – see Paul Loasby's memories.

It was a Friday; doors were to open at 7.30 pm with the support band on stage at 8.00 pm, the usual running order by now. We had dropped the 2.00 am, three or four bands programming format by then. I was getting too old, so were the musicians! Now bands on the road were arriving about 2.00 pm, or rather their PA and road crew were. But here we were, 7.00 pm, no band or equipment. It would take at least two hours to set up – what to do? Cancel? Easier to keep the doors shut than have to clear the hall of 1000-plus disgruntled fans – I know it wasn't metal but 'hippies' can get nasty too, you know!

Then, just as I was going to toss the coin to help me make the 'life-changing' or 'life-threatening' decision, a rather harassed, dishevelled roadie turned up. 7.15 pm!

"Traffic," he pleaded.

"Bloody hell, how long before you're ready?"

"Give us some extra humpers and an hour."

"OK. Done."

We very nearly were!

On the bill that night was a support band called Café Society. Now a close friend – agent, promoter, record shop owner and advisor, Mike Lloyd from Hanley, near Stoke – had phoned me up the previous day, saying that he had noticed I had BJH performing on Friday. Well he had had them on the Wednesday (I think it was, forty years is a long time to remember days, too many pints of Mitchell's in the Ring o' Bells) and he had to tell me about the support band. Café Society, he said, was the worst band he had ever had on (a trifle harsh, I thought afterwards). They had left the stage to deathly silence; a lone voice had sarcastically called out "More." The band returned to the stage. "I didn't mean it," cried the voice. Mike said they were so bad he had refused to pay them their measly £50 fee. Again a bit harsh.

Anyway they played Lancaster and, well, at the end of the night I was settling the BJH account with a cheque and had Cafe Society's £50 cash. They never showed up so I presumed that maybe what had happened in Hanley was happening a lot and they had stopped going in search of their petrol/beer/food money. I wasn't about to chase them, so …

It was several years later that the story reached its conclusion. In 1977 a single by a 'new' punk artist reached No. 5 in the national charts, '2-4-6-8 Motorway'. The artist was Tom Robinson – previously in Café Society. Paul Loasby was doing some dates with him and in a conversation I said I really wanted a date, really fancied it. I would even pay £5000! That was a great deal of money for me to guarantee. Unheard of, believe me.

"He won't do it," Paul said.

"Of course he will," I insisted.

"Look, I'll put you on a conference call if you promise to keep quiet."

So I heard, biting my knuckles, that I had cheated him (Tom Robinson) out of £50 and he wouldn't play for me for any amount. I even suggested to Paul that he go back and offer £5050 but same answer – it was a matter of principal.

Well that was almost a first, a matter of principal in the music business. Sort of impressive, wasn't it?

P.S. A further development, or maybe a conclusion, to this story has occurred in the last couple of weeks. On reading this book, as a preface to his writing of the foreword, Andy Kershaw rang me to query my description of Tom Robinson in my *Regrets* section. I explained that the only thing 'monstrous' about him was his fame; he was selling vast numbers of records and tickets. "Oh, that's OK then," Andy responded, "I was just worried because I'd always found him to be a really great bloke. Tom is a good mate of mine that I see fairly regularly."

I outlined the aforementioned story, explaining that I hadn't realised that he had been in Café Society when I was trying to book him. "I tell you what," Andy gleefully promised, "the next time I see Tom I'll give him £50 and explain it's from you and Lancaster University – it's the money you've been owed for years!"

I really hope he remembers to do that and that Tom buys him a couple of pints with it.

Barry Lucas

Bauhaus

30 October 1981 Support: Natural Scientist

Bauhaus were an English post-punk band, formed in Northampton in 1978.

With their dark, gloomy sound and image, Bauhaus are generally considered to be the first gothic rock group.

Bauhaus disbanded in 1983.

Support came from local Morecambe electropunk and new wave band, **Natural Scientist.**

The band were active from around 1980 to 1984, releasing an EP, *Anaesthetic Of Love*, and a single, 'See Through You/Liar', on Dental Records.

The band lineup was:
Stuart Baldwin – guitar, vocals
Neil 'Fee' Crossley – bass, vocals
Boris Forrest – guitar, vocals
Marek Gabrysch – drums
Pete Marsh – keyboards

Courtesy of Gabor Nemeth www.bauhausgigguide.info

I haven't got a great deal to say about this concert except a short story to help give an insight into a promoter's mind.

Bauhaus were a very interesting, innovative band, or arty-farty, depending on your point of view. Not to everybody's taste but if you were into them, you were, and enthusiastically so.

Paul Loasby, as PLP, was promoting the show and it hadn't done very well. He was losing a lot of money. So, to cheer him up, drown his sorrows etc., I took him to the ASH bar (Assistant Staff House) opposite the Great Hall entrance. In the middle of his second pint, Paul suddenly said that we had to get back to the hall as the band were on in five minutes and we had to watch them. "Hang on, I don't understand this, you're losing money so why would you want to watch it flowing down the drain?" I asked, bewildered.

"But they're bloody brilliant, got to watch them!" Paul was in the music business as a promoter because he loved the music. It set him apart from most of the other promoters at the time, and it certainly would today. It was also why he had great flair as a promoter and probably explains why he had so many financially disastrous gigs!

Barry Lucas

Be-Bop Deluxe

22 January 1977 Support: The Steve Gibbons Band

Be-Bop Deluxe were an English progressive rock band who achieved critical acclaim and moderate commercial success during the mid to late '70s. Be-Bop Deluxe were formed by Wakefield-born Bill Nelson in 1972 and went on to achieve success with five studio albums and three live albums. Their single 'Ships in the Night' reached No. 23 in the UK charts of 1976. Bill Nelson was to return to the Great Hall with his band Red Noise in 1979 after Nelson dissolved Be-Bop Deluxe.

Support on the night came from Birmingham rocker **Steve Gibbons**, still doing his stuff today having extensively toured the UK, Europe and Scandinavia since 1986. His band also provided support to Manfred Mann's Earth Band's November 1973 concert.

BE-BOP
DELUXE
AND THE STEVE GIBBONS BAND
UNIVERSITY OF LANCASTER
SATURDAY JAN. 22 7.30PM £1.75
John Angus

The Beat

15 May 1981 — Supports: Au Pairs | The Mood Elevators
15 October 1982 — Support: Berlin Wales

British ska band The Beat made two visits to Lancaster University.

They were founded in Birmingham in 1978 and are probably best known for their cover of the classic Motown hit 'Tears of a Clown' which reached No. 6 in the UK charts in 1979, followed by 'Mirror In The Bathroom' which peaked at No. 4 in 1980. 'Mirror In The Bathroom' was the first single released in the UK to have been digitally recorded.

The original lineup of the band broke up in 1983, but after many personnel changes two versions of the band continue to tour today; one under the name of The English Beat, and the other The Beat.

The **Au Pairs** were a post-punk band who were formed in Birmingham in 1979 and were compared in style to The Gang of Four. Fronting the band was vocalist/guitarist Lesley Woods who at the time was described as "one of the most striking women in British rock". They released two albums before disbanding in 1983.

A four-piece band from Birmingham, **The Mood Elevators** were invited to support The Beat on their 1981 tour, after the band saw them perform at a pub gig in 1980.

Little is known about 1982 support act **Berlin Wales.**

Beck, Bogert and Appice

19 January 1974 — Supports: Marie Celeste | Upp

Jeff Beck, Tim Bogert and drummer Carmine Appice formed their hard rock trio in 1972, evolving from The Jeff Beck Group, with Bogert and Appice coming from Vanilla Fudge. Their debut album, *Beck, Bogert and Appice*, was their one and only studio album, followed by *Live in Japan.*

This Lancaster concert featured the band performing the song 'Superstition,' originally written for Jeff Beck by Stevie Wonder. The plan was for Beck to release his version of this song first, with his newly formed band. However, due to a combination of the delayed release of Beck, Bogert and Appice's debut album and Motown CEO Berry Gordy's prediction that 'Superstition' would be a huge hit, Wonder ended up releasing the song as the lead single off his album *Talking Book* ahead of Beck's version. It reached No. 1 in the US and peaked at No. 11 in the UK Singles Chart in February 1973. Beck, Bogert and Appice disbanded in 1974.

Marie Celeste were an acoustic five-piece psychedelic/folk band from Wolverhampton, with two female vocalists.

UPP were a four piece band whose first album, *This Way ... Upp*, was released on the Epic label in 1976. The album featured, among the many "friends" guesting, a certain Jeff Beck on guitar.

Bert Jansch

2 March 1978

Following two fabulous Great Hall concerts with Pentangle in the early seventies, Scottish folk musician Bert Jansch returned for a solo performance in the Nuffield Theatre. It was with the folk 'super-group' Pentangle that the highly influential Glaswegian guitarist Bert Jansch made his name, playing alongside his friend and fellow guitarist John Renbourn. Over his career Jansch recorded six albums with Pentangle up to their disbandment in early 1973 and over 20 albums under his own name and several more jointly with Renbourn.

This Nuffield date fell between the release of his 1977 album *A Rare Conundrum* and his beautiful meditative paean to British birds in the 1979 album *Avocet.*

Following a long battle with cancer Bert Jansch passed away in 2011 aged sixty seven; his last appearance was earlier that year for a concert in the Royal Festival Hall in London.

This was the third appearance by Bert Jansch at Lancaster. In 1970 and 1972 he was on the Great Hall stage as part of the amazing Pentangle, for whom his vocals, and more importantly his guitar work, proved so important in establishing the band at the forefront of British folk music. In 1973 he left to concentrate on his own blend of folk and blues and became an iconic performer.

I was to use the Nuffield Theatre on many occasions over the years, as it was an excellent venue for those quality acts that couldn't fill the Great Hall but had a substantial, dedicated following. These were mainly folk and blues acts, although there was the truly memorable night when I had Joy Division as a third-on-the-bill act! Being a theatre club, the Nuffield licence did not have a stipulated audience capacity. It didn't make sense to me then and it still doesn't today, but then there have been many aspects of the UK's public entertainments licensing laws that have been beyond my comprehension. With Ken Parrot, the Director of Nuffield, we worked on a capacity of 550 and it created a terrific atmosphere in there.

Bert Jansch provided one such notable evening, when his guitar work was staggeringly good and that raspy voice was so perfect for the blues. He had, by now, been recognised as one of the great British guitarists: "the innovator of the time … so far ahead of what anyone else was doing" (Jimmy Page); "he was one of the most influential and intriguing musicians to have come out of the British music scene" (Johnny Marr). Other artists influenced by him include Donovan, Paul Simon and Neil Young. It was a great night in the Nuffield!

Barry Lucas

BERT JANSCH
NUFFIELD
THEATRE
LANCASTER
UNIVERSITY
THURSDAY
MARCH 2ND
7.30PM £1

John Angus

Big Country

6 October 1984 **Steeltown Tour** Support: White China

Stuart Adamson, former frontman of The Skids, returned to Lancaster for a concert with his band Big Country, six years after The Skids provided the support to The Stranglers in 1978.

Formed in Dunfermline, they were best known for the single 'Fields Of Fire (400 Miles)' which reached No. 10 in the UK Singles Chart in 1983. After releasing a total of nine studio albums Big Country are still active today.

The band currently features two of the original members: drummer Mark Brzezicki and guitarist Bruce Watson, but sadly without Stuart Adamson, who committed suicide in 2001.

Formed in 1981 **White China** are a five piece band, also from The Skids hometown, Dunfermline.

They disbanded in 1986 then re-formed in 2012 and are still recording and touring.

Bill Bruford's UK

12 May 1978 Support: The Fabulous Poodles

Former drummer with Yes, Genesis and King Crimson, Bill Bruford visited Lancaster University for a second time with his band, UK.

Active from 1977 to 1980 the lineup consisted of:
John Wetton (formerly of Uriah Heep) – bass guitar
Eddie Jobson (from Curved Air) – keyboards, violins
Alan Holdsworth (formerly of Soft Machine) – guitars
Bill Bruford – drums

They produced two studio albums and one live album during their three-year existence.

Bruford had previously appeared as drummer with Yes in the Great Hall in 1970.

Lancaster setlist: 'Alaska', 'Time to Kill', 'The Sahara of Snow', 'Carrying No Cross', 'The Only Thing She Needs', 'Forever Until Sunday', 'Thirty Years In the Dead of Night', 'By the Light of Day', 'Presto Vivace', 'Caesar's Palace Blues'.

Mick Walsh reviewing the concert in *SCAN* newspaper said;

> "UK provided stark contrast to the ribald teen beat love songs provided by support band, The Fabulous Poodles. There was no humour or communication from UK with the audience; just four uncompromising musicians determined to stand or fall on the quality of the music that they produced. I am pleased to report that they stood up quite admirably".

The Fabulous Poodles were a quirky pub rock band formed in 1976, who disbanded in 1980 after releasing two UK albums.

Bill Nelson's Red Noise

16 March 1979 Support: Fingerprintz

After dissolving Be-Bop Deluxe, Bill Nelson formed his new wave band, Red Noise in 1978, along with his brother Ian and one other former member of Be-Bop Deluxe, Andy Clarke. Releasing just the one album, *Sound-on-Sound* in February 1979, and two singles, Red Noise disbanded later that same year.

Lancaster band lineup:
Bill Nelson – guitars
Ian Nelson – saxophone
Andy Clark – keyboards
Rick Ford – bass guitar
Steve Peer – drums

SCAN newspaper reported that, due to adverse weather conditions that afternoon, Bill and his wife Jan did not arrive at the university until 7.45 pm:

> "Without a sound check, Red Noise took to the stage clad in Nelson designed 'Trumpton' soldiers uniforms to a half-filled audience. The opener 'Don't Touch Me (I'm Electric)' set the attack".

Fingerprintz were formed in 1979 by Scottish vocalist Jimmie O'Neill and guitarist Cha Burns. Three albums were released before their disbandment in 1985.

Billy Connolly

1979 **Big Wee Tour**

Billy Connolly was born and raised in Glasgow, Scotland. He left school to work in the shipyards, becoming a welder, and joined the Territorial Army (in the parachute regiment) at around the same time.

He developed an interest in folk music, eventually becoming an accomplished banjo player and a member of the band Humblebums with Gerry Rafferty (later of 'Baker Street' fame). The jokes he told between songs eventually took over his act and he became a full-time comedian. Already a big star in Scotland, he became a household name in the UK after appearing on Parkinson (1971) in the early seventies. Billy has released many recordings and videos of his concert performances over the years and has expanded his repertoire to include acting, appearing in a number of television dramas and films, most recently in the USA. In the '90s he made two documentary series for the BBC, about Scotland and Australia respectively, and in 1997 starred in the award winning film *Mrs Brown*. He is one of the UK's top comedians.

Billy Connolly

"The Big Yin" hit Lancaster on his 'Big Wee Tour'. It was after THE Parkinson interview and THE bike joke. It also marked the very beginning of the era when comedy became the new rock 'n' roll. Promoted like a major music tour, Billy was one of the very first comedians to tour rock venues as opposed to theatres. The show here in the Great Hall was fully seated, so it was limited to 950 tickets, which sold out very quickly.

At this point Billy Connolly was going through his drugs, alcohol and rock 'n' roll period, well documented in Pamela Stephenson's great biography. As she recounted, Billy became very fond indeed of cocaine, finding it a great help to his shows in the early days. I was asked to send someone down to London to pick up an album Mr Connolly urgently required – we weren't told what was being transported back to Lancaster, only that it was a very valuable album and must be guarded accordingly. It wasn't Bing Crosby's 'White Christmas' but maybe it ought to have been!

Billy was a remarkable tour de force and made mincemeat of any hecklers foolish enough to take him on. An outstanding show! I cannot claim that I foresaw the rise of the comedy 'gods' but I did recognise that here was a potentially lucrative market; comedians did indeed provide a good night out.

After the show, Bailrigg Student Television asked if they could have an interview. A TV studio was quickly constructed backstage and Billy gave what turned out to be an hour's performance – it was brilliant but the budding TV producers complained to me afterwards that he was somewhat 'wired' and went on and on when they only wanted a brief ten minutes interview! They had a unique event but I bet they didn't keep it for posterity – what a tragedy.

As a postscript, I heard that Mr Connolly had a great night back at his hotel!

Barry Lucas

Billy Connolly on the Great Hall stage
©Geoff Campbell

Black Oak Arkansas

14 January 1974 Support: Sassafrass

The legendary influential American southern rock band Black Oak Arkansas were formed in 1963 and took their name simply from their hometown of Black Oak in Arkansas USA.

Led by Jim "Dandy" Mangrum, the band reached the height of its fame in the 1970s with ten charting albums released in that decade, the best known being *High On The Hog,* which reached No. 25 in 1974's Billboard Hot 100 Chart. James Mangrum has continued to record and tour with a series of different Black Oak lineups up to the present day.

Reportedly, Black Oak Arkansas hold the world record for the highest number of successive members of a rock band: sixty-one.

Sassafrass from South Wales were formed in 1970 and were described as a kind of Fleetwood Mac/Eagles hybrid. The use of twin guitar solos was a distinctive feature of their music. In the early 1970s they held the record for highest number of gigs in a single year, with their 332 beating Slade by one!

Black Oak Arkansas

Jim Dandy to the rescue! This is not so much the story of a concert but of a relationship which was so important to the history of rock music at Lancaster University.

College Event, a magazine mentioned elsewhere in this book, was a mini-bible for the music business at one time. It was mandatory reading for college social secretaries, agents, record companies and promoters in the '70s. On a page dedicated to music in the North, it mentioned, as an aside, the red telephone line between Leeds and Lancaster across the Pennines. It largely went unnoticed in the business but it was of huge significance for the future.

Leeds University was for years THE college venue, a reputation and programme which could only be dreamed of by all other college venues in the country. But I was determined to change all that and in the early '70s that process started. Lancaster started to be an irritating thorn in Leeds' side, slowly gaining ground then beginning to get the occasional act that they were unable to sign. Why? I am sure it was a mystery to a succession of social secretaries. I loved it; they were growing to hate it and eventually to fear it. Their social secs were faceless names to me, I never met any of them and that's the way I wanted it to stay – it made it easier to beat them. Of course I knew several of them by name but I had little respect for them as promoters; they were at one of the biggest universities in the UK, sat on the main motorway in the country, in one of the biggest cities in the country, and had no public hall or venue in the city to compete with, so obviously they were always going to be offered the biggest acts. However, I did get to know Andy Kershaw later as he phoned me on his election to the post of social secretary and asked for some advice and guidance. He proved to be a very accomplished promoter and I had to (grudgingly) admire his achievements. The summer after he left Leeds I was backstage at Donnington with Geoff Campbell and several agents and promoters when Andy came up to tell us he had been offered a job with the BBC. He proceeded to regale us all for about thirty minutes with the most entertaining stories and anecdotes. Andy then ended with "Can't think why they've offered me a job." We all looked at each other and thought, "We know why."

A few years earlier at Imperial College, London, NUS Social Secretaries' Conference, on the Saturday lunchtime, young agent Richard Griffiths (mentioned elsewhere as the first AC/DC manager) came up to me: "Hi Barry, do you want to meet the Leeds Social Secretary?"

"No," I abruptly replied, and moved to the bar.

"Oh, well, Barry this is Paul Loasby. Paul this is Barry Lucas from Lancaster. "Not interested", I thought, but then he did offer to buy me a beer, and I'm always a sucker for that. Anyway, one beer progressed to two, to ten. Paul was down at the conference with some of his committee, sleeping in the back of a transit van – very rock 'n' roll, but not very big time. "Erm, he might be OK", I thought.

Paul Loasby was more than that; he became my best mate and without him some of the legendary events detailed in this book simply would not have happened. In today's terminology we bonded; in '70s speak we got pissed together.

We formed a friendship that lasts to this day but in those early days we talked, exchanged ideas, he picked my brain and we set up that 'red phone line' between our offices. One day Paul used that line to tell me he had been offered Black Oak for £1500. They were a biggish American rock band who would do business. I phoned the agent and the conversations that followed were priceless.

"Hey I'm interested in Black Oak but I'm the only professional ents officer, I'm not paying £1500 like that amateur social sec. at Leeds."

"Paul, got it for £1250, your turn."

"Hey, this is Leeds University, the best and the most prestigious university gig in Europe, I'm not paying more than other unis."

"Barry, got it down to £1000."

"Hey I told you, this is my job, my career, I'm not in it for a laugh! I have to make money to justify being the only full time ents officer in Europe. I can't be seen to be paying the same as other unis."

"Paul, got it for £750, over to you again."

We both got Jim Dandy to perform for £750, half the fee other colleges were paying. Get in!

Barry Lucas

Black Sabbath

12 June 1970 **"Black Sabbath" Tour** Supports: The Pretty Things | Fat Abbots

Pioneers of heavy metal, Black Sabbath were formed in Birmingham in 1968 by guitarist and main songwriter Tony Iommi, bassist and main lyricist Geezer Butler, singer Ozzy Osbourne and drummer Bill Ward.

On 30 August 1969 Black Sabbath played their first ever live gig in Workington, Cumbria.

Their June 1970 concert in the Great Hall was in support of the band's debut album *Black Sabbath*, released in February 1970, which went on to reach No. 8 in the UK album chart.

Probable setlist: 'Paranoid', 'Iron Man', 'N.I.B', 'Black Sabbath', 'Walpurgis', 'Hand of Doom', 'Fairies Wear Boots', 'Guitar Solo', 'Behind the Wall of Sleep', 'Rat Salad'.

Starting in January 2016, Black Sabbath embarked on their final world tour, entitled The End Tour, and, following eighty-one dates, the band played their final concert on 4 February 2017 in their home city of Birmingham.

The Pretty Things are an English rock band from London, formed by Dick Taylor and Phil May in 1963. Their first album, *The Pretty Things*, was released in 1965 and reached No. 6 in the UK Albums Chart. In June 1970 the university saw the band supporting Black Sabbath and performing numbers from their newly released album *Parachute*. This was a landmark album, receiving rave reviews and was a very mature, serious concept recording. In 1972, The Pretty Things returned to Lancaster in a supporting role to Medicine Head.

The **Fat Abbots** were a short-lived Goth rock band from Leicester and were managed by Barry Lucas' sister.

For a short – very short! – time the Fat Abbots were managed by my sister, Carol. We paid them their petrol money to Lancaster and found them a student's floor to sleep on.

In the summer of 1970, Gaz Taylor and I were flushed with the success of The Who and had already booked acts, such as Black Sabbbath and Family, for the autumn term. So we decided to do a little private promoting to supplement our grants. My family had moved to Oadby, near Leicester, and we toured the area until we found a venue in Coalville, a small, former mining town nearby. We called our promoting company 'Tusk Promotions' – Gaz' idea, not mine – and we did two shows, the first with Van der Graff Generator and the other featuring Black Widow.

As you will have no doubt gathered, they weren't wildly successful – we didn't promote any more as there weren't enough tickets sold to bulk up our grants. But Black Widow, a Leicester-born Goth, black magic, heavy rock band, nearly famous for their legendary single 'Come to the Sabbat (Satan's there)', were supported by another Leicester Goth band, the Fat Abbots.

Barry Lucas

Blonde on Blonde

24 October 1969 Support: Eclection

Blonde on Blonde were a guitar-led psychedelic rock group from South Wales and arrived in North Lancashire for one of the first 'Central Hall' concerts.

The band were formed in Newport in 1967 by vocalist and guitarist Ralph Denyer, drummer Les Hicks, bassist Richard Hopkins and guitarist and sitar player Gareth Johnson. The band were named after Bob Dylan's 1966 album of the same name.

They released three studio albums during their four-year existence: *Contrasts* in 1969 was followed by *Rebirth* in 1970 and *Reflections On A Life* in 1971.

Blonde on Blonde appeared at the 1969 Isle of Wight Festival but achieved only modest commercial success. They disbanded in early 1972.

Support band **Eclection** were a short-lived, British-based psychedelic/folk rock band, originally formed in 1967 in London by Norwegian-born Georg Kajanus. They released the one self-titled album on the Elektra label.

Georg Kajanus returned to Lancaster with his band Sailor, the support act for Mott The Hoople in their 1974 Great Hall concert.

Blondie

27 February 1978 **Rag Ball Concert** Supports: Advertising I Mungo Jerry

Blondie were one of the first American new wave bands to achieve mainstream success in the United Kingdom and arrived at Lancaster University to promote the February 1978 release of their second album *Plastic Letters*. The album gave the band their first two hit singles, 'Denis', which reached No. 2 in the UK charts, and '(I'm Always Touched by Your) Presence, Dear', going to No. 10.

Later in September 1978, Blondie released the album that would make them international stars, entitled *Parallel Lines*. The album went to No. 1 in the UK Albums Chart and spawned several hit singles, including the No. 1 hits 'Heart Of Glass' and 'Sunday Girl'.

Lancaster band lineup:
Debbie Harry – lead vocals
Chris Stein – guitars
Nigel Harrison – bass
Jimmy Destri – keyboards, backing vocals
Clem Burke – drums

Blondie broke up in 1982 and re-formed in 1997, going on to achieve another No. 1 UK hit with 'Maria' in 1999.

A concert-goer at the time, David Summers remembers seeing Debbie Harry and her entourage prior to the concert eating in the nearby Cartmel College refectory. He told me: "She looked like some sort of beautiful alien creature; a queen bee surrounded by her drones."

Mungo Jerry appeared last on the bill around midnight as late replacements for the initially advertised Alberto y Los Trios Paranoias, the Mancunian comedy rock band.

According to a *SCAN* concert review;

> "Blondie were very ordinary on the night with Mungo Jerry later producing a tremendous set that really livened the evening up; the band performing their classics, 'In The Summertime', 'Lady Rose', 'Long Legged Woman Dressed in Black' and 'Alright, Alright, Alright'."

Little is known about the band **Advertising** but Mick Walsh, writing in *SCAN*, noted:

> "... despite the band finishing with a dry rendition of Petula Clark's 'Downtown' the reception was decidedly lukewarm"

In this period, Rag Week ended with the Rag Ball. Unfortunately it was organised by the Rag Committee, a group of individuals who were great at zany stunts – throwing flour, eggs and water over OAPs from rag floats in Lancaster city centre etc. Such jolly japes! But these same people had to research, book and organise a rock concert – the Rag Ball – and they were simply not cut out for that. They continually oversaw disasters, as they overpaid and under drew. I offered to incorporate the Ball into my programme, whereby I would book and run the show and they could have all the profits. Al Gordon, later to be a truly great student union president but at that moment Rag Chairman, agreed and gave me free reign.

I was in 'Ear 'Ere one evening when a record company rep. came in with a new 12" single. Picture disc, beautiful blonde, basque, suspenders, stockings torn and ripped – 'Rip Her To Shreds'. I know, very unPC today, but then …

She was American, coming over for a UK tour and record release. I felt immediately that this would not just generate music paper headlines; this would feature in the red-tops, pages of it. It was going to be a sensation, I knew it for certain. But for some unknown reason very few others in the music business did, whatever they may say today.

So it came to pass that I was able to get a date on Blondie's first tour, £500, straight fee, no percentage. It meant that if the show sold as I thought it would we would make a killing. I didn't even attempt to haggle with the agent, a young guy who didn't really know what he had been given, nor, I suspect, did his bosses. It wasn't his fault, although I believe it was to later cost him his job. Al Gordon and "the committee" said that they had never heard of the band and were very nervous. 'Trust me' was all I could say. Well you can guess the rest: a monstrous sell-out. I had stuck a support band on to appease the Rag brigade and help fulfill the criteria of Rag Ball, the good time band, Mungo Jerry.

That evening I was standing at the back of the hall talking to Debbie Harry when the doors were opened. We were almost knocked off our feet by hoards of desperate young lads, crashing into and past us in their eagerness to get to the front of the stage. I said to Debbie: "Do you realise they're barging us over to get to the front to have a better view of you?"

"Yeah, funny, if only they knew," she laughed.

For some bizarre reason Blondie, like several other new, mainstream bands, were labelled as punk. After the show I had to attempt to reassure a confused Debbie Harry, who was towelling off pints of 'gob'.

"Honest, spitting on you means they really like you!"

"Fucking hell, what would they do if they thought I was crap?!"

Barry Lucas

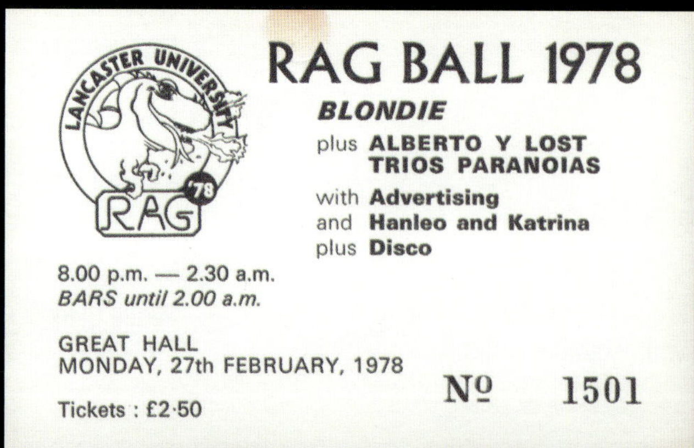

LANCASTER
RAG BALL

BLONDIE

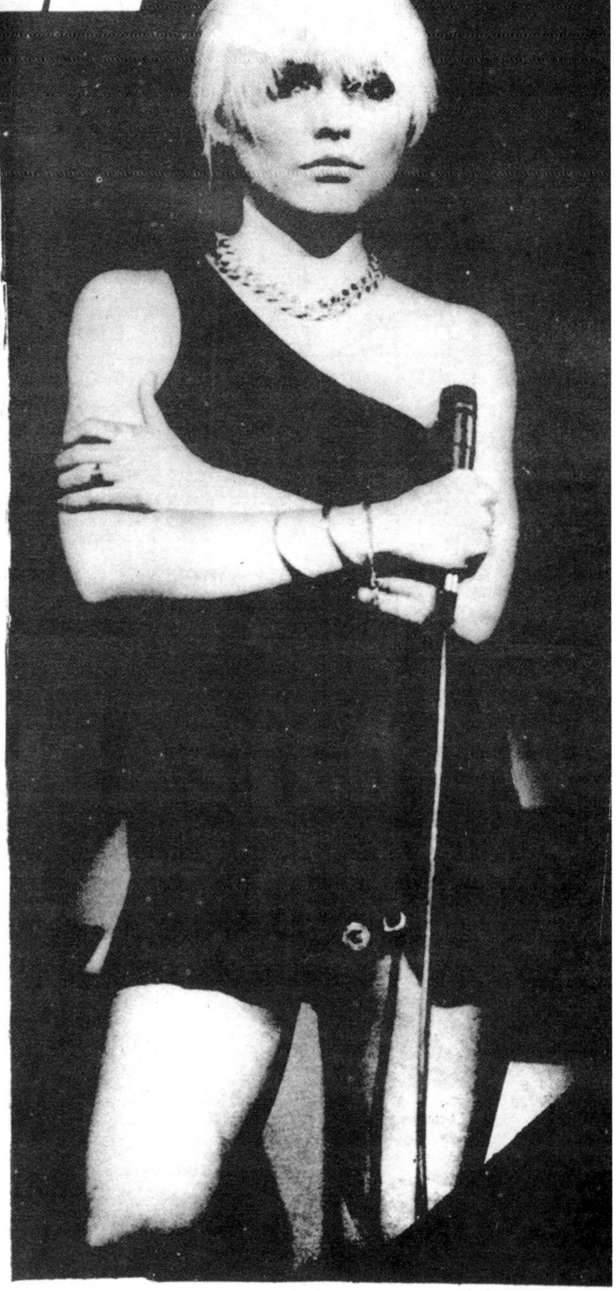

BLONDIE - Have been hailed as the American punk band - but to British audiences that can be a very misleading description, British and American punk are poles apart. Their debut album last year "Blondie" featuring the beautiful Debbie Harry tended to the softer pop side of the market. Her vocals were very reminiscent of The Shangrilas but this 2nd album 'Plastic Letters' plays down that side of their music and concentrates on more complex, powerful musical numbers.

Of course the presence of the classical American blonde beauty of Debbie Harry has meant that when they arrived in London a couple of weeks ago every national paper had full page articles especially The Sun, Mirror and Mail, even The Morecambe and Lancaster Guardian managed half a page. Although this has meant many of the inane "Get 'em off" calls from the front rows Debbie Harry has a great line in put downs. Many a budding young male chauvinist has crawled away from many a hall in Britain and America. A 'nice dumb blonde' proves to be anything but.

MUNGO JERRY with their monstrous hits of a few years ago have developed into a great ball band. Their mixture of jug music and rock 'n' roll has resulted in full date sheets at College, Grad, Summer and Rag Balls. It's dancey good-time music nothing more nothing less.

ADVERTISING: are EMI's 'new white hopes' for 1978 bigtime, supporting Blondie on the whole tour.

HANLEO + KATRINA: a real live circus act featuring knife throwing, snakes, fire eating etc.

MR. WIZARD DISCO: one of the most comprehensive, professional outfits in the N. West.

LATE BAR: 2:00 a.m. drinking.

LATE TRANSPORT: Free buses back to Lancaster and Morecambe at 2:30.

TIMES: 8:00 - 2:30 a.m.

TICKETS: £2.00 from SRC Reception or Ear-Ere Records, Lancaster.

selling fast

Blue Jays Justin Hayward and John Lodge

12 December 1975 Support: Trapeze

During the period of The Moody Blue's three-year hiatus, Justin Hayward and John Lodge recorded and released the album *Blue Jays*, in March 1975. The name *Blue Jays* for the album came from being not only, obviously, the name of a bird but also the fact that the album was put together by the Moody Blues members, all of whose first names began with J; the (Moody) Blue Js.

Originally scheduled for 21 November 1975, this concert was cancelled due to Justin Hayward's laryngitis and rearranged to take place on 12 December 1975.

The live recording of the whole of the Lancaster University performance is available as part of an eleven disc Moody Blues compilation album called *Timeless Flight.*

Lancaster setlist: 'Tuesday Afternoon', 'You And Me', 'My Brother', 'Isn't Life Strange', 'Who Are You Now', 'New Horizon', 'Emily's Song', 'I Dreamed Last Night', 'Nights In White Satin', 'I'm just A Singer', 'Blue Guitar', 'When You Wake Up', 'Question'.

Band lineup:
Justin Hayward – guitar, vocals
John Lodge – bass guitar, vocals
Jim Cockey – violin
Tim Tompkins – cello
Tom Tompkins – viola
Kirk Duncan – piano
Graham Deakin – drums

Support on the night was supplied by the Woverhampton hard rock band **Trapeze.** Formed in 1969, the core members of the band were vocalist John Jones, guitarist/keyboardist Terry Rowley, guitarist Mel Galley, singer/bassist Glenn Hughes, and drummer Dave Holland. In 1973, shortly before this Lancaster appearance, Glenn Hughes left to join Deep Purple. Drummer Dave Holland went on to join Judas Priest in 1979. Trapeze had major musical success in the 1970s and 1980s releasing a total of six studio albums along with a successful 1970 single 'Black Cloud' taken from the album *Medusa*, produced by John Lodge. Trapeze finally disbanded in the eary 1990s.

Blue Jays

The Blue Jays' story started with The Moody Blues – of course it did, I hear you cry, but in the case of Lancaster University it has a significant meaning.

When I booked The Moody Blues for a concert in November 1971 – for £1500, the same price as Pink Floyd and more than for The Who – the band were of legendary status. Several hit albums and one of the defining hit singles of the '60s, 'Nights in White Satin', had established them as major artists of the late '60s and '70s. I can still visualise the tour poster. It was a multi-coloured map of the UK detailing their stops and (thrillingly for me then) naming each local promoter, so I had my name up in lights all over the country! Unfortunately I didn't keep a copy of the poster and generally very little memorabilia from the Great Hall concerts; if only I had known then what I know now.

Tickets went on sale and they flew out. People were coming from Scotland, the North East and the Midlands. It was a major music event. On the day of the show I went down into Lancaster to pick up the ticket stubs and money from the local agents. Arriving back at the Students' Union offices in University House at about 3.30 pm, I found Reception slamming the shutters down and the Union's secretaries fleeing the building to cries of, "Well *I'm* not telling him!" Brave Sue remained though, nervously seated behind her typewriter, smiling, sort of. "What's wrong?" I rather hesitantly asked.

"Well," she said, "we've just had a phone call from London. Tonight's show has been cancelled."

"Ha bloody ha, too busy for jokes, I've got a major sell-out on tonight."

"No you haven't, ring this number."

I rang MAM, The Moody Blues agency. The booker was very apologetic: "John Lodge has been taken ill with gasteroenteritis. We have had to cancel a number of dates and the band cannot perform in Lancaster tonight."

"He can't have!"

"He has and we are sending you the Harley Street certificate. Illness, nothing we can do about it. Contract invalid. Sorry."

Bloody hell, he's sorry! Nothing compared to the state I was in. But there really was nothing I could do about it. I couldn't argue with him, just no point. What to do? Lots of people – especially my wife, Mary, who booked and ran The Platform in Morecambe, a local authority arts/music venue – can't stand the hassle, the pressure when things go wrong. I, on the other hand, love it. I really do get a buzz out of thinking on my feet, in a crisis, sorting out a problem. Here was first problem: I can't stop people travelling to Lancaster so I need to refund them when they arrive; banks closed, phone bank manager, get them to re-open and cash me a cheque for 1500 x £1.25p. I went across Alexandra Square with a big holdall – do you know how heavy 1500 x 5p and 3000 x 10p coins are? No? Very heavy, I can assure you! I had to borrow a porters' trolley from University House.

The second problem; people are coming from miles, I felt I couldn't just say sorry and give them their ticket money back, so I decided to give them a 'free' show of a disco and a live band. I quickly rang Mike Lloyd, an agent in Hanley, to ask if he could get me a dancey, rhythm and blues band for three hours time! He could and he did. Right, now to the Great Hall.

After refunding 1500 tickets and explaining 700 times or more the same story, I could relax. The relief band, ironically called Money, had arrived amidst all the chaos and had set up. Go on lads at 8.00 pm. Play two forty-five minute sets, surrounded by a disco. Thanks.

I then went over to the Lonsdale Bar where John Allen sold me a large bottle of coke and a bottle of Three Pipers Scotch. Back to the balcony in the hall. The evening went surprisingly well and most punters seemed to appreciate the effort we had taken to take as much pain away as possible. A quarter of the way through the whisky and coke, the band came on. Money were good lads, semi-pros from Manchester who did cover versions, and I used them again a year or so later for a rag ball where they appeared with The Tremeloes. But nobody had told them why they were here at such short notice. Oh the irony – and I couldn't make this up – when the first number they played was … yes you guessed it, 'Nights in White Satin'! The audience just stood there: were they taking the piss? Then the booing started, then the throwing of plastic glasses. I sent someone on stage to explain the audience's reaction to the band. Big apologies. Then into a Moodie-free set and everybody had as good a time as they could, considering. I finished the bottle of scotch. Absolutely blotto, I invited the band to crash at my flat in Dallas Road. We had to stop twice, crossing the park, for me to be sick in the bushes. I was so ill the next morning, but I had a five-a-side football match in the gym – not a good idea. To this day, if I smell Three Pipers Whisky, I involuntarily retch.

The Blue Jays were a band formed during The Moody Blue's three-year hiatus, by Justin Hayward and John Lodge. But alas it never really had the same kudos in the public's mind. Here we were, four years on from The Moody Blues cancellation, and history was to repeat itself.

The Lancaster date was scheduled for November 1975 and again cancelled at short notice. This time Justin Hayward was suffering from laryngitis. Happily a date was rescheduled for December.

The show did reasonable business but wasn't a total sell-out. However, that night, at about 8.30 pm a limo drew up outside the Great Hall and out got John Conteh, the then world light heavy-weight champion, with several of his brothers. They had just been involved in an investigation into an armed robbery. Unfortunately Jeremy Oppenheim, the sabbatical editor of *SCAN*, didn't know this. Jeremy knew nothing of sport; he was a great guy, a good friend, but if it came to a fight my money would be on the wet paper bag! He said that he didn't care who they were, they were not coming in without tickets and as they didn't want to pay Jeremy was going to stand his ground. I had to pull him away and quietly explain that if he wanted to take them on he would be on his own. They got in!

At the end of a heavy night I arrived home and poured a drink, settling down to watch a movie in bed. Around 1.00 am the phone rang; it was Geoff Campbell from the Great Hall asking if I could get back there ASAP as Jack Nicholson, the senior porter, was fighting with the road crew. Bloody hell, where was John Conteh when you needed him? I arrived back at the hall just in time to see Jack boot a box of Blue Jays programmes out of the porters' lodge, scattering them across the foyer. It wasn't the roadies but the merchandising crew that Jack was after. All his Second World War submariner's skills had come to the fore. He might have been forty years older than them but he'd fought in the war. After half an hour I had calmed him down, reminded him that they were young lads, footloose and fancy free on tour – a bit like him and his mates away in the war. Did they never do anything stupid? Jack conceded and he drank the pint I'd got him from the dressing room. I could now go back to bed but no Sky pause or catch up in those days. I'd missed my film.

Barry Lucas

The Bluebells

4 October 1985 Support: The Tempest

Following their support slot for Haircut 100 in 1982, Scottish indie band The Bluebells were back in the Great Hall for one of the last university concerts.

The band were active between 1981 and 1985, enjoying three Top 40 UK hits and releasing one studio album, *Sisters*. Their best known hit single was 'Young at Heart' which reached No. 8 in the UK Singles Chart on its original release in 1984. 1993 unexpectedly saw the single achieve the No. 1 slot in the UK Singles Chart following the use of the track in a TV advert for Volkswagen cars.

The Tempest were a 1980s acoustic pop band from Merseyside signed to Magnet Records and were produced by Glenn Tilbrook of Squeeze.

The Blues Band

5 October 1980 Support unknown

Paul Jones, former lead vocalist and harmonica player with Manfred Mann, formed his own outfit in 1979 along with vocalist and slide guitarist Dave Kelly. Kelly had formerly played with the John Dummer Blues Band, Howlin' Wolf and John Lee Hooker among others. Also in the band's lineup at Lancaster were former Manfred Mann bassist Gary Fletcher, guitarist Tom McGuinness and drummer Hughie Flint, the two having previously been the mainstay of the band, McGuinness Flint.

The band arrived at the university to promote the release of their first album, *The Official Blues Band Bootleg Album.*

More recent albums releases for the band include *Back For More, Brassed Up, Fat City* and *Thank You Brother Ray*, the last being a set of cover versions of Ray Charles songs, recorded as a tribute.

After a brief break-up in 1983, The Blues Band are now in their thirty-seventh year and still performing across Europe with the same lineup, apart from Rob Townsend, who replaced Hughie Flint on drums in 1982.

Bob Marley and The Wailers

28 April 1973 **Catch a Fire Tour**

The legendary Jamaican singer/songwriter, guitarist and activist Bob Marley was the most widely known writer and performer of reggae music and more specifically roots reggae, to emerge from Jamaica.

The Wailers, with Bob Marley, were formed in 1963 and after recording extensively in Jamaica the band were signed to Island Records, which issued its label debut album, *Catch a Fire*, in April 1973, quickly followed by *Burnin'* in October of the same year.

The Wailers arrived in the UK in the spring to embark on a twenty-eight date tour promoting the album, *Catch a Fire*, Lancaster University being the first date following a warm-up gig in Nottingham the night before.

For the sake of accuracy, this was a performance by The Wailers featuring Bob Marley. 'Bob Marley and The Wailers' came into existence in 1974 following the departure of Peter Tosh and Bunny Wailer.

The band appeared very late in the evening following a Great Hall disco and by the time the band took to the stage a large portion of the crowd had drifted away with only a lucky few remaining to unwittingly witness an historic Great Hall concert.

Band lineup:
Bob Marley – vocals, rhythm guitar
Peter Tosh – vocals, lead guitar
Bunny Wailer – vocals, percussion
Aston Barrett – bass
Carlton Barrett – drums
Earl 'Wya' Lindo – keyboards

Later that same year The Wailers were to return to the UK for an ill-fated tour and scheduled to include another date at Lancaster University to promote the October 1973 release of the album *Burnin'*.

Barry expands on this in his piece on the next page.

The release of the album *Exodus* in 1977, quickly established Bob Marley's worldwide reputation and he became one of the world's best-selling artists of all time, with sales of more than seventy-five million albums and singles.

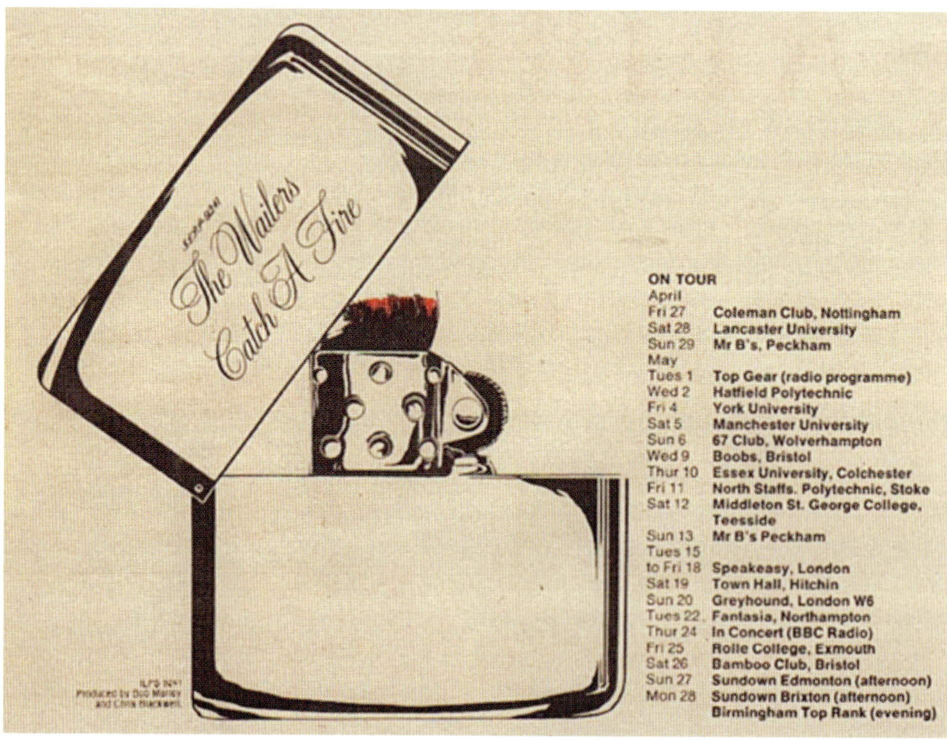

Bob Marley and The Wailers

For a few hundred people this was a special night, a unique moment in rock 'n' roll history and they could say that they were there.

Throughout the '70s I had a good understanding with Island Artists. Robb Winn, who booked The Who for us in 1970, had moved from the small agency in Hull (McCloud Holden) to Island Artists and we had formed a close business relationship, but we also became good friends. Island spent several years trying to persuade me to leave Lancaster and join them. They even left an empty desk in their offices which they said was mine every time I went down to London, but I saw what working in London did to people and I didn't want to become like that. Anyway Robb got me some excellent acts and occasionally I had to do him a favour in return.

This was one of those favours. He phoned me to ask if I would put on one of their new acts. Chris Blackwell, owner of Island Records, had signed this Jamaican reggae band and was certain they would be massive.

"A reggae act? Robb, no one pays to see a reggae act. Sure, they'll dance to the music in a disco, but they wouldn't buy an album or a ticket," I said. Not only were they unheard of, I would have to take the first real date on the tour (although they were playing a warm-up at the Coleman club in Nottingham on the way), so even if they were good, word would not have got out.

Robb said that I wouldn't have to pay a fee, only some petrol and hotel rooms. I explained to Robb that the only way I'd get a crowd would be to put on a disco in the Great Hall and stick the band on after – pay for a disco, 50p, and get a band for free. So that is how Bob Marley and the Wailers came to play Lancaster University.

We managed to get about 1000 to the disco and at midnight I went onto the stage to explain to everybody that there was now a band coming on whom they won't have heard of, but honestly, please stay, as they will be stars some day. I pleaded and about 600 stayed to see the first major date in the UK of Bob Marley.

I had sent a steward to get the band on stage. He had disappeared in a fog of sweet smelling, blue smoke, so I sent another and finally a third, who returned, grinning inanely, with the band and the missing, floating stewards.

"Ladies and Gentlemen, Bob Marley and the Wailers! Thank you!"

A year later Robb phoned me again asking if I would like a date on the next Bob Marley tour – I snapped his hand off – then heard the unbelievable news that the 'support' act would be the American southern rock band, Little Feat – WHAT!

Unfortunately that was the, now legendary, concert that never was. Upon arrival in the UK the tour started chaotically, with Marley's concerts cancelled due to Peter Tosh's food poisoning and further disruption due to heavy snow, which resulted in the early abandonment of the tour in late November '73, including our scheduled date here in Lancaster. A sell-out European Tour as well – Robb had one hell of a time cancelling that one! And Lancaster never did see, what would have been, a truly amazing concert.

Barry Lucas

Bonzo Dog Doo-Dah Band

14 November 1969 Supports: Opel Butterfly I Cleveland Fox

This concert was one of the first in the newly opened 'Central Hall' as it was originally called.

The Bonzo Dog Doo-Dah Band were created in the 1960s by a group of British art students.

The core members of the group for most of the band's career were:
Vivian Stanshall – trumpet, lead vocals
Neil Innes – piano, guitar, lead vocals
Rodney "Rhino" Desborough Slater (saxophone), Roger Ruskin Spear (tenor sax and various contraptions) and Larry "Legs" Smith (drums).

'I'm the Urban Spaceman' produced by Paul McCartney and Gus Dudgeon was a hit for the group in 1968 before they split in 1970 for the first time. Following three splits and subsequent reunions, the Bonzos continue to perform today.

Opal Butterfly were an English psychedelic rock band, from Oxfordshire, active between 1967 and 1970. Interestingly the band featured two future members of Hawkwind, Lemmy and drummer Simon King.

Cleveland Fox were a six-piece band formed in the late 1960s in the Bolton/Atherton area of Lancashire. Described as a soul band, they disbanded in the early 1970s.

Boomtown Rats

18 November 1977		Support: The Bernie Tormé Band
8 December 1978	**Seasonal Turkey Tour Xmas '78**	Support: The Vipers
23 April 1982	**V Deep Tour**	Support: Matt Fretton
8 February 1985	**The Long Grass Tour**	Support: Zerra One

Veterans of four appearances, the Boomtown Rats' 1978 concert holds the record for the largest audience in the Great Hall. They are credited with twelve Top 40 singles and six studio albums.

The members of the original Boomtown Rats lineup were:
Bob Geldof – vocals
Garry Roberts – lead guitar
Johnnie Fingers – keyboards
Pete Briquette – bass
Gerry Cott – rhythm guitar
Simon Crowe – drums

All six members originated from Dún Laoghaire, Ireland. The Boomtown Rats broke up in 1986, but re-formed in 2013, without Johnnie Fingers or Gerry Cott, and continue to tour.

The Bernie Tormé Band were a punk band formed in 1976 and led by the singer, songwriter and rock guitarist from Dublin, Bernie Tormé. Tormé revealed that he secured the supporting band slot with the Boomtown Rats by agreeing to go around London putting up posters advertising the tour. Later in his career, Bernie went on to play lead guitar in Ian Gillan's band, Gillan, and most likely appeared on stage with him for his 1980 Lancaster concert.

The Vipers were an Irish new wave band active in the late 1970s who also toured with The Jam and The Clash. Not to be confused with The Jam's support act for their 1979 appearance, who were The Vapors, of 'Turning Japanese' fame.

Support for The V Deep Tour 1982 may possibly have been **Matt Fretton,** who was probably best known for being a support act for Depeche Mode in the Early 1980s. He had a hit in May 1983 with 'It's So High', which reached No. 50 in the UK Singles Chart, and was performed on Top of the Pops.

Zerra One are another Irish outfit, active between 1982 and 1987. The band were also utilised as openers for U2 and The Cure on various tours.

Buzzcocks

16 March 1978 Supports: The Slits | F Church

A concert with its problems on the night.

The Buzzcocks were formed in Bolton in 1976 and were led by Pete Shelley alongside singer/songwriter Howard Devoto.

The band were a major influence on the Manchester music scene with their best known single 'Ever Fallen in Love (With Someone You Shouldn't've)' peaking at No. 12 in the UK charts of September 1978.

Following the departure of Devoto from the Buzzcocks in February 1977, he appeared again in November 1978 for a concert in the Great Hall with his new band Magazine.

Continuing fights and disturbances during the support acts resulted in the Buzzcocks playing the gig with house lights turned on. Barry Lucas has written more about this gig in his 'Punk' chapter.

The Slits were a female British punk rock/post-punk/ reggae band, formed in London in 1976 and were originally an all-female outfit led by Arianna Forster (aka Ari Up). The lineup also featured Viv Albertine (guitars), Tessa Pollit (bass) and Palmolive (drums). Prior to arriving in Lancaster for this gig the band had backed-up The Clash on their 'White Riot' tour in 1977 along with The Buzzcocks. The Slits released a total of four studio albums with the best known probably being their debut album *Cut*, on the Island label. Since the band's first split in 1982, The Slits have had many different lineups but finally dissolved following Aris' death in 2010.

Local Lancaster band, **F Church** were first up on stage that night. F Church had evolved out of The Kassels; Lancaster's first true punk band and were fronted by my old mate from art school, Neil Thompson on vocals. The band on the night also featured China Street bassist Adam Williams on drums with John Elles (guitars), Alan Greenwood (bass) and Steve Normanton (keyboards) completing the lineup. Some month's later F Church's Adam Williams and Steve Normanton moved on, with the band adding Oscar (Chris) Heywood (guitars) and Baz on electric violin and becoming known as The Permanents with John Elles taking up the full time drumming role.

Camel

25 October 1975 Support: Wally

Camel are an English progressive rock band formed in 1971 and for this concert were fronted by the former keyboard player of Van Morrison's Them, Peter Bardens. Completing the lineup were founder members Andy Latimer, Doug Ferguson and Andy Ward.

The concert featured Camel performing their epic masterpiece *The Snow Goose*.

Supporting act **Wally** are a progressive rock band which originated in Harrogate in the early 1970s. They have been described as having a sound somewhere between Dire Straits and Pink Floyd.

Wally were led by singer-songwriter and founder Roy Webber and in 1973, after playing the northern UK pub rock circuit, the group entered a new act competition organised by the music paper *Melody Maker*. The band made it to the finals held at London's Roundhouse Theatre, but did not win. They did however catch the eye of one of the judges, "Whispering" Bob Harris, legendary DJ of The Old Grey Whistle Test. The runners-up prize was the opportunity to record a session for Harris's BBC radio show *The Monday Program*. Taking Wally under his wing, Harris secured a recording contract with Atlantic Records. "I really liked them," recalls Bob Harris. "I liked the swirling sound they made ... acoustic guitar, electric guitar, fiddle, Fender Rhodes piano and pedal steel guitar. I liked their harmonies, the way their voices matched. I liked their influences ... David Crosby, Jackson Browne and Neil Young. But most of all I liked Roy Webber's songs."

Many a concert hall in the 1970s echoed to random shouts from the audience of "Wally" during the wait for the bands to appear on stage. The shouting on this evening was particularly loud and frequent!

A couple of stories exist about the origins of the shouting of "Wally" at concerts. One being that it started at the Reading Festival in 1972 with a guy looking for his lost dog and shouting his name with the crowd joining in; the other that it originated from the 1970 Isle of Wight Festival with someone shouting trying to locate his lost mate in the crowd.

In 2009, the surviving members of Wally's original line-up (Roy Webber, Paul Middleton, Pete Sage, Roger Narraway and Nick Glennie-Smith, augmented by Frank Mizen on pedal steel and Will Jackson on guitar) reunited and performed to a sell-out crowd in their hometown of Harrogate.

Wally continue to tour and record.

Top: Camel, bottom: Wally, both ©David Bradbury

Caravan

23 April 1976 Support: Stars

Caravan are a Psychedelic jazz rock fusion outfit formed in 1968 in Canterbury, Kent, and were an important band on the Canterbury scene alongside other bands such as Soft Machine, Gong, and Hatfield and The North.

Caravan are veterans of fourteen studio albums, the most critically acclaimed being *In The Land of Grey and Pink*, released in 1971. Their seventh album, *Blind Dog at St Dunstan's*, was released on the day of this Great Hall concert.

Caravan remain active on the live scene still fronted by the original founder member Pye Hastings.

During a concert in 1969 at The Marquee Club, London, Pye Hastings was dramatically electrocuted on stage, although thankfully he went on to make a full recovery.

Stars were an Australian country and rock band from Adelaide that were active between 1975 and 1979.

The Chieftains

18 November 1978 Support unknown
16 November 1982 Support unknown

The Chieftains, formed in 1962, have been around for over fifty years, entertaining audiences with their mainly instrumental Irish sounds. The group released a string of successful records throughout the 1970s and 1980s and their work with Van Morrison in 1988 resulted in the critically acclaimed album *Irish Heartbeat*.

Still at the helm is founder Paddy Moloney, the uillean piper from Dublin. Two tracks by The Chieftains feature on the Martin Scorsese film *Gangs of New York*.

Chuck Berry

22 March 1972 Support: The Roy Young Band

The legend and pioneer of rock music that is Chuck Berry visited Lancaster on one of only five UK dates as his famous hit 'My Ding-a-Ling' was on its way to the No. 1 slot in the UK Singles Chart of 1972. Originally written in 1952 by David Bartholomew, it was Chuck Berry's only No. 1, both in the UK and the US.

Berry penned classic hits such as, 'Roll Over Beethoven', 'Sweet Little Sixteen' and 'Johnny B Goode'. Berry also wrote the hit 'You Never Can Tell' which featured in the movie Pulp Fiction, with John Travolta and Uma Thurman dancing to the song at Jack Rabbit Slims restaurant.

Despite his advancing years, he continued playing one-night concerts and embarked on a European tour in 2008 at the age of 82.

John Lennon famously said "If you tried to give rock and roll another name, you might call it Chuck Berry."

Chuck berry died in March 2017 aged 90.

Roy Young is a British rock and roll singer and keyboard player who recorded with David Bowie on his *Young Americans* and *Low* albums. Active since 1958 he has toured with the likes of Cliff Richard and The Shadows, Ian Hunter and Mick Ronson. He formed The Roy Young Band in 1969 and in 2006 released an album entitled *Still Young*.

Chuck Berry

Over the years Lancaster played host to several legends of the music business, names that have gone down in history, but arguably none as big as Chuck Berry. He had just had his only British chart success with the appalling, 'My Ding-a-Ling' (just compare it to his back catalogue) and he was coming to the UK to play just five dates – one of which was to be at Lancaster. Historic – definitely one to say you were there, one to say I saw that man live to your grandchildren. A sell-out then? No! Inexplicably Lancaster again had one of those nights, about nine hundred and fifty people with less than half the tickets sold. Why? Don't ask me, I've no idea. Suggestions on a postcard please.

Ripped off by record companies and promoters, even gaoled by a racist American Southern State legal system, Chuck Berry's history was such that he was never going to trust anybody again at his age. A hit record meant that he could cash in at last, even in his advanced years. At £1500, the fee was high enough in those days, but I had to lodge £750 before he would leave the shores of the USA and agree to give him the balance, in cash in his hand, before he went on stage. Even if I hadn't understood the reasons (which I did) I would have agreed. If you can't get Elvis you get, arguably, the next most influential figure in modern pop music, don't you?

Unfortunately, the tour was just that, a chance to earn some swift bucks. We had the first date so when he landed at Heathrow he was driven in luxury straight up to Lancaster. The backing musicians were just a cheap rock 'n' roll band of young lads from London. One minute they are playing in London pubs, the next they are preparing to play with one of the legends of rock music. They stood nervously in the dressing room awaiting the arrival of what must have been their hero, a rock 'n' roll god. He got out of his limo at the back of the Great Hall, walked up the corridor, took the cash off me and went into the dressing room, saying "Hi, let's go!"

"But what's the set order?" they asked.

"You know my songs, I'll start, you follow, now let's go."

The guys slowly followed him out of the dressing room. I must say, I felt so sorry for them. Their big moment, their moment in the sun – how would it go now? Well you can probably guess. Maybe the missing audience already knew something I didn't, but at least I can tell my grandchildren I saw that guitarist live at Lancaster.

Barry Lucas

The Clash

23 January 1980 **16 Tons Tour Europe** Supports: Mikey Dread I Interference

The Clash released the album *London Calling* in December 1979 and played the Great Hall in January 1980 in support of the album with the classic lineup:
Joe Strummer – lead vocals, rhythm guitar
Mick Jones – lead guitar, lead vocals
Paul Simonon – bass guitar, vocals
Nicky 'Topper' Headon – drums

London calling was awarded *Rolling Stone* magazine's best album of the eighties and peaked at No. 9 in the UK Albums Chart.

The Clash were formed in 1976 and originally included Keith Levene on guitars, who was fired soon after their formation and went on to form Public Image Ltd with John Lydon in 1978. After releasing six studio albums, The Clash disbanded in early 1986. Johnny Green, The Clash's long time road manager, is a Lancaster University alumnus.

Lancaster Setlist: 'Clash City Rockers', 'Brand New Cadillac', 'Safe European Home', 'Jimmy Jazz', 'London Calling', 'The Guns of Brixton', 'Train in Vain', 'Protex Blue', 'Koka Kola', 'I Fought the Law', '(White Man) In Hammersmith Palais', 'Bankrobber', 'Clampdown', 'Wrong 'em Boyo', 'Stay Free', 'Police and Thieves', 'Capital Radio', 'Janie Jones', 'Complete Control', 'Armagideon Time', 'English Civil War', 'Garageland', 'Tommy Gun', 'London's Burning'.

Michael George Campbell aka **'Mikey Dread'** was a Jamaican singer, producer and broadcaster who became great friends with The Clash and was involved in producing the band's single 'Bankrobber'. Mikey also performed on a number of tracks on the Clash's 1980 album, *Sandinista!*

First up on stage that night were local Lancaster four piece punk outfit **Interference**. The band was fronted by vocalist Jed Heggerty.

©Geoff Campbell

Clash sound check ©Geoff Campbell

Cliff Richard

Early 1972 Support unknown

An eventful concert for Cliff Richard, 'The Peter Pan of Pop', at Lancaster University, resulting in disruption due to protests by gay rights demonstrators.

Cliff Richard is the most successful British male solo artist of all time. He also has the distinction of being the only artist to have achieved UK No. 1 singles throughout five consecutive decades, in the 1950s, 1960s, 1970s, 1980s and 1990s.

He was made an OBE in 1980 and was knighted in 1995.

Cliff Richard

1970s, Cliff at Lancaster University, the home of rock 'n' roll in North West England – doesn't sound quite right does it? But it happened, and how …

Of course even I would not have been brave enough to book Cliff into Lancaster University in the 1970s. The booking was arranged by an organisation called Nationwide Festival of Light, a Christian movement which was campaigning against the Permissive Society. As the date drew closer, the University authorities advised the organisers to contact me and use the Students' Union's expertise to help stage the show. I readily agreed; after all Cliff was (is), whatever you think of him artistically, a legend.

The show date approached and I became aware of a problem: the Gay Liberation Front was planning to organise a major demonstration during Cliff's performance. They had obtained a block of tickets and were to attend the actual show in force. I doubled my stewards but I knew we were going to have problems. The concert was to be an acoustic set, with a talk element, it couldn't drown out a section of the audience determined to disrupt like an amplified, band-driven set, could.

The concert was a seated sell-out, obviously, but artistically it was a disaster. The GLF came in full drag to demand that Cliff 'came out'. It destroyed the show, without a battle which would devastate the evening; I couldn't control that element of the audience.

At the end of the show I had a meeting in the dressing room with Cliff. At this point in the story I must say that he is one of the nicest, most genuine, people I have ever met in the music business. I still think there is a painting in the attic though – he looked like a teenager! He was clearly upset about the destruction of the evening which was about his Christian beliefs and how they governed his life. He said that he would like to meet the leading figures in the GLF, but not now, just after the show, as it was too raw. He asked me to ask them if they would come back next week to meet him to discuss their issues. I was impressed.

They agreed and the following week Cliff arrived, in a very flash sports car, at The Chaplaincy Centre and met with the representatives of the GLF. What was discussed is confidential and I have to respect that. All I can say is that Cliff Richard is a very impressive human being and when I am asked about who were the nicest stars I ever met, he is among the first I mention.

Barry Lucas

CLIMAX
BLUES BAND
+ THE JO ANN KELLY BAND
7.30PM FRIDAY 15 OCTOBER. UNIVERSITY OF LANCASTER. TICKETS: £1.00

John Angus

Climax Blues Band

15 October 1976	Support: Jo Anne Kelly
5 May 1978	Support: Dire Straits
30 January 1982	Support: The Look

Climax Blues Band are a British band formed in Stafford in 1968 and were originally called Climax Chicago Blues Band. In 1972, due to pressure from an American band called Chicago Transit Authority, the group dropped the Chicago tag.

With seventeen studio albums to their name and a 1976 No. 10 UK chart hit with 'Couldn't Get It Right', they were a popular draw for the Great Hall. The band continues to tour.

Jo Anne Kelly was an English blues guitarist and singer. During her career she worked with Tony McPhee of The Groundhogs and The John Dummer Band.

Dire Straits were a treat for anyone lucky enough to have emerged from the bar area and get their money's worth on the night. The set would have featured tracks from their debut album *Dire Straits*, released in October 1978. The album produced the hit single 'Sultans of Swing', which reached No. 8 on the UK Singles Chart.

Writing his concert review in *SCAN* newspaper, Mick Walsh pointed out that *Melody Maker* had tipped Dire Straits as one to watch in '78, "So don't be surprised if they turn up on the rock 'n' roll scrapheap in a couple of years, alongside previous *MM* favourites such as Deaf School, Staa Max etc"

The Look are a UK pop band who had a No. 6 hit single in the UK Singles Chart in 1981 with 'I Am The Beat'. The band are still performing and touring.

Climax Blues Band

It may come as a surprise to some readers but Climax were a big band around this time. They had had a little success in the UK as Climax Chicago Blues Band when they went to the States, getting rave reviews there and Canada, and enjoying chart success when their single 'Couldn't Get It Right' reached No. 3 in *Billboard*. This Great Hall show had an audience of approximately 1500 but those that had tickets will still be kicking themselves if they arrived late or stayed in the bar and missed the £50 support act – Dire Straits.

However, there are a couple of other stories about Climax and Lancaster. This was their second appearance. Previously they had headlined the Freshers' Ball. Don't ask me why but for some reason I hadn't been able to use the Great Hall that particular Freshers' Week, so the end of the week extravaganza was held in the Lower Ashton Hall Lancaster. Climax were headlining, along with two or three other bands whose names escape me now, and Bernard Manning – I know, but it seemed like a good idea for a Ball (?) at the time!

In those days bands arrived around six o'clock in a transit van with a couple of roadies, got the gear in, set up the PA, sound checked and were ready to play by 7.30 pm. I hold my hand up. I didn't read the contract properly where the rider did say 12.00 noon get in and three humpers for the gear. I was living in Dallas Road at the time and wandered casually down at 6.00 pm. I was met by an irate band. I hadn't bothered to ask the Beadle to unlock the Town Hall or to arrange for any humpers. "Where's the fucking social sec.?" the band demanded, ranting about being stood around for six hours.

Quickly thinking on my feet I said, "Oh, he's a well known prat. Totally disorganised and couldn't organise a piss-up in a brewery. Look, I'm not doing anything, I'll get the hall opened and help you with the gear down those steps."

"Thanks mate, that's great of you, but how can we get our hands on that jerk of a social sec.?"

"Don't know. Would you believe he has been known not to turn up at some gigs and left the treasurer to pay the band?"

"Unfucking believable. What an arse."

"Yes, I agree – I'll get the Beadle sorted out with the keys."

"Thanks mate, there's a beer waiting for you."

"Great, be back soon." Phew. Drank on the band that night. Great show though. But Bernard went down so badly, heckled so mercilessly that he wouldn't play another college gig for ten years.

Now fast forward twenty years. I had a club in Morecambe, The Gardens, and promoted a lot of rock. Climax were on at the 350-capacity venue and I had sold about 150. There was only one member of the original band left, the rest were eager young blues musicians. In the bar at the end of the night we were having a post-gig beer and chat when I asked if he could remember the last time he was playing in this area at the Great Hall. He said he did vaguely. "Do you remember your support act?"

"No, who were they?"

"Dire Straits."

It was priceless to see the looks on his young band members' faces – a 'where did it all go wrong?' moment!

Barry Lucas

Cockney Rebel

19 October 1974 Support: Life

Fronted by the horse-racing pundit Steve Harley, his band Cockney Rebel played the Great Hall shortly before his best-known hit, 'Make Me Smile (Come Up and See Me)', charted at No. 1 in the UK Singles Chart of 1975.

One of Cockney Rebel's first ever gigs was as a support act to The Jeff Beck Group in a concert in London in 1972. Steve Harley and Cockney Rebel are still actively touring, with original band members violinist Barry Wickens and drummer Stuart Elliot.

Not much is known about support act **Life**.

Steve Harley was at the height of his fame but I can safely say that I certainly would not 'come up and see' him and neither could I ever ever envisage me 'making him smile'. When I get those questions –you know, "Who were the nicest artists?", and "Who were the most unpleasant?" – Mr Harley springs instantly to mind as an answer. Can you guess to which question?

Barry Lucas

Colosseum

27 November 1970 Supports: Brian Davison's Every Which Way I Anno Domini

Colosseum were founded in 1968 by legendary drummer Jon Hiseman, along with sax player Dick Heckstall-Smith and bass player Tony Reeves. Soon they were joined by Dave Greenslade.

They released three studio albums, including the highly acclaimed double album, *Colosseum Live* in late 1971. Colosseum's lineup for this 1970 concert in the Great Hall included Chris Farlowe (later a member of Atomic Rooster) on vocals and Dave "Clem" Clempson (later of Humble Pie) on guitars.

Soon after the release of *Colosseum Live* the band separated, with Dave Greenslade going on to form his band Greenslade.

Brian "Blinky" Davison was a British drummer and former member of The Nice, who, after their breakup, formed his band **Every Which Way**. The band were short-lived, releasing just the one album. Blinky Davison returned to perform in Lancaster in 1973 with the band Refugee.

Anno Domini were a Northern Irish band who toured Germany with Rory Gallagher and Taste.

Country Joe and the Fish

5 May 1972 Supports: JSD Band I Smith Perkins and Smith

Country Joe and the Fish were an American psychedelic rock band formed in California in1965. The band was fronted by "Country" Joe McDonald and Barry "The Fish" Melton and were best known for their rendition of the song 'Don't Bogart Me'. The band Little Feat also covered the song, the original being written by sixties psychedelic country rockers Fraternity of Man.

Joe's is also well remembered for his song "The "Fish" Cheer/I-Feel-Like-I'm-Fixin'-to-Die Rag", a dark comedy novelty song about the Vietnam War, whose familiar chorus was ("One, two, three, what are we fighting for?"). The track was written in about 20 minutes for an anti-Vietnam War play and performed at the Woodstock festival on the Saturday and the Sunday in August 1969.

The JSD Band were a Scottish-based Celtic and folk rock band, active from 1969–1974.

Brothers Steve and Tim Smith, along with Wayne Perkins, came together in the early 1970s to form **Smith, Perkins and Smith**. They recorded just the one album and toured in England on the same bill with Free, Family, and Vinegar Joe with Robert Palmer. They were to appear later that same year in the Great Hall, as support act to Free. Later in their careers Steve Smith worked alongside Robert Palmer, with brother Tim, going on to work with Lynyrd Skynyrd.

I was a student of the '68 generation. I came to the university in the autumn of that year, the year of student revolts around the world; demonstrations in London, Paris, Mexico, Berlin, Rome, Prague, Brazil, Spain, Poland, China, Havana, Boston, Canada, Carolina, LA, New York, Chicago and Sweden. Many were violent, with a youth movement seemingly dedicated to changing society. As Jim Morrison sang, "They've got the guns but we've got the numbers. Come on we're taking over. We want the world and we want it now!"

One band could, and indeed does, claim to be the one that ended the Vietnam War: Country Joe and the Fish. Their 'Vietnam Song' became the anthem of the anti-war movement:
And it's one, two, three,
What are we fighting for?
Don't ask me, I don't give a damn,
Next stop is Vietnam;
And it's five, six, seven,
Open up the pearly gates,
Well there ain't no time to reason why,
Whoopee! We're all gonna die.

How could I, a revolting student of 1968, not take a date on Country Joe and the Fish when it was offered? However, there is another aspect to this concert's story which was significant. The support act was an American band, 'Smith, Perkins and Smith', who were later to support Free at Lancaster. They were a nice country rock band, featuring two brothers. Good time music, terrific guys.

I had a phone call from the USA asking me to get one of the brothers to call home because it was urgent. When the band had finished their set I relayed the message. In order to phone the States and to give him some privacy I took him to my office in Alexandra Square, where he tragically discovered that his wife had suddenly died.

Sometimes you realise that the music isn't the be all and end all.

Barry Lucas

The Cure

15 November 1980 Support: Tarzan 5

The Cure played the university following the release of their second album, *Seventeen Seconds,* in April 1980.

Formed in Crawley, West Sussex, in 1976, the band was fronted by guitarist, vocalist and principal songwriter, Robert Smith. The Cure were one of the first alternative bands to have chart and commercial success in an era before alternative rock had broken into the mainstream. In 1979 The Cure played as a support band for a UK tour with Siouxsie and The Banshees. Partway through the tour, The Banshees lost their lead guitarist and Smith was invited to stand in for the rest of the tour, playing in both bands on the night.

The Cure are still active, with the band enjoying a European tour in 2016 which ended in three dates at London's Wembley Arena.

Lancaster band lineup:
Robert Smith – vocals, guitar, keyboard
Lol Tolhurst – drums
Simon Gallup – bass
Matthieu Hartley – keyboards

Tarzan 5 were an eighties indie dance band.

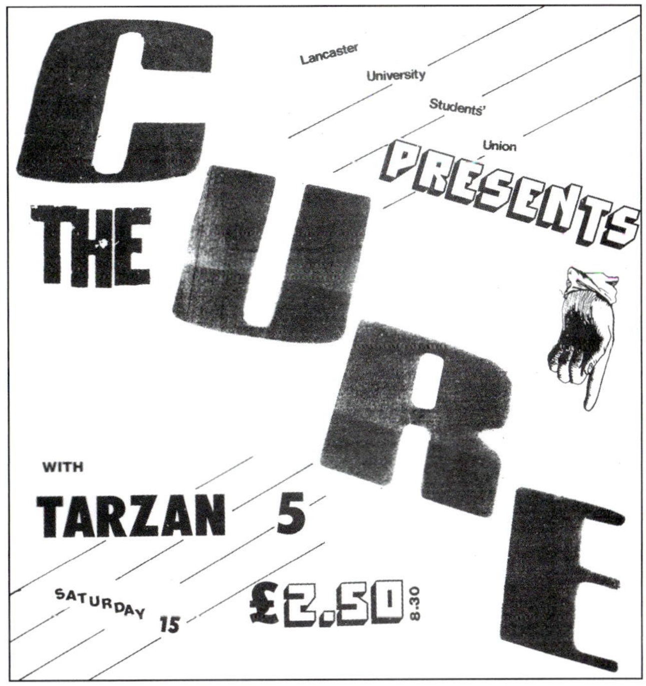

Simon Gallup of The Cure

Curved Air

29 January 1972 — Support: Sunshine
6 December 1975 — Support: possibly Banco or Halfbreed

Curved Air, the highly acclaimed progressive folk rock band visited the university twice with the charismatic Sonja Kristina on lead vocals. Curved Air were one of the first rock groups to use an electric violin, played by Darryl Way.

They released eight studio albums and their single 'Back Street Luv' peaked at No. 4 in the UK Singles Chart of 1971.

In 1974 Curved Air recruited Stewart Copeland as their road manager. Eventually he moved on to drumming for the band in 1975, subsequently leaving to join up with The Police in early 1977.

In 2008 Curved Air were re-formed and continue to record and perform internationally.

Little is known about **Sunshine**, other than that they may have been a folk rock band from Belfast.

Possible support act Banco del Mutuo Soccorso, or **Banco** for short, are an Italian progressive rock band formed in the 1970s in Rome, inspired by the likes of Gentle Giant and Jethro Tull. They are still currently active.

There may also have been a support slot by a band called **Halfbreed**, of which little is known.

Curved Air: The classical prog-rockers are just launching into their party-piece (Summer from Vivaldi's Four Seasons), when their violinist slips and falls flat on his back bringing Summer to an end. The audience with commendable maturity are restrained; the rest of the band thinks it's hilarious.

Maurice Hubbard (Pink Custard Light Show)

A terrific show, with the one and only Sonja Kristina belting out those songs, accompanied by Darryl Way's violin in such a unique style. Towards the end of the set, her furious solos were performed with one stockinged leg braced on the front of stage monitors while eager fans ran their hands up and down.

In the dressing room after the show, the band had done their scheduled encores and were looking forward to relaxing back at the hotel. In came Sonja:

"Let's go back out!"

"No!" was the chorus.

"But lads, I'm having sooo much fun," she smirked.

Barry Lucas

The Damned

27 June 1977 Support: The Adverts

The Damned are an English punk band formed in London in 1976 by lead vocalist Dave Vanian, guitarist Brian James, bassist Captain Sensible and drummer Rat Scabies. Along with the Sex Pistols and The Clash, they helped to spearhead the punk movement in the United Kingdom.

The band appeared for a date at the university between the release of their February 1977 debut album *Damned Damned Damned* and the November 1977 album *Music For Pleasure.*

Punk band **The Adverts** provided the evening's support, returning to Lancaster as headliners in February 1978.

Punk by Barry Lucas

This period of the Great Hall concerts deserves dealing with as a whole rather than as a series of events. The list of punk bands that played the Great Hall is impressive. Punk truly shook up the rather complacent music world in the mid '70s. It was a movement that was sorely needed. The pretentiousness of the major established artists and their failure to tour around the country had made a mockery of rock 'n' roll as the music of working class youth. Tours of twenty to thirty dates, to all corners of the UK, were a thing of the past. Bands ensconced themselves in one of four or five big cities, camping down in an arena and saying to the fans, "If you want to see us, we're here." Fans had to buy ever more expensive tickets, then catch trains, coaches or cars, adding even more expense to the privilege of seeing their favourite artists. These artists were in that position because those very fans, who they now treated with disdain, had bought the tickets for previous shows, together with albums, shirts, merchandise, programmes etc. They had put the bands in their positions of wealth and power and how were they rewarded? With ever increasing indifference by the bands, which often flew in from tax exile or country estates to play live once every year or two.

However, I do have to confess that I wasn't instantly a disciple of punk. Of course I liked and could see the quality of bands like Costello, Blondie, Rats, Stranglers etc., but some of the younger, angrier bands … One evening, after work, I drove down to meet the staff of 'Ear 'Ere Records in the Slip Inn, conveniently next door to the shop. As we all consumed the Mitchells (or for the more discerning, any lager that was available) sat around 'The Barrel', we started discussing the relative merits of this new wave of music, punk. There was Nigel, Roger, Malcolm, Eric, Kevin, myself and a couple of others.

The critique followed this course:

"They can't play their instruments."

"You can't make out the lyrics."

"It's just a wall of noise."

"It'll never last."

Then I suddenly stopped the conversation.

THE DAMNED
+ THE ADVERTS
UNIVERSITY OF LANCASTER
£1.00
7.30PM MON. JUNE 27

John Angus

"Do you know, that's exactly what my mum and dad said about The Beatles and The Stones? When did we become our parents, we're only in our twenties!" Everybody laughed and agreed, little knowing at the time how wrong we were. Except Malcolm, I think he knew exactly what was going on; after all he was the youngest there. A little while later he was to write to Patti Smith via 'Ear 'Ere, suggesting she release the track 'Because The Night' as a single. It became a hit and she had the good grace to write back to 'Ear 'Ere thanking the staff, and Malcolm in particular, for the advice.

Lancaster had, by the end, a good punk pedigree: Stranglers, Damned, Costello, Hazel O'Connor, Ian Dury, The Jam, Siouxsie and the Banshees, Adverts, Buzzcocks, The Clash, The Slits, Boomtown Rats, two Stiff Records tours, Pretenders, Public Image Ltd, Ramones, Ultravox, Undertones, Rezillos, Stiff Little Fingers, Skids, Toyah, Magazine, and who could forget the legendary Dick Envy!

Not a bad list but there is a conspicuous omission. Anybody spot the deliberate mistake? Ask anyone about Punk, even those not born when it happened, and the one band they will all come up with, is missing: The Sex Pistols. Why didn't they ever play the premier college venue in the country? Well, they didn't actually play many live gigs but that's not the story. For the first time I will explain the real reason, or rather I will *confess* the real reason.

University House had decided, in their wisdom, that punk had to be banned from Lancaster University. Paula Richardson, the hall booker and a close friend, had to tell me the news. She was embarrassed, to say the least, but explained that when I completed a hall booking form I had to state the act and describe what type of music they would perform. The information would be sent through to Arthur Gray, a lovely ex-policeman, but sixty-odd years old and a real old-fashioned gentleman. He was to decide on the musical merits of the acts I had booked. It lead to some brilliant moments: I persuaded him that The Stranglers were a country and western band and The Undertones were an Irish folk act etc. You really couldn't make it up, the incompetence of University House was unbelievable.

The Pistols were booked into Lancaster, but as the date approached I was getting increasingly concerned about the growing violence surrounding punk shows in the Great Hall. With the smaller bands went smaller crowds and I still felt able to control the shows, but The Pistols would be taking things to a whole new level. Audiences of eight hundred to a thousand were all the punk bands were generally pulling. I knew The Pistols would sell out and draw many more, I anticipated 2500 plus, many of whom would not just say, "Sold-out, I haven't got a ticket, I'll go home, fifty or sixty miles or so. Thanks, good night!" Increasingly Pistols' shows were degenerating into violence, the stage show orchestrated it and I didn't feel Lancaster needed any help to descend into a riot. Punk shows had become an excuse for football gangs from Barrow, Preston, Blackpool and Lancaster to meet and have a ruck in the Great Hall. Bloody stupid, I know, but the music was an irrelevance where it could be used as an excuse, a background, for a ritualistic battle.

But I didn't want to be the one to call a halt on one of the most important bands, in the most important movement in music, since Elvis. Morally, intellectually, I didn't want the image or the legacy of a censor. I went to see Maggie Gallagher, who was the first female Students' Union President. She was a Trotskyist but we got on extremely well and I liked and respected her. I showed her the press cuttings of whips, leather, bondage, the 'defilement' of women etc., plus the threat – or as I put it, the promise of violence at a Students' Union gig. She thought that we shouldn't be seen to be supporting this kind of event. I 'reluctantly' agreed.

"Cancel it," she said.

"If you're sure," I said.

If you are reading this, sorry Maggie, I conned you, but for the best of reasons.

The Buzzcocks were a band I loved. I had travelled to Blackpool to watch them in a small club/bar – I was a real fan. But at Lancaster the concert became problematic. The violence, the mayhem, it was totally out of control during the support acts. The Buzzcocks got on stage but I had to put on the house lights midway through their first number, with the remainder of their set played in full illumination. Let me show you how silly and dangerous, it got. One of my stewards, from the left hand stage fire doors, dragged a young lad into the porters' lodge. He was antagonised and holding a steel bar, "This prat was laying into people with this and tried to belt me."

I told the lad that I was going to call his mother to come and get him. He just broke down sobbing, "Don't tell my mum, she'll kill me." I missed my calling. I should have been an interrogator at Guantanamo Bay.

Seriously though, the Buzzcocks was the end. I would not put on any more punk shows, it was too dangerous.

I knew that the next weekend Preston Polytechnic had The Vibrators on. Out of professional courtesy I phoned the Entertainments Manager (I had been on the interviewing panel, creating that particular professional post at Preston

Polytechnic in the past). I explained what had happened at Lancaster over several months and my decision to cancel all future shows. I advised her to cancel her show next weekend. She told me that she felt she could handle it. I said that that is what I thought, but it was getting too dangerous. However, she felt confident in her, and her staff's ability, to handle any situation. I was sadly, so tragically, proved right. The concert resulted in the death of one person and serious injuries to three others, being reported in the press the next day with the headline 'RIOT AT PRESTON GIG'.

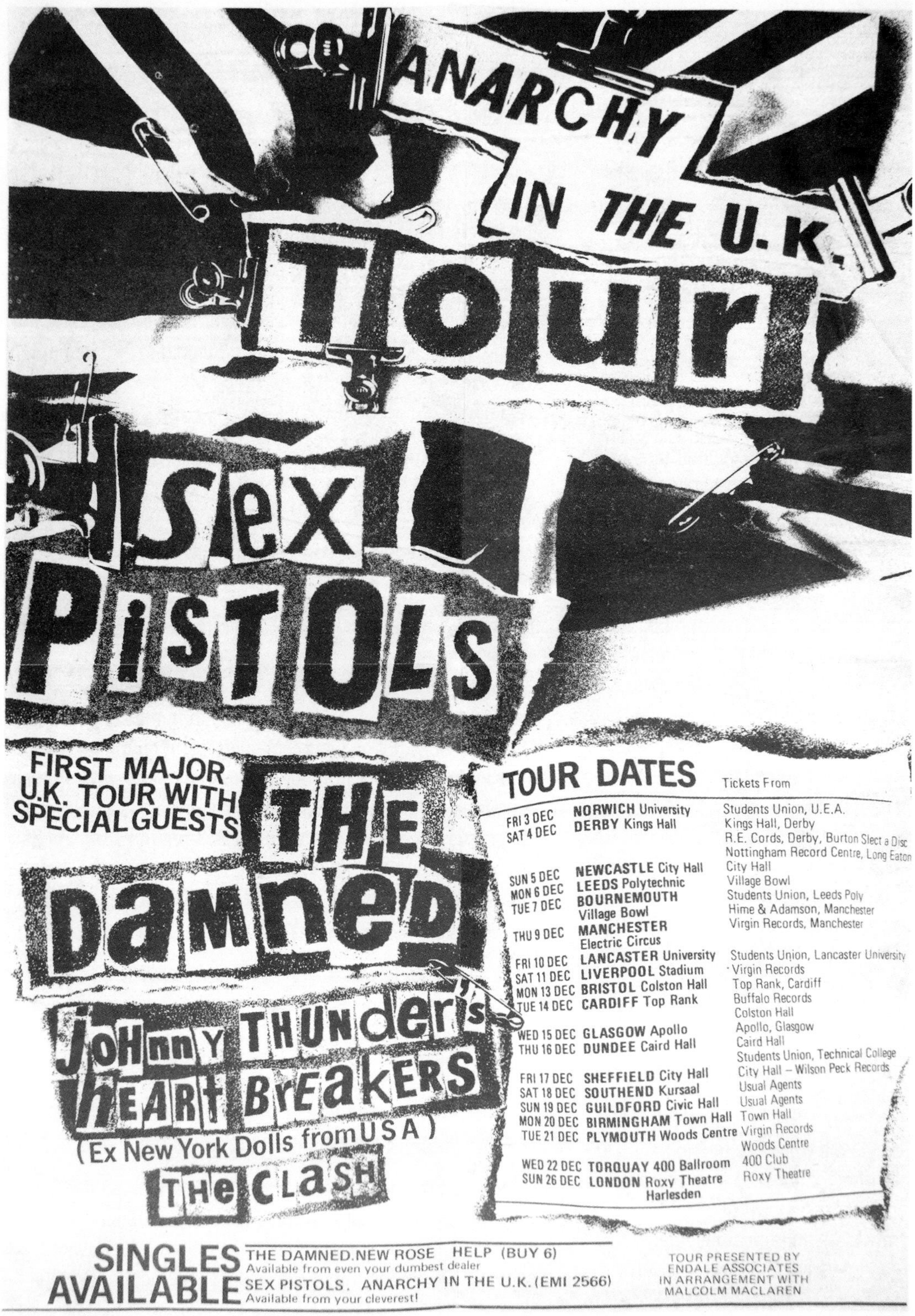

Darts

26 February 1979 — **Rag Ball Concert** Supports: Dave Berry and The Cruisers | The Late Show

20 February 1982 — Support: Weapon of Peace

Doo-wap revival band Darts are a nine piece band assembled by lead singer Den Hegarty in 1976. They had a string of chart successes in the late '70s and early '80s, the best known being 'The Boy From New York City' and 'Duke of Earl'.

In 1981, Hegarty became a television presenter, including being part of the team fronting the children's programme *Tiswas*.

The band re-formed in 2006 for occasional appearances which consistently sell out.

Dave Berry from Sheffield is a 1960s pop singer who was popular in Belgium and The Netherlands. Berry was noted for writing the song 'The Crying Game', which was covered by Boy George and was the soundtrack of the film of the same name.

Little is known about **The Late Show**.

Weapon of Peace, the reggae band from Wolverhampton, were the unusual undercard to Darts in 1982.

This turned out to be a nightmare of a show. I had forgotten all about this particular evening – I think that I had somehow wiped it from my memory for self-preservation. But unfortunately Maurice Hubbard, of Pink Custard Light Show fame, reminded me all about the evening and so it all came flooding back, I'm shuddering as I write this even now, 38 years later.

The event was a Rag Ball, which meant that the Rag Committee wanted a variety of acts and more importantly, a late bar. Darts were a very successful, popular band at the time and were on a conventional, city hall type, tour. They did not want to be going on to half-pissed students at 12.30 at night, playing a set and leaving the venue around 2.00 am. Their road crew certainly were not looking forward to a get-out at that time, meaning that they wouldn't be hitting the road until something like 4.00 am. So obviously they refused to go on as the headline act, that is, closing the show. They insisted on taking the stage at around 9.00 pm and not only that but they also required that their crew took their equipment off stage immediately after they finished their set.

Quite simply, a nightmare. I knew what would happen but actually it was even worse than I could have foreseen. The band finished a great set, left the stage after an encore or two and then their roadies took over to a deafeningly silent Great Hall. Dave Berry was to follow but his only big hit was 'The Crying Game' way back in 1964. I think Maurice describes it best, "They finish their set and the audience watch for nearly an hour, in silence, as their gear is broken down and removed. The road-crew become the main attraction. Dave Berry has to follow this, playing to people, most of whom had probably never heard of him."

You know when people say that they wanted the ground to swallow you up? Well …

Barry Lucas

Dead or Alive

12 May 1984 Support unknown

Liverpool dance group Dead or Alive, fronted by Pete Burns, achieved the first ever No. 1 hit for the production trio of Stock Aitken Waterman in March 1985, with the single 'You Spin Me Round (Like a Record)'.

Following Pete Burns' appearance in 2006 Celebrity Big Brother, the hit from the 1985 *Youthquake* album was re-released and once more reached the top five in the UK Singles Chart. Having got twenty-eight singles and seven studio albums under their belt they completely disbanded in 2011.

Pete Burns died following a sudden cardiac arrest on 23 October 2016 at the age of fifty-seven.

Deaf School

4 December 1976 Support: The Count Bishops

Deaf School assembled their lineup at Liverpool Art School in 1973 and had some interestingly named members:
Bette Bright – vocals
Enrico Cadillac – vocals
Cliff Hanger – guitars
Eric Shark – vocals
Max Ripple – keyboards
Steve "Average" Lindsey – bass guitar
Tim Whittaker – drums

Between 1976 and 1978 the band recorded three albums for the Warner Brothers label, in an art rock style that had its roots in cabaret, moving towards a harder punk rock sound.

Following splits and reunions over the years Deaf School are currently still active, having released the album *Launderette* in 2015.

Pub rockers **The Count Bishops** were formed in 1975 and existed up to 1980, along the way releasing four studio albums and being described as a grimier version of Dr Feelgood.

1977 saw the band playing support to Motorhead on their first tour.

DEAF SCHOOL
plus
Count Bishops
UNIVERSITY OF LANCASTER
7.30pm SATURDAY 4th DECEMBER TICKETS £1.00

John Angus

Deep Purple

23 January 1970 **European Tour** Supports: Farm I Urbane Gorilla

Another early concert in the 'Central Hall' featuring Deep Purple with the classic lineup of:
Ian Gillan – vocals
Ritchie Blackmore – guitars
Jon Lord – keyboards
Roger Glover – bass guitar
Ian Paice – drums

The band performed tracks from the upcoming *In Rock* album.

Possible Lancaster setlist: 'And the Address', 'Kneel and Pray', 'Into the Fire', 'Kentucky Woman', 'Child in Time', 'Mandrake Root', 'Wring That Neck (aka Hard Road)', 'Ritchie's Blues', 'Paint It Black, instrumental', drum solo.

Richard 'Dick' Dixon, currently a County College porter at the university, recalls being unable to gain entry to the concert on the night due to its being a total sell out. "Basically we stayed and listened to the gig outside the Great Hall. It was loud enough to enjoy out there"

In 1972 Deep Purple were recognised in *The Guinness Book of World Records* as the loudest band in the world. A gig at London's Rainbow Theatre registered 117 decibels and rendered three members of the audience unconscious.

Farm, who also supported Procol Harum and Argent at Lancaster University, were a rock band who originated in Aylesbury, Buckinghamshire.

Band members were:
Bill Stallwood – vocals
Nigel Harrison – bass
Mick Barnard – guitars
Paul Hammond – drums
Pete Tyson – sax, flute

Nigel Harrison went on to become Blondie's long-serving bass guitarist, joining them in late 1977.

Mick Barnard, for a brief time, was the guitarist of the band Genesis, following the departure of founding member Anthony Phillips. Barnard was eventually replaced by Steve Hackett.

Originally called Urban Gorilla, this was a Lancaster band that went through various singers and guitarists but were essentially built around steel guitarist Henry Ayrton, sax player Julian Holt and bass player Jeff Dade. Henry was a student at Lancaster University and under the influence of Captain Beefheart, the seed of the band was planted around 1967. At some point later, the band changed their name to **Urbane Gorilla** before disbanding in 1971. Billed as Urban Gorilla the band also made a Great Hall appearance providing support to Family for their October 1970 Great Hall date.

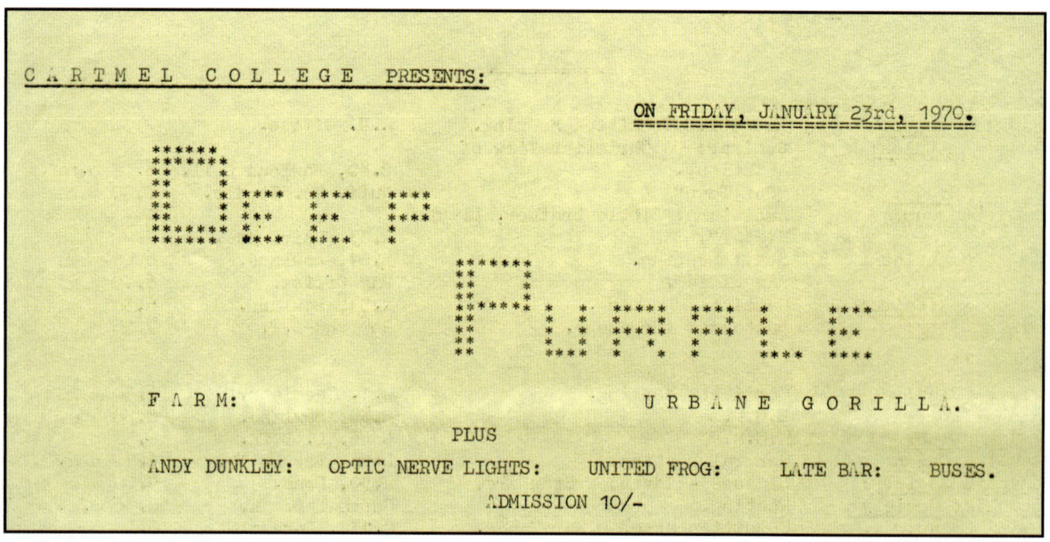
CARTMEL COLLEGE PRESENTS:

ON FRIDAY, JANUARY 23rd, 1970.

DEEP PURPLE

FARM: URBANE GORILLA.

PLUS

ANDY DUNKLEY: OPTIC NERVE LIGHTS: UNITED FROG: LATE BAR: BUSES.

ADMISSION 10/-

Dire Straits

12 December 1980 **The On Location Tour** Support unknown, possibly no support act

Following their 1978 appearance in a support slot for Climax Blues Band, the band revisited Lancaster University for a date on their On Location tour to promote the October 1980 release of the album *Making Movies*.

Band lineup:
Mark Knopfler – guitar, vocals
John Illsley – bass
Pick Withers – drums
Alan Clark – keyboards
Hal Lindes – guitar

Lancaster setlist: 'Once Upon a Time in the West', 'Expresso Love', 'Down to the Waterline', 'Lions', 'Skateaway', 'Romeo and Juliet', 'In the Gallery', 'News', 'Sultans of Swing', 'Les Boys', 'Portobello Belle', 'Angel of Mercy', 'Tunnel of Love', 'Wild West End', 'Where Do You Think You're Going'.

It was during the recording of *Making Movies* that musical differences between the Knopfler brothers surfaced, resulting in the departure of David prior to the tour.

Dire Straits finally broke up in 1995, after releasing a total of six studio albums.

Like many of the bands who appeared in the '70s and early '80s, many colleges could say that they had them on as support acts, as up and coming acts, as breaking headliners. But NO colleges had a list of acts that played there as major international arena and festival headliners. No college, that is, except Lancaster.

Dire Straits had played Lancaster as a £50 support act. But here they were – post 'Sultans of Swing' – world superstars playing a smallish college; something that was unique to Lancaster and which would never be repeated anywhere in the world on the regular basis, it occurred in North West England.

Barry Lucas

©Geoff Campbell

Dr Feelgood

10 October 1975 — Support: GT Moore and The Reggae Guitars
10 December 1979 — Support: Phil Rambow Band

British pub rock band Dr Feelgood were formed in Canvey Island, Essex, by the late Lee Brilleaux, Wilko Johnson, John B. Sparks on bass guitar and John Martin, aka "The Big Figure", on drums.

Dr Feelgood were known primarily for their high energy live performances and both of these uni gigs were no letdown on the night. The set of the 1975 concert would have featured songs from the album *Down by The Jetty*, released in 1974, and the 1975 classic Feelgood album *Malpractice.* Their 1976 album *Stupidity* reached No. 1 in the UK Albums Charts. Shortly afterwards, in March 1977, due to conflicts with Lee Brilleaux, Wilko Johnson was to leave the band and did not appear on stage at their 1979 gig. 1979 also saw the band hit the Top 10 of the UK charts with the single 'Milk and Alcohol'.

A version of the band (featuring none of the original members) continues to tour and record to this day.

GT Moore and The Reggae Guitars were the incarnation of Gerald Thomas Moore, his band sometimes featuring two drummers along with congas and a three-piece brass section. The band featured ex-Gentle Giant drummer Malcolm Mortimore. During his career, GT Moore has performed and recorded with such illustrious artists as Joan Baez, Johnny Nash and Lee 'Scratch' Perry. Undoubtedly one of the greatest guitarists in the world, Gerald Moore died in 2011 aged fifty-eight.

Canadian-born pub rocker **Phil Rambow** emigrated to England in 1973 and immediately formed an outfit called The Winkies, playing as backing band to Brian Eno on his first and only solo tour in early 1974. The Winkies were to disband in 1975, after which Phil Rambow assembled his own Phil Rambow Band. He performed at the tribute concert in 2002 to the late Kirsty MacColl following her accidental death.

Lee Brilleaux 1979 ©Geoff Campbell

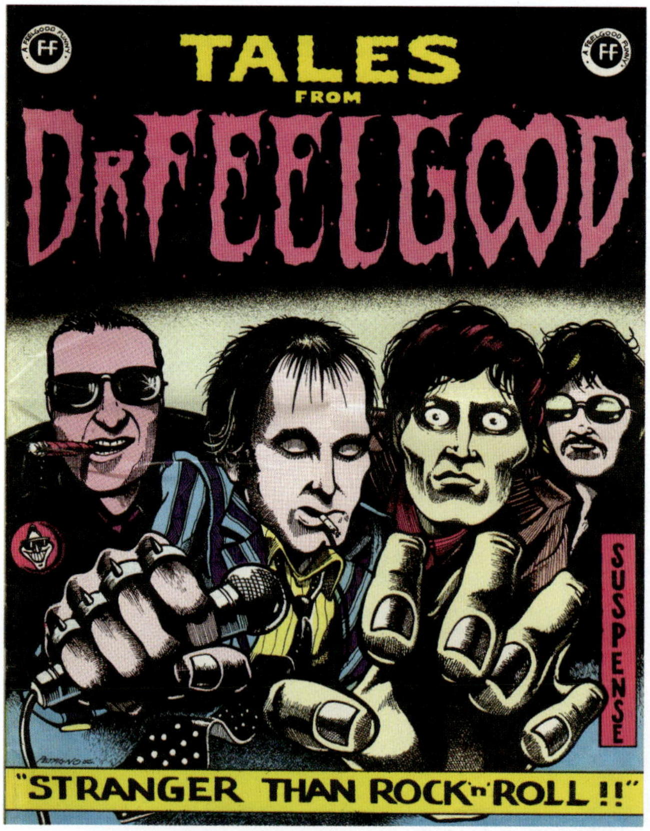

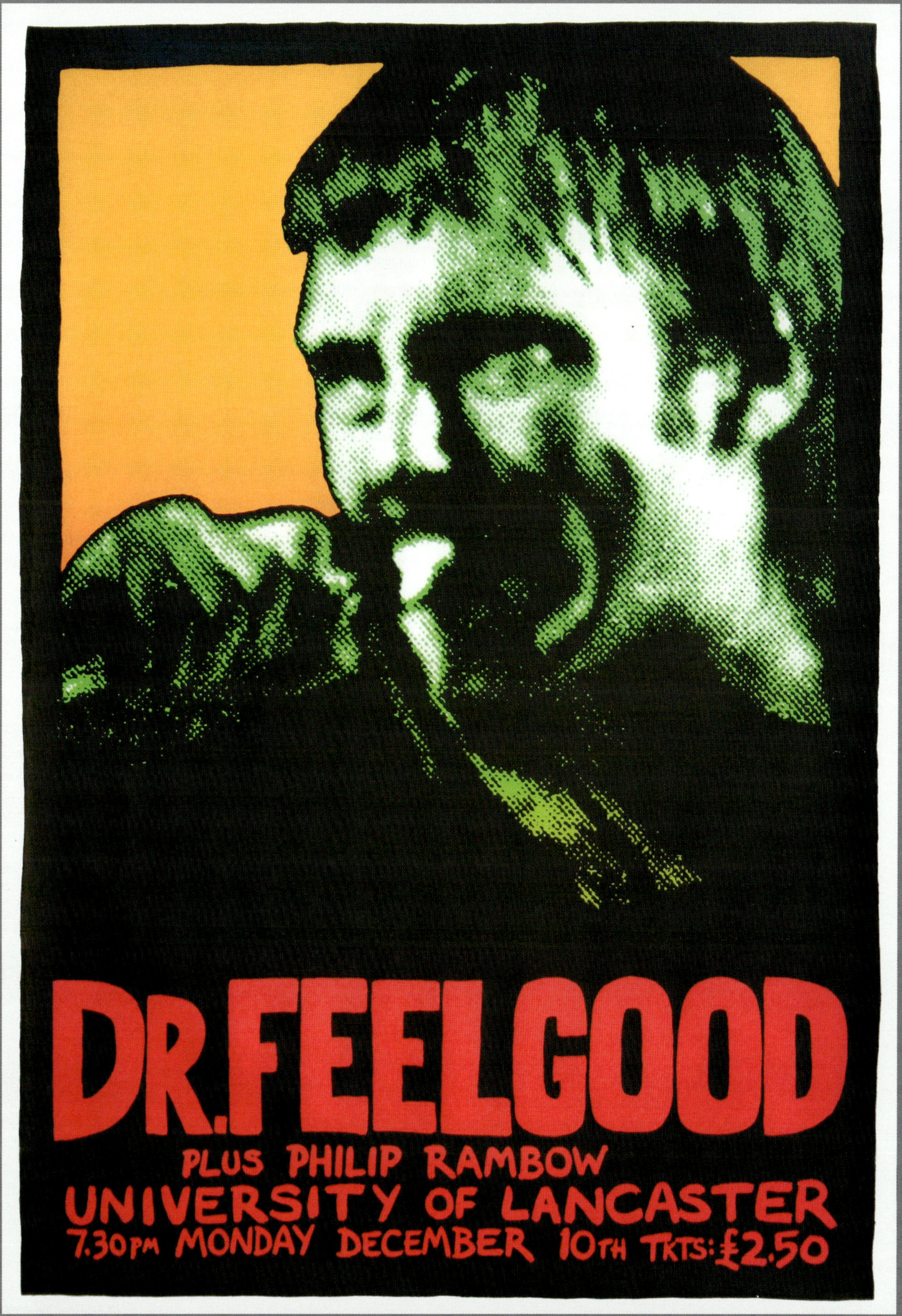
DR.FEELGOOD
PLUS PHILIP RAMBOW
UNIVERSITY OF LANCASTER
7.30PM MONDAY DECEMBER 10TH TKTS: £2.50

John Angus

Echo & The Bunnymen

1 May 1981 — Support: Blue Orchids

21 October 1984 — **Ocean Rain Tour** — Support: The Triffids

Formed in 1978, the original lineup of Liverpool band Echo & The Bunnymen was frontman and vocalist Ian McCulloch, Will Sergeant on guitar and Les Pattinson on bass guitar. The Bunnymen did not feature a drummer but instead used a drum machine. By 1980 the drum machine had been replaced by real-life drummer Pete de Freitas.

Their first Great Hall concert featured songs from the band's second album release, *Heaven Up Here*, which reached No. 10 in the UK Albums Chart.

1984 saw The Bunnymen return for a second concert, this time with four studio albums and ten singles to their name, including 'The Killing Moon' and 'The Back of Love'.

Following a complete split of the band in 1993, McCulloch and Sergeant regrouped with Pattinson in 1997 and returned as Echo & the Bunnymen, having a UK Top 10 hit with 'Nothing Lasts Forever'.

But maybe some things do, as Echo & The Bunnymen are still active today.

Manchester post-punk band **Blue Orchids** were formed by ex-Fall guitarist Martin Bramah in 1979 and are still active today.

The Triffids were an Australian band active from 1978 to 1989 and have been described as Australia's best-loved post-punk group.

Echo & The Bunnymen 1984 ©Geoff Campbell

EDDIE + THE HOT RODS
PLUS:
NO DICE
7.30PM
SAT. OCT. 15TH
£1.50
UNIVERSITY
OF LANCASTER

John Angus

Eddie and The Hot Rods

15 October 1977 Support: No Dice

Hailing from the same neck of the woods as Dr Feelgood, Eddie and The Hotrods were formed in 1975 in Canvey Island, Essex, and were initially called The Rods.

They are best known for their Top 10 hit of 1977 'Do Anything You Wanna Do'.

Still touring and recording today, they originally split up in 1981, but have re-formed several times since, with lead singer Barrie Masters the only constant member.

The Hotrods on this evening featured ex-Kursaal Flyers lead guitarist Graeme Douglas.

January 1976 had previously seen The Hotrods in the Great Hall as guests of The Kursaal Flyers.

No Dice were a four-piece band from North London who released two albums, *No Dice* and *2 Faced.* They toured extensively from 1976 until the early '80s.

Eric Clapton

EC was here. Yes, "Old Slow Hand" actually played a university date as a world superstar, not once, but twice. By now even Leeds could only sit back and wonder, why? How?

Well, in the summer of 1976 Paul Loasby, ironically an ex-Leeds Social Secretary, who was now running Harvey Goldsmith's office, phoned to ask if I could see the sea from Lancaster University. I explained that if you went to the top of Bowland Tower you could. "That'll do," he said. "Do you want Eric Clapton in August? He's doing a traditional seaside resorts tour so I'll tell him Lancaster is a seaside town." I thought, "well it is sort of, but do I want Clapton?" Is the Pope a Catholic? I would have some explaining to do to the returning students – "Er, by the way while you were at home one of the greatest rock stars in the world was here, shame you missed him". But I'd live with that.

I'd had to help Paul with some crew and security for his date in Blackpool, a small seaside resort rivalling Lancaster! Consequently I was well prepared for the staging requirements of the show. Eric Clapton had managed to rid himself of the terrible heroin problem he'd had, but by this time he had replaced it with Courvoisier brandy. It didn't prevent an outstanding show though. In the afternoon he had placed a bet on a horse and I had to send somebody down to the bookies pick up his winnings of £500. He was ecstatic – it was amazing, all that fame and fortune he enjoys and he was over the moon about that £500.

We managed to do another gig with him, this time in term time, luckily for the student population … and me.

However this had an other story. Although Paul Loasby had put several dates from Harvey Goldsmith tours into Lancaster by now, this date was the first that the great man himself, Harvey Goldsmith, had ventured up to the wilds of Lancaster. It was vitally important to me (and Paul) that he was impressed with the show and with the organisation of the venue, so we were both walking on eggshells all night. Sat in the porters' lodge in the Great Hall foyer, Harvey, behind Jack Nicholson's desk (head porter), said how great the show was and then suggested to Paul that they put a night at Lancaster on all their tours. "Great idea, Harvey, I never thought of that," agreed Paul sycophantically. Everything brilliant. Then … In stormed the tour manager, screaming, "The bloody bouncers have nicked Eric's bottle of Southern Comfort!" I just prayed for the ground to swallow me up. My regular three dressing room stewards were a bit, well, you could say they were 'characters', you know, local lads, salt of the earth – that kind of crap. But surely they wouldn't, surely not that … Oh yes. I went theatrically nuts but what would Harvey say? Just, "Sack 'em!" The gig was such a success and Harvey made so much money though, that a little thing like a bottle of whisky was not going to alter his opinion. Phew, close one though.

I didn't sack them and lived to regret it – see Tina Turner.

Then worse(?) was to follow. Geoff Campbell came to see me in the foyer: the humpers wanted a pay rise or they were not going to do the get out. They knew I was vulnerable, Harvey Goldsmith himself being there, and it was a massively important gig, arguably the biggest we had ever staged and it was 11.00 pm. I couldn't find other humpers, the majority of the stewards had left and the road crew wanted to get the gear out and get back to the hotel bar. I was furious but fairly helpless. I pointed out to them that they had done bigger get outs without any complaints, but they were leaving me with no alternative but to give in. "Right," I told them, "I will pay you more, but you will never work a show here again." They had obviously gone away triumphant, but then talked. Geoff returned to say they would do the get out at the usual rates. Once again, phew, I desperately did not want Harvey, back in the hotel, talking about breweries and piss-ups.

Barry Lucas

Hi Paul,

I was interested to read about your book being written about the Lancaster University concerts, a great place for a gig and I saw quite a few there. My name is Mark Thornley.

I worked at a record shop in Blackpool called Music Mania in 1978 for a couple of years when I was seventeen. We were also ticket agents for the concerts and also used to get some stock from 'Ear 'Ere Records in Lancaster and if I remember correctly, Barry Lucas had something to do with them.

I remember meeting him a few times when I used to go with the guy who used to pick up the records.

They would keep promotional stuff for me relating to Eric Clapton as I was a big fan and I still am. One of the best gigs I saw was Clapton in 1980 on the Just One Night tour. I was desperate to meet him after the gig and managed to get myself right outside the door of the dressing room, but could not get in. Maybe Eric was busy with his brandy at the time. But I did speak to him during the gig though!

I was right at the front and having smoked something exotic before the gig was in a fine mood, at a quiet moment I shouted "play Blues Power Eric," to which he replied "already played it mate," and then somebody else shouted back "well play it again then". Great gig and Eric was on top form and looking liked he was having a great time. He inspired me to start playing the guitar when I was fifteen. I also remember having a pint with Phil Mogg of UFO when I saw them just after their sound check. I was in early because I knew the guys on the door and asked him if being the singer in a rock band was all it was cracked up to be, "oh yes" was the answer. It would be wouldn't it!

I also remember Bad Company was a particularly good gig in 1979.

Anyway, hope you don't mind me dropping you a line. Happy memories from those days and I am still playing myself, being fortunate enough to have played some good gigs over the years. Notably supporting Peter Green with his first incarnation of the Splinter Group including the late great Cozy Powell on drums, when I was in a band called The Healers.

All the best

Regards,

Mark.

Eric Clapton and Marcy Levy in 1976

1980 ©Geoff Campbell

ROBERT STIGWOOD ORGANISATION LTD.
IN ASSOCIATION with HARVEY GOLDSMITH

presents at

LANCASTER UNIVERSITY

ERIC CLAPTON

AND HIS BAND

plus

MR. PUGH'S Puppet Theatre

Saturday, 7th August Doors 8 p.m.

TICKETS £2.20 Nº 5738

The Europeans

10 October 1983 — Support: Annabel Lamb

From London, The Europeans were a British new wave group formed in 1981 and disbanded in 1985. They released three albums, two studio and one live, none of which achieved much in terms of chart position. In 1989, their former keyboard player and lead vocalist from Kendal, Cumbria, Steve Hogarth, also known as "h", joined Marillion as their lead vocalist.

Annabel Lamb is an English singer and songwriter. She had a British Top 30 hit in 1983 with her cover version of The Doors song, 'Riders On The Storm', her only hit in the UK Singles Chart. She has released eight albums and is still active, having worked with, in the past, Kiki Dee.

Fairport Convention

4 October 1969 — Supports: Indo-Jazz Fusions | Brett Marvin and The Thunderbolts | Duffy Power
10 March 1973 — Support: Claire Hamill
20 November 1974 — Support: Bryn Haworth
14 October 1975 — Support: David Lewis
9 December 1976 — Support: Arbre

Veterans of five Great Hall appearances Fairport Convention were formed in April 1967 by a group of folk musicians, Richard Thompson (guitarist), Ian Matthews (singer) and Ashley Hutchings (bassist), in Muswell Hill, London.

Fairport Convention are regarded as one of the most important groups of the folk rock movement.

By the time the band made their first appearance at Lancaster, to play what was the first concert in the newly opened Central Hall, they already had three albums under their belt.

Their first album was *Fairport Convention*, a mixture of original songs and covers from American folk singers. Following the suggestions of their producer, Joe Boyd, the band recruited singer Sandy Denny (who had briefly played in the Strawbs) in 1968, with 1969 seeing the addition of highly regarded songwriter and violin player Dave Swarbrick, who was to emerge as Fairport Convention's leading figure, guiding the band through a series of important albums until its disbandment in 1979. Dave Swarbrick passed away in 2016 at the age of seventy-five.

With the band now stretching to over five decades in the music business and having gone through numerous lineup changes, the Fairports are undoubtedly the greatest British folk group of all time. Since the band's reformation in 1985, they have hosted the Cropredy Festival in Oxfordshire, which is the largest annual folk event in England.

Individually and collectively the members of Fairport Convention have received numerous awards recognising their contribution to music and culture and, as of 2017, they continue to record and tour.

In what was probably the first "big gig" in the newly opened Central Hall, folk-rockers Fairport Convention were bizarrely supported by the eccentric British pub blues band, **Brett Marvin and the Thunderbolts.**

Formed in 1968, curiously the band did not and never have featured a Brett Marvin amongst the lineup but on the night did feature Jona Lewie, famous for his 1980 hit single 'You'll Always Find Me in the Kitchen at Parties' and the perennial Christmas number, 'Stop the Cavalry'. Jona returned to the Great Hall, almost ten years later, as part of the Be Stiff Tour in 1978.

The Indo-Jazz Fusions were a British-based outfit formed in the mid-sixties that fused jazz and Indian sounds. The band was the creation of classically trained Indian composer John Mayer and the Jamaican-born jazz saxophonist Joe Harriott.

The Joe Harriott-John Mayer partnership composed the distinctive theme tune, 'Acka Raga', for the early episodes of the BBC quiz show *Ask the Family*, which was broadcast between 1967 and 1984. The theme featured Mayer on sitar.

The Fall

9 November 1985 Support unknown

Originally formed in 1976 in Manchester, The Fall have over forty years of recording and performing under their belt with their founder and sole constant leader Mark E. Smith (not to be confused with the current Vice Chancellor of Lancaster University!).

The Fall continue to release new music and have constantly toured during the whole of its lifespan. To 2015, there have been 30 studio albums, almost double that number of singles and 85-odd live albums and compilations. The bands most recent studio album being *Sub-Lingual Tablet* from 2015.

Lancaster setlist: 'Cruiser's Creek', 'Clear Off', 'Rollin' Danny', 'The Man Whose Head Expanded', 'Couldn't Get Ahead', 'Barmy', 'Draygo's Guilt', 'Stephen Song', '2x4', 'Gut Of The Quantifier', 'What You Need', 'I Feel Voxish', Spoilt Victorian Child', 'My New House', 'God Box', 'LA.', 'No Bulbs'.

Family

16 October 1970 Supports: Nothineverappens I Urban Gorilla

The earliest and most well-known of the Leicester rooted prog bands, Family assembled in 1967, mixing beat with psychedelic, classical, folk and experimental music. They were adept at both chart hits and being weird in their early days. Fronted by the gruff, gargly voice of Roger Chapman, the rest of the band comprised Charlie Whitney (guitar), Rick Grech (bass, violin), Jim King (woodwinds) and Rob Townsend (drums). Their debut album *Music In A Dolls House* came out in 1968 and is an oddball mixture of pop hits, prog and eccentric stuff and went some way to hinting at their finest, 1969's *Family Entertainment,* where they pulled out all the creative stops and really went for it. Of course it wasn't until they pretty much left Leicester for good that they became internationally famous, getting into the charts with singles like 'The Weavers Answer' and 'Burlesque'. The band didn't exist long beyond 1973 though, with Chapman & Whitney forming Streetwalkers, who later changed into Roger Chapman & The Shortlist. Rick Grech is, however, the most prolific member, having been involved in the super group Blind Faith and a wealth of other bands.

Yorkshire's finest ever psychedelic rock/folk rock band from Kingston upon Hull, **Nothineverappens** were formed in the late 1960s and disbanded in 1972.

Billed here as **Urban Gorilla** the local Lancaster band were onstage again having previously backed Deep Purple earlier that year.

Family were a great band, doing some amazing stuff and, in Roger Chapman, they had one of the most unforgettable rock voices, although I remember the show mainly for one thing; a personal nightmare. It was the first and only time I went on stage unprepared to make an announcement. You must never, ever, ever not know what you want to say, word for word. There had been some technical problems with the PA, the mixer in particular, and a delay had ensued. The band's manager had asked me if I would go on stage, explain, apologise and say it wouldn't be much longer before the show started. No problem!

I went on stage. "Ladies and Gentlemen er, er …" The "ers" echoed around the hall through the PA. More stuttering, "Erm" – "Erm" came back at me like the ponderings of The Almighty (and not the band either). "There's been a mix-up with the mixer and the … er … mix-up should be sorted soon and the mixer sorted so the mix-up is fixed," I babbled. Oh no, so many sonorous 'mix-ups' – if only the stage had had one of those old fashioned trap doors I could have disappeared down. I swore, as I crept shamefully off the stage, that I would never again walk onto a stage without a script.

Barry Lucas

Fanny

18 May 1973 Supports: Heads Hands & Feet | Fumble

Fanny were one of the first notable all-girl rock bands to be signed to a major label and achieved two Top 40 UK hits. They were formed by Jean Millington, who played with David Bowie and is married to Bowie's lead guitarist Earl Slick.

They influenced bands from Joan Jett and The Blackhearts to Courtney Love.

From 1974 the band included guitarist Patti Quattro in the lineup, sister of Suzy.

This visit to Lancaster was in support of the release of their fifth album, *Mother's Pride.*

> "One of the most important female bands in American rock has been buried without a trace. And that is Fanny. They were one of the finest ... rock bands of their time, in about 1973. They were extraordinary ... they're as important as anybody else who's ever been, ever; it just wasn't their time. Revivify Fanny. And I will feel that my work is done."
>
> —David Bowie

Heads Hands & Feet were a country-influenced six-piece band featuring the legendary Albert Lee on guitars and Chas Hodges on keyboards. Heads Hands & Feet became a popular live band in the UK, making appearances on The Old Grey Whistle Test and also in Europe, where they appeared on the German music programme Beat-Club. They disbanded in 1973.

Albert Lee was to play alongside Eric Clapton at his 1980 Great Hall appearance, when Chas Hodges and Dave Peacock provided Eric Clapton's support act on the night.

From Weston-super-Mare, **Fumble** were originally formed in 1967 by Des Henly (guitars and vocals), Mario Ferrari (bass), Barry Pike (drums) and the late Sean Mayes on piano. Originally known as The Baloons (sic) they became Fumble in 1972 and specialized in covering rock 'n' roll classics, releasing two studio albums over their career. Their debut *Fumble* in 1972, was followed-up with *Poetry in Lotion* in 1974. Fumble arrived in Lancaster fresh from a tour supporting David Bowie on the US leg of his Ziggy Stardust tour.

One of the first, probably THE first, all-girl heavy rock bands. I still don't really believe it but, by the time they reached Lancaster, the Americans hadn't been made aware of the difference in meaning of their name on both sides of the Atlantic. It was a fun discussion!

Barry Lucas

Albert Lee is one of my favourite guitarists. His mastery of country rock is wonderful and I have seen him in an amazing array of venues. Later that year I was given a box at the Royal Albert Hall by Island Records for their concert with Mott the Hoople, on the condition that I and my party launch a couple of hundred frisbees into the audience. Then came the Clapton gig. Then about eight years ago he was at The Carleton in Morecambe, where only about sixty people (including comps) were there to hear a remarkable twenty-minute version of his iconic 'Country Boy'. Do you know, sometimes I just don't understand. Only sixty people for a legend and yet many bemoan the fact that venues don't promote live music any more! Thanks, Mike O'Brien, for a great night.

Barry Lucas

The Flying Burrito Brothers

4 December 1970

Supports: Hard Meat | The Greatest Show on Earth

In 1968, ex-members of The Byrds, Chris Hillman and Gram Parsons, formed what some people considered to be the greatest country rock band of all time: The Flying Burrito Brothers. Joined by Sneaky Pete Kleinow on pedal steel guitar and Chris Ethridge on bass, along with Michael Clarke on drums, The Burritos performed tracks in the Great Hall from their seminal 1969 album *The Gilded Palace of Sin.* The band sounded like nothing else around at the time and also looked like nothing else. Regular stage attire was smart country and western style suits, with Parson's suit being decorated with marijuana leaves and naked women on the lapels.

Gram Parsons tragically died in 1973 at the age of 26 as the result of an overdose of morphine and alcohol. His death at a motel in The Joshua Tree National Park in California was followed by incredible events including the theft of his body from Los Angeles International Airport by friends and their subsequent cremation of Parsons in the desert, according to Parsons' wish.

The Burritos played the infamous Altamont Free Concert headlined by The Rolling Stones in 1969.

Hard Meat were a UK psychedelic progressive rock band consisting of:
Mick Dolan – electric Guitar, acoustic guitar, lead vocals
Steve Dolan – electric bass, string bass, vocals
Mick Carless – drums, congas, percussion, assorted loud noises

The band made two albums released by Warner Bros in 1970: *Hard Meat* and *Through a Window.*

The Greatest Show on Earth were a UK progressive rock band active from 1968 to 1971. They recorded two albums on Harvest Records in 1970: *Horizons* and *The Going's Easy.* The band was also notable for its album covers, designed by the artist group Hipgnosis.

> This band were quite simply the greatest country rock act, and they played the Great Hall on a very early tour. For me it was memorable for the best forged tickets I came across – unfortunately well after the concert!
>
> Barry Lucas

UNIVERSITY OF LANCASTER № 7792
proudly presents from AMERICA
The Flying Burrito Brothers
(formerly with the BYRDS)
with their guests **HARD MEAT** and
THE GREATEST SHOW ON EARTH
THEIR ONLY LIVE APPEARANCE IN THE NORTH
CENTRAL HALL 8—1
FRIDAY, 4th DECEMBER, 1970
Tickets **15s.** At the Door **£1**

For their last 'Do' of term . . .
Lancaster University Social Committee
proudly presents from the USA . . .
THE FLYING BURRITO BROS.
This Group was formed by two ex-members of the Byrds.
This is one of only four dates in Britain with these guests:
HARD MEAT
+ THE GREATEST SHOW ON EARTH
FRIDAY 4th DECEMBER
CENTRAL HALL - 8—1 a.m.
LATE BAR AND BUSES
SPECIAL GUEST APPEARANCES FROM
GAS "I'll get 'em back" TAYLOR
ADVANCE TICKETS 15/- ★ £1 AT DOOR

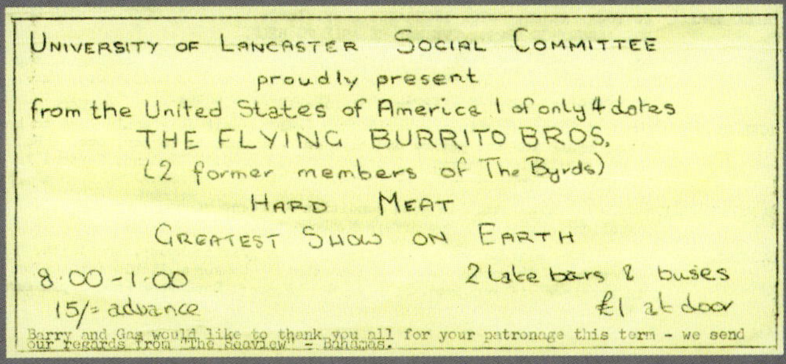

UNIVERSITY OF LANCASTER SOCIAL COMMITTEE
proudly present
from the United States of America 1 of only 4 dates
THE FLYING BURRITO BROS.
(2 former members of The Byrds)
HARD MEAT
GREATEST SHOW ON EARTH
8·00-1·00 2 late bars & buses
15/= advance £1 at door
Barry and Gas would like to thank you all for your patronage this term - we send our regards from "The Seaview" - Bahamas.

Focus

28 February 1976 Support: Charlie

Focus are a Dutch progressive rock band formed in Amsterdam in 1969 by Thijs van Leer.

Based around the technical mastery of van Leer on keyboards, flute and vocals, and Jan Akkerman on guitars, Focus were on the whole an instrumental group. The band achieved their popularity following the huge success of their 1971 album *Focus II,* which contained the hit single 'Hocus Pocus'.

On the night Jan Akkerman failed to appear on stage following his sacking from the band in early 1976 by Thijs Van Leer, and much to the disappointment of fans, Akkerman had been replaced on the night by Belgian guitarist Philip Catherine.

Jan Akkerman returned to the Great Hall a year later with his own band.

Focus continue to record and tour, with Thijs Van Leer and drummer Pierre van der Linden in the lineup. In 2014, Focus released their eleventh studio album *Golden Oldies*, a collection of newly re-recorded versions of some of their most popular songs, including 'Sylvia', 'House of the King' and 'Hocus Pocus'.

Charlie were a British rock band that were formed in 1971 by singer-songwriter Terry Thomas, and included former Argent guitarist John Verity. Although success in the UK eluded Charlie, they had luck with four minor hit singles in the US.

UNIVERSITY OF LANCASTER
FOCUS
PLUS
CHARLIE
8.00PM SATURDAY 28TH FEBRUARY TICKETS £1.25

John Angus

Frankie Miller Band

23 November 1977 Support: Meal Ticket

Born in 1949 in Glasgow Frankie Miller was once described by Rod Stewart as "… the best white soul singer in the world"

In 1975 Miller formed The Frankie Miller Band with Henry McCullogh (guitar), Stu Perry (drums), Chrissie Stewart (bass) and Mick Weaver (guitars). They recorded the album *The Rock* in 1975, which was greeted quite positively by the critics but sold only moderately. June 1977 saw the release of Frankie's fourth album, *Full House*, and Frankie visted Lancaster in support of its release. 'Be Good to Yourself', a composition by Andy Fraser of Free, was issued as a single from the album *Full House* and reached No. 27 in the UK Singles Chart, becoming Miller's first chart hit.

Henry McCullogh had previously been on stage in the Great Hall as guitarist in Paul McCartney's new band Wings for their 1972 concert.

Meal Ticket were a country rock band that played the London pub circuit in the 1970s. Reviewing the concert in *SCAN* newspaper, Paul Johnson wrote: "Meal Ticket were by far the better act on the night".

A great bill – Meal Ticket were an excellent band – that saw the only appearance at Lancaster of one of the best R&B singers in history. If you haven't heard Frankie Miller I beg you to find some back catalogue and give it a go – he is really special.

The concert was fantastic – oh it made a loss, only about 500 people, if I remember rightly, and I sat in the balcony feeling a tremendous kinship with those discerning souls down in the hall enjoying truly great music. In my mind I was composing a rant for *SCAN*, lecturing all those Philistines who didn't attend. Never sent the letter though – their loss, I decided, not mine. But actually on ticket sales, it was mine also!

Barry Lucas

Free

8 October 1970 Support: Wishbone Ash
6 October 1972 Support: Smith Perkins and Smith

Legendary rock band Free were formed in London in 1968 by Paul Rogers, Andy Fraser, Paul Kossoff and Simon Kirke. The remarkable fact about this group of lads was their ages at the time: Rogers and Kirke were eighteen, Kossoff was seventeen and Andy Fraser was fifteen! The band were best known for their signature hit single 'All Right Now', which spent a total of five weeks at No. 2 in the UK Singles Chart of summer 1970. Their first appearance in the Great Hall featured the classic lineup of Free, including Paul Kossoff, with support provided by a fledgling Wishbone Ash, who by all accounts produced a fantastic performance, almost blowing Free off the stage. In October 1972 Free returned to Lancaster but with a changed lineup. During a period of chaos for the band in mid-1972, mainly due to Paul Kossoff's unreliability and drug addiction, Andy Fraser had left Free, to be replaced by Tetsu Yamauchi on bass and John 'Rabbit' Bundrick had been added as keyboard player.

Free finally disbanded in 1973 with lead singer Paul Rodgers going on to become the frontman of Bad Company, together with Simon Kirke on drums, and bassist Andy Fraser assembling his band Sharks. Lead guitarist Paul Kossoff went on to form Back Street Crawler but tragically died from a drug-induced heart attack at the age of twenty-five, in 1976.

Exactly a year after their formation, **Wishbone Ash** took to the Great Hall stage as a support band to Free, performing tracks from their debut album, *Wishbone Ash,* released in December 1970.

Smith Perkins Smith, the American country-rock band of the early 1970s who included guitarist and singer Wayne Perkins, together with Tim Smith and Steve Smith, were back again following their May 1972 support slot for Country Joe and The Fish.

Free

After The Doors, this band is my favourite. A collection of fifteen, sixteen and seventeen year olds put together an album, 'Tons of Sobs', which I still play, and can sing along to, to this day. It truly is a class album.

So in 1970 I had booked Free to perform. They had just been hailed as one of the great acts at the Isle of Wight Festival that summer, playing in front of an estimated 600,000 people. They had released one of the great rock anthems – featured to this day on virtually every classic rock collection – 'All Right Now'. Despite all our memories it only reached No. 2 – I wonder if you can remember what kept it off the No. 1 spot? Look it up!

The support act that day was a little-known band: Wishbone Ash. They had a sponsorship deal with a PA company (Orange) and on the 60ft-wide stage were a handful of small orange (the colour, not the contents) boxes. They looked almost laughable, as by now PAs were becoming macho big, but what sound they produced – wonderful. Unfortunately you sort of knew they wouldn't catch on, because for the rock gods of the '70s size really did matter! And what a set the band produced, the battling guitars just blew me away. I didn't think it possible but I didn't want it to end, even if that meant Free not walking onto stage to replace them. It wasn't only me either, the whole audience went crazy.

Free followed, did their set, leaving 'All Right Now', the massive current hit single, as their anthem encore. I stood with them in the corridor at the side of the stage. It was strangely quiet, no applause, no stomping, nothing. Paul Rodgers and I slowly opened the doors to find that the audience had left. Free could not follow their support act that night.

The next time I had Free on was a nightmare from start to finish (almost). Don't get me wrong, this time Free were brilliant, the show fantastic, truly memorable, only … I had booked the band for the Freshers' Ball, in those days the first concert of Freshers' Week, the first weekend in October. Word obviously got out and I released tickets to the nine agencies covering the NW, plus obviously mail requests. Don't ask me how, I don't know to this day, but demand was such that it sold out in a week. What was I thinking about – as in, Freshers' Ball 1972 sold out before the first years had even arrived? Talk about cock-up, that must rank as the daddy of them all. So good news freshers: your introductory week is climaxed by one of the biggest bands in the UK. Bad news: it's already a sell-out. I suppose it didn't do my advance ticket sales for future shows any harm, as first years quickly appreciated that if you wanted to see an act in the Great Hall you had better get your ticket early – even if that was two weeks before you knew it was on!

The second part of my personal nightmare was the middle support act – a circus knife thrower. Mick Cater (later to become UB40's manager) was the booker at Island Artists. The company had finally employed Mick in exasperation, fed up of waiting for me to take up their job offer. Mick and I got on really well and had many escapades. We were to become close friends, although perhaps never as close as that night.

He had, earlier that year, booked a tour for Mott the Hoople's Rock 'n' Roll Circus. The evening featured bands plus two unlikely supports, the legendary old-time comic genius Max Wall, and a certain circus knife thrower. Mick asked me to look after their date in Carlisle Market Hall. Now, that could be a chapter in itself. I had to bring up some of the Great Hall's stewards and humpers, for the venue was not used to this sort of event and couldn't cope. If you want to know what it's like doing a show there, read George Melly's autobiography where there is a brilliant description which was as valid for Mott as it was when it was written several years before – nothing had changed, I promise you. Anyway Mick now informed me that he had booked the same knife thrower for the Free bill – again, I've no idea why but it was the kind of crazy thing done occasionally in the '70s. They were called La Vivas and, after this night I can't imagine why I booked them again but by this time they had changed their name to Hanleo and Katrina. I think I know why!

Now, the knife thrower was a legendary drinker and when I arrived at the hall at 5.00 pm for the sound checks he was already on his second pint in the ASH house. I said hello and asked him where his wife was, as she was his usual partner on stage. He said that she was in hospital as he had had rather too many at the last show and put a 8" Bowie knife through her thigh. Unbeknown to me, the climax of his act was when he "arranged" for the promoter of the show to be his on stage "victim". So after he had finished with his audience participation bit, a signal to the in-the-know stewards saw Mick and me frog marched to the small stage which had been set up in the middle of the hall. We had to remove our shirts and then stand back to back. It was all a bit of a laugh until he leant forward to me and whispered, hand over mic, that I had to put my arm behind my body and pull my stomach in – bloody cheek! Suddenly an 8" knife was vibrating 3" from my stomach. And I knew how long he had been in the ASH bar. Gulp. Then came a real gasp from the audience. Mick uttered a funny squeak and I turned around to see a similar instrument of death quivering AGAINST Mick's groin. The rest of the act was conducted with Mick's – and my – eyes firmly shut and our bodies squeezed as close as we could possibly get.

Barry Lucas

Genesis

23 February 1973 **Foxtrot Tour** Support: String Driven Thing

Genesis were formed at Charterhouse School, Godalming, Surrey, in 1967 and were one of the most successful rock acts of the 1970s, 1980s and 1990s.

Genesis' first album, *From Genesis to Revelation*, was released in March 1969, followed by *Trespass* (1970) and *Nursery Cryme* (1971).

In February 1973 the classic Genesis lineup of Peter Gabriel, Tony Banks, Mike Rutherford, Steve Hackett and Phil Collins (on drums) visited Lancaster in support of the October 1972 release of their fourth studio album, *Foxtrot.*

Over the years, Genesis have enjoyed a longevity exceeded only by the likes of the Rolling Stones and the Kinks, and in the process provided a launch pad for the superstardom of Peter Gabriel and Phil Collins.

The band's first live album, *Genesis Live*, was released later the same year in August of 1973 and is formed from the recordings of shows straight after the Lancaster appearance, at The Free Trade Hall, Manchester, on 24 February and De Montfort Hall, Leicester, on 25 February 1973.

Possible Lancaster setlist: 'Watcher Of The Skies', 'Happy The Man', 'Fountain Of Salmacis', 'Get'em Out By Friday', 'The Musical Box', 'The Return Of The Giant Hogweed', 'Supper's Ready', 'The Knife', 'Harold The Barrel'

Peter Gabriel returned to Lancaster University in 1978 to perform as a solo act.

String Driven Thing are a folk rock band formed in 1967 in Glasgow and were part of the famed Charisma stable, alongside Genesis, Lindisfarne and Van Der Graaf Generator.

Led by husband and wife Chris and Pauline Adams, they featured the electric violin of Graham Smith. In April 2009, String Driven Thing re-formed with Chris, Pauline and Graham playing gigs in 2012 to coincide with the fortieth anniversary of their *Foxtrot* tour, with Genesis.

Gentle Giant

17 March 1972 Support: T2

Gentle Giant were a British progressive rock band active between 1970 and 1980. The band were known for the complexity and sophistication of their music and for the varied musical skills of its members.

Gentle Giant were considered to be one of the most experimental rock bands of the 1970s and all of the band members, except Malcolm Mortimore, were multi-instrumentalists. Although not commercially successful, they did achieve a cult following.

Shortly prior to this concert, drummer Malcolm Mortimore was seriously injured in a motorcycle accident and was replaced by John Weathers.

Lancaster lineup:
Gary Green – guitar, mandolin, vocals, recorder, bass, drums, xylophone
Kerry Minnear – keyboards, lead vocals (on recordings only), cello, vibraphone, xylophone, recorder, guitar, bass, drums
Derek Shulman – lead vocals, saxophone, recorder, keyboards, bass, drums, percussion
Phil Shulman – lead vocals, saxophone, trumpet, clarinet, recorder, percussion
Ray Shulman – bass, trumpet, violin, vocals, viola, drums, percussion, recorder, guitar
John "Pugwash" Weathers – drums, percussion, vibraphone, xylophone, vocals, guitar

London band **T2** returned to Lancaster a year after their appearance with The Groundhogs.

First up on stage was the former Bonzo Dog Doo-Dah Band multi-instrumentalist **Roger Ruskin Spear and his Giant Kinetic Wardrobe Show** (a.k.a Giant Orchestral Wardrobe). Roger's repertoire of instruments included saxophones, clarinet, piano, guitars and percussion.

A feature of his one-man show was a female tailor's dummy fitted with proximity switches, which produced increasingly high-pitched screams when a hand neared her chest (or 'sensitive zone').

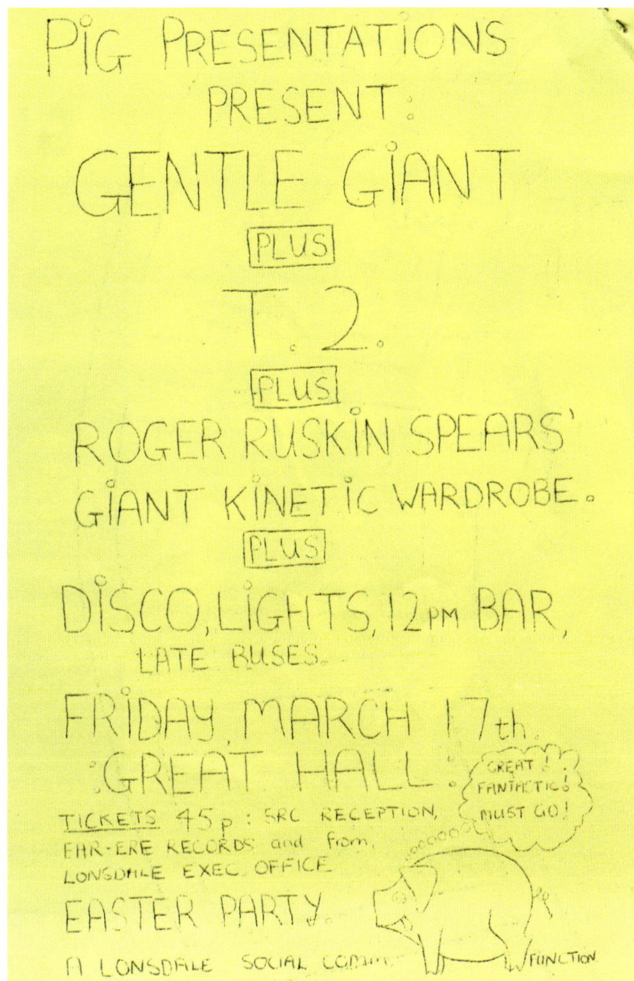

Gillan

When I left the Students' Union at the end of 1984, one of the first projects I became involved with was the world tour of the newly re-formed Deep Purple. The only date they were to perform in the UK was Knebworth. That was, if Knebworth could get its entertainments licence back that it had lost as the result of a few operational problems when it staged The Rolling Stones some years earlier. Paul Loasby was able to achieve that and so Deep Purple at Knebworth in 1985 actually happened.

I was primarily responsible for the dressing room areas and the backstage 'ambience', as the American production company called it. Yes, I hadn't the faintest idea what they were talking about either at that first meeting. Anyway, it transpired that I had to create a 'medieval fayre' for all the guests, record companies and general music business dignitaries – you know, all those people who were getting in without paying. But, more importantly, I was specifically responsible for the dressing room area. A nightmare. The backstage area set aside for artists' dressing rooms was a fairly large, fenced-off field but when I received Deep Purple's rider it had to be dramatically expanded. They wanted a separate area for them, away from the other bands, not a usual requirement I must say. Each band – and there were about seven – had one or two Portakabins to act as dressing rooms. However, although Deep Purple had just re-formed, there was obviously no love lost between the band members. I had to provide each member with their own dressing room, each desperate to be away from the others and individually fenced off. Indeed, Ritchie Blackmore insisted that every window in his particular room be covered in kitchen foil so that none of the other band members could see him. I wonder why they got back together – couldn't have been the money, could it?

A year or so later, I opened The Gardens in Morecambe. It was formally a 350-capacity nightclub/disco, The Blue Rhapsody, which I, in partnership with Jean Yates, turned into a rock music venue. Although, to be fair, we featured a really wide range of live music, not just rock. My old contacts enabled us to 'punch above our weight' and we featured many artists who should not have been playing in a three hundred and fifty capacity, seaside venue: Jools Holland, Humphrey Lyttleton, Ronnie Scott, Ted Hawkins, Shakespears Sister, Napalm Death, Terence Trent D'arby, and Joe Louis Walker. And Ian Gillan. Paul Darwin (of Great Hall flying points fame – see Ultravox) rang me one day to ask if I wanted Ian Gillan in my rock club. Well, arguably one of the greatest rock singers in the world, leader of arguably one of the greatest rock bands in the world – of course I didn't! But there was a caveat – and it was a beauty. Ian was going out with some very old friends from his youth – proper mates, not rock 'n' roll legends – and he was not doing dates in order to play the superstar. Very commendable I hear you say but . . .

The band were to perform under the name of, Garth Rocket and The Moonlighters. A name so catchy I could not remember it and have had to look it up for this piece. The words 'Ian Gillan' and 'Deep Purple' etc. were not to appear in any publicity, posters, flyers or ads. Once again I see you nodding in agreement; what a nice chap. As a fan I can agree, but as a promoter it was a nightmare. I pleaded with Paul, "How can I sell tickets to see an act nobody has ever heard of? I can sell it on Gillan's name but a load of unknown lads in a pub, rock band (£5 a ticket I think it was) – no chance. Paul, give me a break."

Paul was very sympathetic, he understood but he was adamant – any mention of the star, or his pedigree, and the gig wouldn't happen, even if that was as the doors were opening.

As I said, a dilemma! What would you have done? After all, it was my actual cash involved now. So, yes you've guessed it, the area was covered in posters reading "From Deep Purple – the legendary singer Ian Gillan in . . . at The Gardens, Morecambe."

On the morning of the gig, Paul rang me to ask how it was doing. I told him that it had been sold out for several weeks. "Bloody great! Hang on, how did you manage that? Nobody else is selling out." I knew Paul well enough to be honest. I read him out a poster. "Struth, Barry, it'll never happen. I told you and I wasn't joking."

"Ok Paul, how are you coming into Morecambe?"

"From the north, off the motorway at the Carnforth junction and then down the coast road." Paul had tour-managed many acts into Lancaster University and he was from the NW. "Ok, leave it with me," I reassured him. Quick phone call to two of my club bouncers, Hughie and J.C., one bucket, one sponge, one scraper and all the posters from Carnforth to The Gardens on Morecambe seafront were carefully removed. Nobody was any the wiser.

Ian Gillan actually congratulated me on getting a sell-out, he thought that I must be a brilliant promoter.

Sweaty, steamy rock club, 350 (or so) bodies crammed in – rock 'n' roll as it was meant to be, courtesy of Ian Gillan on a night of making Morecambe rock.

Barry Lucas

Gong

12 March 1976 Support: Wigwam

A psychedelic rock band formed by Australian Daevid Allen, formerly of Soft Machine and Gilli Smyth in France in 1969. Gong became pioneers of a new brand of psychedelia/space-rock/trip-rock with a conceptual ethos involving aliens and alternative realities and are probably best known for their 1971 album *Camembert Electrique* and 1973's *Flying Teapot*. As a truly international outfit, Gong became increasingly linked to other bands of the Canterbury scene at the time and many musicians came and went.

Following the departure of founder Daevid Allen in 1975, the band continued on with Steve Hillage as leader for a short while before morphing into the more jazz-rock styled Pierre Moerlen's Gong around 1978. There have been many other versions of Gong over the years and no other band has such immediate word association with 'hippies' as Gong. The band visited Lancaster on the first date of their 1976 tour and featured Gong's long serving French percussionist Pierre Moerlen and saxophonist Didier Malherbe in a new Gong line-up, following the release a month earlier, of the band's sixth studio album *Shamal*; the first to be recorded without Allen. A version of Gong are still active today with the album *Rejoice! I'm Dead!* released in September 2016.

Support act **Wigwam** are a Finnish progressive rock band formed in 1968 and presently still touring and recording. In Finland they have a loyal and lasting (although limited) following and their influence on Finnish rock music is still widely recognised.

Graham Parker and The Rumour

11 November 1977 Support: Clover
10 March 1979 Support: Sports

Graham Parker and The Rumour were formed in London in 1975 with a sound bridging new wave with the earlier pub-rock scene.

The band built a reputation as incendiary live performers and these two university appearances were, according to reports, no exception. The Rumour were recording artists in their own right and released three albums before teaming up with Parker in 1976 as his backing band. They recorded five albums together until they split in 1980. In early 2011, Parker reunited with all five original members of The Rumour to record a new album entitled *Three Chords Good*, which was released in November 2012 with a further album, *Mystery Glue* following in 2015.

Grahams Parker's 1977 visit to Lancaster was a memorable one for him. Not for the great reception the Great Hall audience gave him, but for the great storm that raged during the night as they stayed in their Morecambe seafront hotel. The huge tide that night washed into the hotel and also destroyed one of Morecambe's piers.

Huey Lewis and his band **Clover** appear for the third time in the Great Hall in a supporting role.

Support for the 1979 concert were the Australian band **Sports,** hailing from Melbourne. They were invited over to the UK after being spotted by Graham Parker during a tour of Australia.

GRAHAM PARKER
+THE RUMOUR
PLUS
CLOVER
LANCASTER
UNIVERSITY
FRIDAY
NOVEMBER
11TH
£1.50

John Angus

Graham Parker and The Rumour

A concert at Lancaster University which was an incredible, unforgettable night for Morecambe. And it was all recorded in the national press.

Graham Parker was another artist who, for some unfathomable reason, was labelled as punk. It was a good show, with the excellent Clover (later to become Huey Lewis and the News) as support, although having a steward with a mop and bucket at the side of the stage to rush on and clean up the audience's spit, was slightly disconcerting for Huey! It wasn't easy explaining to him, as he was towelling off pints of spittle in the dressing room, that this was a sign that the fans really liked him.

But the evening was also memorable for another outstanding event: the destruction of Morecambe! It was a Friday night and the bands were staying at The Strathmore Hotel on the sea front in the town. On tour with the bands was a journalist from *Sounds* – one of the big three weekly music newspapers – and what a story he had to file about a night of mayhem on the road with a rock'n'roll band. It was the night that Morecambe was hit by one of the fiercest storms in living memory, and it was combined with a massive high tide. One pier was completely destroyed, and the promenade was battered and flooded, as indeed was a major part of the town. The Strathmore and all the hotels and shops on the promenade were flooded. The band and crew had to decamp to the first floor to drink and watch the ensuing mayhem. The next morning the town looked like a battle scene as children scavenged on the beach to collect coins that had spilt out of the wrecked one-armed bandits lying on the sands. But what a great story for the travelling journalist. Under the banner headline the next week, 'Graham Parker Hits Town, £500,000 Worth of Damage Done', were pictures of Morecambe's mass destruction. The Stones could only destroy hotel bedrooms, Graham Parker could destroy towns!

Barry Lucas

Graham Parker 1979 ©Geoff Campbell

Brinsley Schwarz, Graham Parker & Andrew Bodnar 1979 ©Geoff Campbell

The Groundhogs

22 January 1971 — Support: T2
25 February 1972 — Supports: CCS | Johnny Johnson and the Bandwagon

Active now for over fifty years, The Groundhogs, fronted by Tony McPhee on guitar and vocals, are a top progressive blues rock group. Emerging in the early sixties as a blues band and noted for backing visiting American blues artists such as John Lee Hooker, the band evolved in the latter part of the sixties into a heavy rock group, scoring a hit with their fourth and possibly most popular album *Split.* Through the '70s the band continued to record and play live as a trio, albeit with changing band members, and towards the end of the seventies they were recording as a four-piece with the addition of a second guitar. The band disbanded in the late seventies, to reform once again a year or so later as a trio but with new members. The Groundhogs continued through the '80s, with many personnel changes through to 2004 when Tony McPhee laid the band to rest.

In 2007 Tony McPhee once again put The Groundhogs together for live concerts. To date the band is still working, still fronted by Tony despite his having suffered a stroke. Tony "T.S." McPhee is regarded as one of the very best blues guitarists to come from these shores.

From London, **T2** were a British progressive rock band, best known for their 1970 album *It'll All Work Out in Boomland.* They were a spin-off from a band called Please. T2 returned to Lancaster a year later as the support act for Gentle Giant.

Alexis Korner was a British blues musician and radio broadcaster who has sometimes been referred to as "a founding father of British blues". A major influence on the sound of the British music scene in the 1960s, Korner was instrumental in bringing together various English blues musicians, including Peter Thorup, a Danish guitarist, singer, composer and record producer. Peter joined up with Alexis for this concert and they would have been known at the time as Collective Consciousness Society, aka **CCS**.

CCS are best known for their instrumental version of Led Zeppelin's 1969 track 'Whole Lotta Love', which got into the UK Singles Chart in 1970 and was used as the theme music for the BBC pop programme *Top of the Pops* for most of the 1970s. CCS also found UK chart success with the single 'Tap Turns On The Water' reaching No. 5 in September 1971.

First up on stage were **Johnny Johnson and the Bandwagon**. They were an American vocal soul group formed in 1967 and were originally known simply as The Bandwagon. They featured Artie Fullilove, Billy Bradley, Terry Lewis and lead singer Johnny Johnson.

Gypsy

16 January 1970 — Support: Mighty Baby

An early concert in the Great Hall, Gypsy were a British band from Leicester influenced by late '60s Californian folk-psychedelic rock. They made two LPs and issued a few singles. Their debut album *Gypsy* came out in 1971.

Band lineup:
John Knapp –guitar, keyboards, vocals
David McCarthy – bass, vocals
Robin Pizer – guitar, vocals
Rod Read – guitar, vocals
Moth Smith – drums

After United Artists cancelled their contract in 1973 the band, in dismay, split up.

Psychedelic rock outfit **Mighty Baby** were formed in 1968 from the ashes of a band called The Action. They released two albums, *Mighty Baby* in December 1969 and *Jug Of Love* in October 1971.

Mighty Baby performed on the first day of the 1970 Isle of Wight Festival.

Haircut One Hundred

6 March 1982 Support: The Bluebells

Haircut One Hundred are a British new wave group formed in 1980 by frontman Nick Heyward. The band had four UK Top 10 hit singles between 1981 and 1982, including 'Favourite Shirts', 'Love Plus One' and 'Fantastic Day'.

They released two studio albums and continue to tour with Nick Heyward still at the helm.

Scottish indie band and 1985 Great Hall headliners **The Bluebells** had three Top 40 hit singles in the UK, all written by guitarist and founder member Bobby Bluebell (real name Robert Hodgens): 'I'm Falling', 'Cath', and their biggest success, 'Young at Heart'.

I have got to be brutally honest here; I cannot really remember anything about the show. To be fair to the band I probably spent most of the evening in the ASH bar. Phil McIntyre (ex-Preston Polytechnic Social Secretary mentioned elsewhere in the book) was promoting the tour. Phil was, and still is, a brilliant promoter, but that evening he had his brother, Nigel, and his right hand man, Paul Roberts, on the show. So Phil, who in those days liked a beer, was not needed in the hall and therefore dragged me, kicking and screaming, to the bar as soon as the band walked on stage.

At the end of the night, Phil wanted the settlement, ninety per cent of the net ticket sales, paid to him in cash. I think he needed to pay the band something and have 'on-the-road' cash available. So after the invoices etc. were agreed, Phil took the cash balance and stuffed it into his lumberjack shirt, announcing, "Let's go and get something to eat. Where's open at this time?" Well, 'this time' was about 11.00 pm. I used to always recommend The Steak and Kebab but it had changed hands and then closed, re-opened and closed again etc. etc. So there was only really Pizza Margherita in Lancaster at that time in the area. Nigel was told to stay and oversee the 'get-out' and the rest of us, about six or seven, went to have the meal. As pizza restaurants go it's all right, but they gave us funny looks arriving at 11.15 pm. Phil splashed the cash and, surprise surprise, we were treated really well, but poor old Nigel arrived at about 11.55 pm looking a bit harassed after getting the band away from their fans and supervising as the gear was loaded onto the trucks. He was starving (Nigel likes his scran). But the manager of the restaurant said no food could be ordered after 11.30 pm. We couldn't believe it, we had only just started our meals so a quick pizza wasn't going to hold the staff up for any longer. The manager was insistent, 'rules is rules, we can make no exceptions'. We all pleaded on Nigel's behalf to no effect. Phil, who remember was paying the bill, started to get really annoyed but nothing would change their minds. It was very like an experience I had had at The Steak and Kebab with John Martyn, and that lost them hundreds of pounds in future business as well.

Accepting defeat, we shared our food with Nigel, but Phil turned to me, patting his bulging stomach, and said "I wouldn't mind but I've probably got enough money to buy the bloody place stuffed inside me shirt!".

Barry Lucas

Hawkwind

17 November 1972	**Space Ritual Tour**	Support: Magic Muscle
8 February 1974	**The Ridiculous Roadshow Tour**	Support: Alberto y Los Trios Paranoias
31 January 1975	**A Dead Singer Tour**	Supports: Liquid Len & The Lensmen I Andy Dunkley
14 October 1977	**Spirit of The Age Tour**	Support: Bethnal
17 November 1978	**Hawklords Tour**	No support
16 December 1980	**UK Christmas Tour**	Support: Vardis

From London and formed in November 1969 by guitarist and singer Dave Brock, guitarist Mick Slattery and saxophonist/flautist/singer Nik Turner, Hawkwind have gone through many incarnations and styles of music over the years. Dozens of musicians, dancers and writers have worked with the group since their inception.

Even though essentially an underground/festival band, they had major commercial success with their 1972 hit 'Silver Machine'. The single spent a total of twenty-two weeks in the UK charts in 1972 and reached No. 3.

Over the decades the band has been variously known as Hawkwind Zoo, Hawkwind, Hawklords and then, again, Hawkwind. The 1980 university Christmas concert featured Ginger Baker on drums and ex-Comus and future Toyah drummer Keith Hale on keyboards.

In February of 2014, Hawkwind performed *Space Ritual* at a benefit concert entitled Rock 4 Rescue. English actor Brian Blessed performed on the track 'Sonic Attack' and a studio recording was subsequently released as a single. The concert was eventually released as a CD/DVD set called *Space Ritual Live* in March of 2015.

Veterans of six appearances in the hall, many concert goers have great memories of the gigs, although some have none at all!

At the time of writing, Dave Brock is still at the helm of Hawkwind and busy recording and touring.

Magic Muscle were a psychedelic space/rock group from Bristol, formed around 1969. Following their support slot for Hawkwind on the Space Ritual Tour they earned themselves the nickname "Bastard Sons of Hawkwind".

Master of Ceremonies for the evening was DJ Andy "The Living Jukebox" Dunkley. Hawkwind's lengthy Space Ritual show also included contributions from a naked dancer with a 52" bust named Stacia Blake, the poet Robert Calvert, and the sci-fi writer Michael Moorcock.

Alberto y Lost Trios Paranoias were formed in Manchester in 1972 and were a comedy rock band, in the same vein as the Bonzo Dog Doo-Dah Band. During the period of the band's existence up to 1982 they achieved success in their own right, moving on to being a headline act and being supported by up and coming bands of the time, such as The Police, The Stranglers and Blondie.

Liquid Len & The Lensmen provided the lightshow for many Hawkwind gigs of the early years. Len also worked with Traffic, Free, Mott The Hoople and Black Sabbath.

Andy Dunkley was once again MC for the evening.

For the 1977 Spirit Of The Age Tour Hawkwind employed the support act services of **Bethnal**, who were a British proto-punk/rock band formed in 1972. In 1978 they released two albums on Vertigo Records.

Hawkwind's 1980 Christmas tour saw **Vardis,** an influential three-piece hard rock band from Wakefield, West Yorkshire, as guests. Vardis enjoyed hits between 1978 and 1986. Their second album, released in April 1981 and called *The World's Insane*, featured a cover version of Hawkwind's 'Silver Machine'.

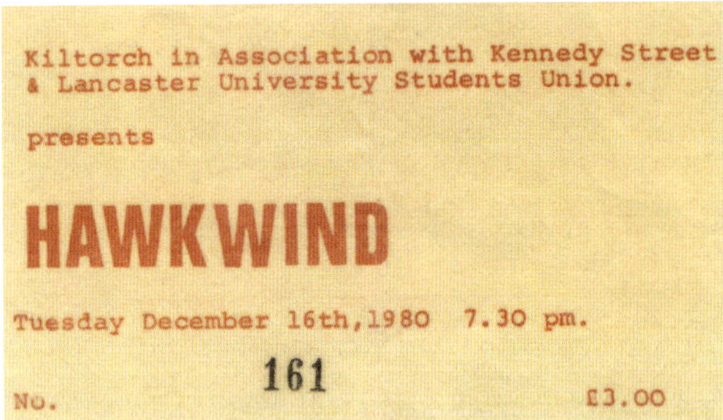

Silver Machine – there, said it all. No, that's not fair. Hawkwind are a really hard working, honest, rock band, who I had on many occasions in many guises. At times they boasted the unforgettable 6ft plus Amazonian stripper/exotic dancer Stacia, and then with Michael Moorcock, the acclaimed sci-fi writer who walked onto stage in a long flasher-type raincoat and who I had to save from bouncers who wanted to forcefully remove "This weird bloke from the audience who had wandered on stage", and finally the legendary rock drummer, Ginger Baker. Hawkwind were also responsible for one of the more outlandish rider demands – that their dressing room be painted totally green. I refused to do that one and it was never mentioned on the night but I wonder how many venues had had to call in the decorators.

Hawkwind wanted to play their final date in the Christmas holidays. I knew there would be very few students about but I also knew that the band had a strong local following. I said that out of term time I couldn't justify risking students' money on a concert, so the band agreed to play on a straight percentage. I was therefore in no danger of losing money, so why not?

On the evening, the tour manager asked if I had planned to open the balcony. I said that, as I had only sold 800 tickets, I probably wouldn't in order to help create a good atmosphere. "Oh good," he said. I asked why? "Well, drink and drugs have taken their toll on Ginger and he frequently needs the toilet during the set, so we have a bucket by the bass drum. Probably not the best sight from the balcony."

I agreed, no viewing from the gods that night.

Barry Lucas

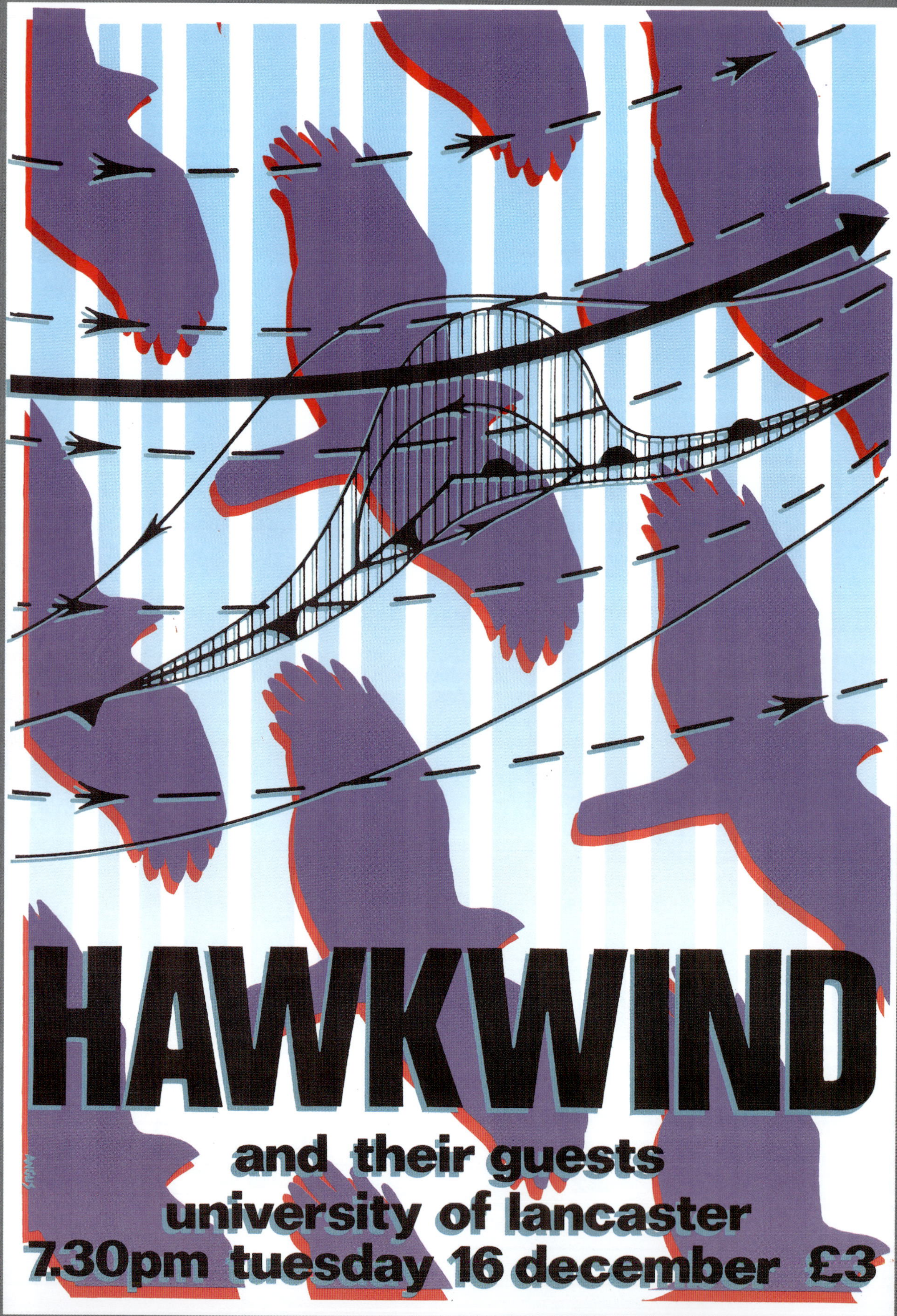
HAWKWIND
and their guests
university of lancaster
7.30pm tuesday 16 december £3

John Angus

ANGUS
HAWKWIND/
HAWKLORDS
+ SUPPORT BAND
7.30PM FRIDAY NOV. 17
UNIVERSITY OF LANCASTER TICKETS: £2

John Angus

Hazel O'Connor

22 November 1980 Support: Duran Duran

English singer-songwriter and actress Hazel O'Connor became famous in the early 1980s with her hit singles 'Eighth Day', 'D-Days' and 'Will You', and was also to become prominent as an actress when she played the role of Kate in the critically acclaimed 1980 film *Breaking Glass.*

Hazel O'Connor, with her backing band Megahype, visited Lancaster for a date on her UK tour in support of her UK No. 5 album *Breaking Glass*. For the tour she selected as her opening act a then-unknown group called Duran Duran; it was the band's first opportunity to play to large audiences in the UK and gave them the exposure they needed to secure a recording contract, although they were a support act that concert goers may have missed whilst in the Great Hall bar!

Hazel O'Connor continues to record and tour and released her twentieth album *See You Again* in 2017.

Duran Duran, the British pop/rock band from Birmingham. John Taylor, Nick Rhodes and Stephen Duffy formed Duran Duran in 1978. The band took their name from villain *Dr Durand Durand* in the cult science-fiction film *Barbarella,* starring Jane Fonda.

Since the 1980s, they have had fourteen hits in the Top 10 of the UK Singles Chart and twenty-one in the Billboard Hot 100, and have sold more than 100 million records.

Lancaster band lineup:
Simon Le Bon – vocals
John Taylor – bass
Andy Taylor – guitar
Nick Rhodes – keyboard
Roger Taylor – drums

Horslips

10 May 1974 Support: Bees Make Honey

Horslips, founded in Dublin in 1970, are generally regarded as the founding fathers of Celtic rock and were one of Ireland's leading rock groups of their era.

Often compared to early Fairport Convention, Horslips drew on their distinctly Irish roots and were capable of playing straight folk material when the moment called for it, but weren't afraid to turn it up loud and hard on the right songs, in the best art-rock style.

They released nine studios albums and one live one before disbanding in 1980.

2004 saw some of the members re-forming Horslips and they still perform intermittently today.

1973 had seen Horslips in the Great Hall as guests of Steeleye Span.

Irish band **Bees Make Honey** were one of the original pub rock groups of the early '70s. The band included Bob Siebenberg, who was later to become Supertramp's long-serving drummer. They disbanded in 1974 after recording two albums on the EMI label.

HAZEL O'CONNOR
HAZEL O'CONNOR
HAZEL O'CONNOR
AND
MEGAHYPE
MEGAHYPE
MEGAHYPE
+
DURAN DURAN
7.30PM SAT. NOV.22
LANCASTER UNIVERSITY
TICKETS 2.50

John Angus

Hot Chocolate

7 November 1975 — Support: D'Dancer
3 March 1978 — Support: Smiling Hard

Hot Chocolate were a pop and soul band originally from Brixton, London, who were most popular during the '70s and '80s. Formed by frontman Errol Brown, who passed away in 2015, the act had at least one hit every year between 1970 and 1984, with their iconic song 'You Sexy Thing' becoming the only track to make the British Top 10 in the 1970s, 1980s and 1990s.

In 1997 'You Sexy Thing' reached the No. 1 slot in the UK charts after it was featured in the movie *The Full Monty.*

An article in *SCAN* newspaper about the upcoming 1975 gig described support band **D'Dancer** as "… a superb funky rock outfit discovered by Chris Squire of the band Yes". They had an English vocalist, backed by a Latin American, a West Indian and a bassist from Los Angeles.

Smiling Hard were a five piece disco/soul band from Portsmouth.

Mike Igoe, *SCAN* Review 25.4.78: "The support band was Smiling Hard who were lifted from the lowest rung of the musical ladder by their interesting use of saxophones and flutes".

At a recent reunion Mark Lane, my head of stewards (see Stiff Tour), told me the full details of a back stage incident this night.

For a period of a couple of years I had quite a few problems with Lancaster's "Satan's Slaves". These were the city's very own Hell's Angels but not quite the impressive Californian breed. They had obviously seen the film of The Altamont Festival and decided that they too would provide 'security' at local concerts. The only problem was that, unlike the promoters and bands at Altamont, I wasn't going to employ them – I'd seen the film as well! However, it didn't stop them attending and causing quite a few problems and feelings of unease and intimidation amongst my audiences. Little did the other concert goers realise, but these Angels couldn't afford a bike between them. They caught the bus up and the last bus back, sitting upstairs in the front seats, making engine noises and pretending to drive the bus home. I don't know whether they made the bus do imaginary wheelies but I wouldn't be at all surprised.

Their leader was called "Edge" – he gave himself the nickname to indicate his preference for knives in fights. At this concert, for some reason that nobody could fathom, he decided that he was going to kill Errol Brown, Hot Chocolate's lead singer. Mark saw him marching down the Great Hall corridor towards the dressing rooms, knife in hand. He and a couple of others grabbed Edge and Mark held his knife hand above his head. The police were called and arrived about fifteen minutes later. All this time Mark had held Edge's arm up above his head, knife and all. Edge was frog marched out of the hall and I almost felt sorry for him. He looked terrified as he was thrown into the back of a police van. I only hope Edge was a dog lover, although he didn't look like one as he saw he would have two companions on the journey back to Lancaster. It would be nice to think that he was able to claim a refund on his return bus ticket.

Mark had to appear in court as the prosecution's main witness. He said that he was ever so slightly nervous as he had to push through hoards of angry Angels milling around outside the court. Luckily, Mark wasn't called as Edge pleaded guilty and received a custodial sentence.

Barry Lucas

HOT CHOCOLATE
PLUS SUPPORT
UNIVERSITY OF LANCASTER
7.30PM FRIDAY 3RD MARCH £2.00

John Angus

The Human League

22 November 1981 Support: Debonair

The Human League are an English electronic new wave band formed in Sheffield in 1977. The band arrived at Lancaster for a concert in support of the October 1981 release of *Dare*, the band's most popular album.

Dare yielded the single 'Don't You Want Me' which was the band's best-known and most commercially successful recording, and was the 1981 Christmas No. 1 in the UK. In total it has sold over a million copies.

The only constant Human League member since 1977 has been vocalist and songwriter Philip Oakey. Joining the band in 1980 were The Human League's two female vocalists, Joanne Catherall and Susan Ann Sulley, who along with Phil Oakey continue to tour today.

Since 1978, The Human League have released nine studio albums, four EPs, thirty singles and several compilation albums. They have had five albums and eight singles in the UK Top 10 and have sold more than twenty million records.

SCAN newspaper reviewer Mike Gould reported that: "throughout the concert images from feature films such as *Nosferatu*, *The Texas Chainsaw Massacre* and *Psycho* were projected onto three black screens behind the band".

Another interesting happening was the apparent disappearance of Phil Oakey prior to the concert. Following a disagreement about the stage setup with his manager, he threw his toys out of the pram and stormed out.

SCAN newspaper reported: "Search parties were dispatched and the man with the Veronica Lake hairdo was eventually found in Garstang, a town eight miles south of the university".

Little is known about support act **Debonair**.

©Geoff Campbell

This was a band who were to describe themselves, only a year later, as bigger than The Beatles. Well I'm not one to argue with superstars but …

On this tour they were certainly a huge draw, selling out very quickly. I had been asked, in advance, for the stage and roof clearance sizes. Lancaster's stage was certainly a large frontage at 60ft, but was only about 30ft deep, although we could, and frequently did, enlarge it with an in-house stage extension. The height of the hall's roof above the stage was massive, again 60ft I think. I relayed this information to the band but forgot to tell them about the sloping roof. It was a slope that meant at the very back of the stage there was only 15ft clearance. However, this had never been a problem in fourteen years.

Well it was this time. The band had brought along a mate who was to provide projected images onto a backdrop and needed to do this from behind said backdrop. Thinking of our stage dimensions I could see their problem; not enough clearance at the rear of the stage. An impasse ensued as it was going to be impossible to achieve this setup. The only solution would be to maybe use front projection. Later that afternoon the bands manager strode into the hall to announce that the gig was off as back projection was an integral part of the whole show. I said to him that actually the band and the music was the show and not some static images but he just stormed off. Then later at around 6.00 pm he phoned me from his hotel in Garstang, some eight miles south of Lancaster. He wanted me to drive there and grovelingly apologise to himself and Phil Oakey and if I did the band would then perform.

Alan Murray said, "You're not doing that, tell them to get stuffed." But we had a sell-out show, people had travelled miles, I really didn't have an option. So Alan drove me down to Garstang, though I made him stay in the car while I did the dirty deed – I could see the scouser in him surfacing and him flattening somebody! The band really made it uncomfortable for me but the concert went ahead and none of the audience had any idea how close it had been to disaster. So, in the end, front projection it was. And do you know, I bet nobody walked out of the hall saying, "If only the images had been projected from behind the backdrop it would have been a fantastic show".

Barry Lucas

LANCASTER UNIVERSITY STUDENT UNION

Presents

HUMAN LEAGUE

+ Guests

SATURDAY NOVEMBER 22nd AT 7.30 p.m.

No. 1467 £3.50

Jack Bruce

2 October 1970 — Supports: Matthews' Southern Comfort | Edgar Broughton Band
8 March 1977 — Support: Hunter

The legendary Scottish ex-Cream bassist Jack Bruce graced the Great Hall twice in the 1970s.

It was in July 1966 that Jack Bruce, Eric Clapton and Ginger Baker formed the three-piece British super group Cream. Cream combined Clapton's blues guitar playing with the powerful voice and intense bass lines of Jack Bruce and the manic drumming of Ginger Baker at the rear. Bruce wrote and sang most of Cream's songs, including 'Sunshine of Your Love' and 'White Room'. When Cream broke up in 1968 after a successful two-year run, he released albums and collaborated with other musicians, launching a solo career that lasted more than forty years.

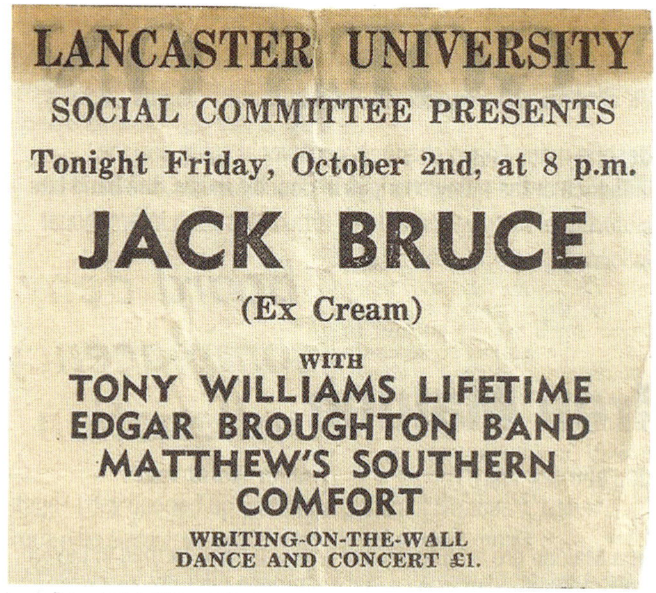
LANCASTER UNIVERSITY
SOCIAL COMMITTEE PRESENTS
Tonight Friday, October 2nd, at 8 p.m.
JACK BRUCE
(Ex Cream)
WITH
TONY WILLIAMS LIFETIME
EDGAR BROUGHTON BAND
MATTHEW'S SOUTHERN COMFORT
WRITING-ON-THE-WALL
DANCE AND CONCERT £1.

Jack's first visit to Lancaster was with drummer Tony Williams, guitarist John McLaughlin (Mahavishnu Orchestra) and organist Larry Young, together forming the band Tony William's Lifetime. The group recorded two albums, with Bruce joining on the second album, *Turn It Over*. However, Lifetime did not receive much critical or commercial acclaim at the time and the band broke up in 1971.

Almost seven years later in 1977, Jack Bruce returned to Lancaster University with his new band, consisting of drummer Simon Phillips and keyboardist Tony Hymas. Then Phillips returned to Lancaster as drummer for Toyah in 1982 and later moved on to become the full-time drummer for American band Toto. Classically trained keyboardist Tony Hymas went on to work extensively with Jeff Beck. The group recorded Jack Bruce's fifth studio album, called *How's Tricks*, which was released in March 1977 to coincide with the tour.

Five months after their headlining gig, folk rock band **Matthews' Southern Comfort** were back again to provide the support for Jack Bruce.

Completing a fabulous value-for-money triple bill was **Edgar Broughton Band.** Edgar and his brother Steve, on drums, returned a month later for their own headlining concert.

Little is known about 1977 support act **Hunter.**

UNIVERSITY OF LANCASTER PRESENTS
THE JACK BRUCE BAND
PLUS HUNTER
7.30PM TUES. MARCH 8TH
£1.25
938 DD 30

John Angus

THE JAM
JAM
JAM
JAM
JAM
JAM
JAM
JAM
This most delicious and appetising Preserve is decidedly better than any Black Currant Jam for soothing a Sore Throat and Checking a Cold, and its remedial properties are really wonderful. Made by a secret process known only to the Proprietors.
No other preserve is anything like it. Ask your Grocer to keep it in stock for you.
PLUS NEW HEARTS AND China STREET
7.30PM
WEDNESDAY
14TH DECEMBER
UNIVERSITY OF LANCASTER
£1.50

John Angus

The Jam

Another of the truly great bands thrown up by the punk revolution. Like several others, The Jam would have always broken through and established themselves as major stars, punk just made it quicker and easier for them.

They were touring extensively and I had a date on the 1977 tour, which was a great show. I was talking to Paul Weller's Dad, John, who was their manager, all afternoon and evening. He was a tremendous guy; I don't know if he actually was from a market trader background but he could easily have been a memorable character from *Only Fools and Horses* or *Minder*. He obviously wasn't sure how long this fame and accompanying fortune would last, but he was going to look after his lads and make it as profitable as possible for them. He was a "diamond geezer", terrific bloke and we got on well.

In 1979 I noticed that the band were doing some dates. All were to be major venues and noticeably, for the first time, no university dates were in the schedule. I phoned their agent to request a date, only to be told, "Sorry but the band are too big to play universities now. They wouldn't even consider a gig at Lancaster". So I asked him to phone John Weller and to say that Barry Lucas at Lancaster University wants a date, he'll pay you cash on the night. The agent rather snootily replied, "I don't know what you're talking about. Waste of time. They won't play universities – too big. I'm not going to waste my time, it's too valuable". But I was convinced I knew what would appeal to John Weller.

"Just make the call," I insisted. I knew he would have to put the offer in front of the band's manager because if he didn't and John was to find out, then he would most probably lose the band and at that stage of their career that was not something he, or his bosses, would want to contemplate.

About an hour later (instantaneous in music business terms) the agent called me back. "I just don't understand it. We all agreed they wouldn't do any more colleges, they're too big, it would be a backward step and it could damage their careers ... We had all agreed."

"So what did he say?" I asked.

"He told me to ring you and fix the date. I just don't understand it ..."

I do remember smiling ... I understood and so would Del Boy.

P.S. The agent never forgave me for, in his eyes, making him look foolish and he tried for years to get his revenge, avoiding offering me bands, but by that time Lancaster was too important to need any agent's goodwill.

Barry Lucas

Jan Akkerman and Kaz Lux

4 March 1977 Support: Kayak

Jan Akkerman, along with Thijs Van Leer, was an original member of the Dutch progressive rock band Focus, from 1969–1976.

Following his sacking and the disappointment of his non-appearance in the Great Hall for Focus' 1976 concert, the Dutch jazz fusion guitarist visited Lancaster with his newly formed band.

A musician of near legendary prowess, Jan Akkerman for a time eclipsed Eric Clapton, Jimmy Page and Jeff Beck in the music press readers' polls in England for top guitarist in the world. *Melody Maker* readers voted him best guitarist in the world in a 1973 poll.

After his departure from Focus, Akkerman teamed up with Dutch vocalist Kaz Lux to create a concept album named *Eli,* which was released in 1976 on Atlantic records.

The concert was a real treat for all fans of Dutch jazz fusion music, featuring former Focus drummer Pierre van der Linden, classically trained concert pianist Joachim Kühn and bass player Cees van der Laarse.

Now in his seventieth year, Akkerman continues to tour and released his latest album, *North Sea Jazz*, in 2013.

Kayak are a Dutch progressive rock band, still active today, formed in 1972 in the city of Hilversum by Ton Scherpenzeel and Pim Koopman.

A month after Queen's Great Hall concert of November 1974, Queen invited Kayak to be their support act for a concert in The Hague, Netherlands, on 8 December 1974.

JAN AKKERMAN
AND THE KAZ LUX BAND
FEATURING:
PIERRE VAN DER LINDEN
CEES VAN DER LAARSE
JOACHIN KUHN
PLUS KAYAK
UNIVERSITY OF LANCASTER
7.30 PM
FRI. MARCH 4TH
TICKETS £1.50

John Angus

Joan Jett and The Blackhearts

22 October 1982 **I Love Rock and Roll Tour** Support: The Smart

Born Joan Larkin on 22 September 1958, in Philadelphia, Pennsylvania, Joan Jett entered the music business at the age of fifteen with the punk-pop band The Runaways.

One of the top women in rock, Joan Jett had a string of hits during the 1980s and 1990s.

Joan Jett and The Blackhearts were formed in 1981. Soon after the success of her Billboard Hot 100 No. 1 hit 'I Love Rock and Roll' Joan and her Blackhearts played a fabulous gig in the Great Hall. 'I Love Rock and Roll' is Billboard's No. 56 song of all time.

Joan, now aged fifty-eight, continues to perform and has also had a career in film and television.

The Smart were a UK rock band formed in Chelsea, London, that existed from 1980 to 1984. They released one single in 1981, titled 'Mr Right'.

John Cale

24 November 1975 **Slow Dazzle Tour** Support: Nasty Pop

John Davies Cale, OBE, is a Welsh musician, composer, singer-songwriter and record producer who was a founding member of the American experimental rock band the Velvet Underground. John Cale played the university on his Slow Dazzle Tour to support his 1975 album of the same name.

Cale's band featured Chris Spedding on guitar, who in 1973 had appeared at the university with Andy Fraser's band, Sharks.

Spedding had a Top 20 solo hit single in the UK with 'Motor Bikin' in 1975.

Liverpool band **Nasty Pop** existed from 1975–1978 and were notable for member Keith Wilkinson, who was to become bassist for Squeeze from 1985–1997.

John Cooper Clarke

19 June 1979 Supports: Joy Division I Fàshiön Music

The "Bard of Salford" Dr John Cooper Clarke, arrived at the university for a second visit, this time in a headlining role for a concert in The Nuffield Theatre alongside, Fashion and Joy Division. He had previously performed in the Great Hall, on the same bill as Third World for a Rock Against Racism concert in November 1978. John Cooper Clarke became famous as a "punk poet" during the punk rock era of the late 1970s, with his best known work being the classic 1980 album *Snap Crackle and Bop*, spawning tracks such as 'Beasley Street' and 'Evidently Chickentown'.

In July 2013, Clarke was awarded an honorary doctorate of arts by the University of Salford as "acknowledgement of a career which has spanned five decades, bringing poetry to non-traditional audiences and influencing musicians and comedians" Upon receipt, Clarke commented: "Now I'm a doctor, finally my dream of opening a cosmetic surgery business can become a reality".

He released several albums in the late 1970s and early 1980s and continues to perform regularly. In 2016, in a collaboration with ex-Strangler, Hugh Cornwell, the pair released the album, *This Time It's Personal.*

Fàshiön Music were a British new wave band consisting of Dee Harris, Al "Luke Sky" James, Alan Darby, John Mulligan, Marlon Recchi and Dik Davis. The band released the album *Product Perfect* in 1979, and between 1978 and 1980 they played shows with many bands such as Toyah Willcox, UB40, Hazel O'Connor and Billy Idol. The band also were used as openers for the B-52s on their UK tour. Being re-formed in 2008, Fashion, as they are now known, are still active.

Joy Division were an English post-punk band formed in 1976 in Salford, Greater Manchester. Originally named Warsaw, the band consisted of singer Ian Curtis, guitarist and keyboardist Bernard Sumner, bassist Peter Hook and drummer Stephen Morris. Joy Division is considered to be the pioneering band of the post-punk movement of the late 1970s and the early 1980s.

The band released two studio albums but is best remembered for their single 'Love Will Tear Us Apart'. The song was first released as a single in June 1980 and became the band's first chart hit, reaching No. 13 in the UK Singles Chart.

The band dissolved in May 1980 after Ian Curtis' suicide. The remaining members re-formed as New Order and went on to achieve much critical and commercial success, with a Great Hall concert in March 1985.

JOHN COOPER
CLARKE
WITH FASHION
+JOY DIVISION
NUFFIELD THEATRE
UNIVERSITY OF LANCASTER
7.30PM TUES. JUNE 19
TICKETS: £1.25

John Angus

Joy Division never played in the Great Hall but they did appear as part of a triple bill in the Nuffield Theatre on 19 June 1979. As the Nuffield is part of the Great Hall complex I feel justified in mentioning this show in this book. I used the theatre several times for acts that would benefit from a more intimate atmosphere, such as Sonny Terry and Brownie McGee, Al Stewart, and a terrific series of lectures on film by Philip Jenkinson (the BBC's film critic and presenter of the very successful *Film Night*).

But here I used it because I realised that the show would not command a large audience, as only people who were sufficiently "in the know" about the developing Manchester music scene would be there.

Joy Division are seen now as one of the most influential bands of the late '70s.

It is hard to believe today but they were third on the bill! Below Fàshiön Music and under headliner, poet John Cooper Clarke. They made for a memorable night. Well, the 300 who attended had a night to remember. It was less than a year later that Ian Curtis, their charismatic lead singer, would commit suicide.

The re-incarnation of the band as New Order would prove impossible for me to pin down to a date, despite a couple of years trying. Well, they were for me; Geoff Campbell, my successor for six months before he headed south to Exeter University and a very successful promoting career, managed it in 1985. A real triumph!

Barry Lucas

The Bard Of Salford in The Great Hall Third World concert 1978

John Martyn

9 May 1973	Support: John Renbourne and Jackie McShee
8 March 1974	Support: David Elliot
8 January 1975	Support: Brown's Home Brew or Lucas & McCulloch
30 April 1976	Support: Brian Robertson Band (with Herbie Flowers)
29 November 1977	Support: Prelude
22 November 1978	Support unknown
1979	Exact date or support unknown
1980	Exact date or support unknown
27 October 1981	Support unknown
6 October 1982	Support unknown

Iain David McGeachy (aka John Martyn, OBE) was a Scottish singer-songwriter and guitarist whose music reflected influences of jazz, blues and rock.

John Martyn was the first white solo act to be signed by Island Records, who released his debut album *London Conversation* in 1968 and started a career that spanned four decades. He went on to release a total of twenty-one studio albums working alongside artists such as Eric Clapton, David Gilmour and Phil Collins.

Martyn was described by *The Times* newspaper as "an electrifying guitarist and singer whose music blurred the boundaries between folk, jazz, rock and blues". He sadly passed away in Kilkenny, Eire, in 2009.

Five months after the January 1973 split of Pentangle, former members **John Renbourne** and **Jackie McShee** teamed up and provided John's support on the night.

David Elliott is a folk rock singer-songwriter who had two solo albums released in the UK on Atlantic Records in the '70s, *David Elliott* and *Solid Ground.*

1975 support may have come from either Joe Brown's **Home Brew** or **Robin Lucas & Drew McCulloch**, who were a Scottish songwriting duo originally from Ayrshire, Scotland. They were signed to British Lion Music, writing songs and touring with a number of acts, including John Martyn and The Pretty Things, often playing at The Marquee Club in Wardour Street, Soho, London.

Brian Alexander Robertson is a Scottish musician, actor, composer and songwriter, from Glasgow, better known as **B. A. Robertson**.

He had a string of hits in the late 1970s and early 1980s, characterised by catchy pop tunes and jaunty, humorous lyrics, most notably his 1979 single 'Bang Bang', which spent twelve weeks in the UK Singles Chart and peaked at No. 2. He also penned hits for Cliff Richard, including 'Carrie' and 'Wired for Sound'.

Renowned bassist Herbie Flowers featured in Brian's band on the night. During the mid '70s Herbie had worked in a writing and production partnership with Brian Robertson.

John's guests for his 1977 concert were **Prelude** who had previously appeared with Ralph McTell in March 1976.

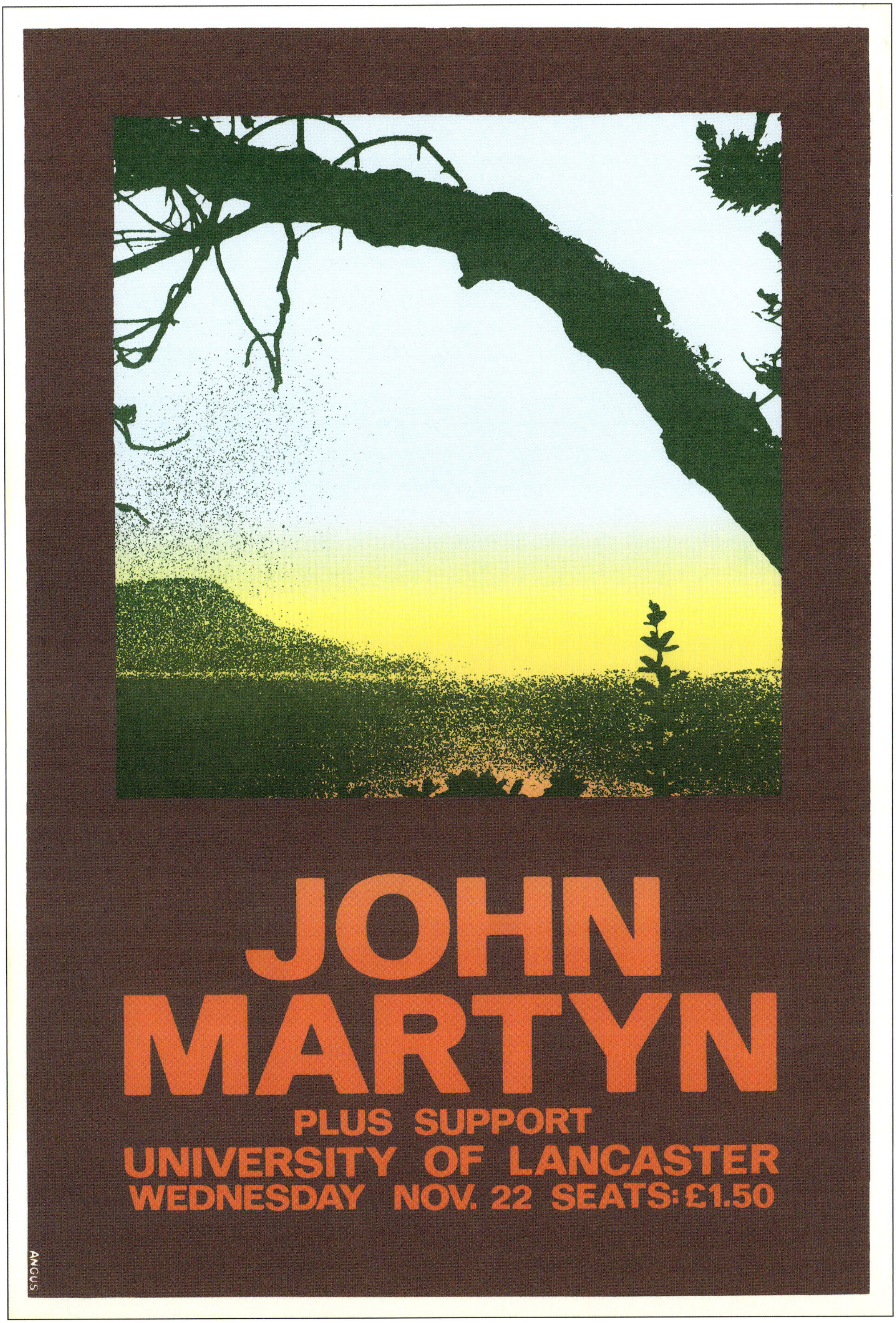
JOHN
MARTYN
PLUS SUPPORT
UNIVERSITY OF LANCASTER
WEDNESDAY NOV. 22 SEATS: £1.50
ANGUS

John Angus

John Martyn

That the album *John Martyn Live* was made at Leeds University, was probably one of the biggest mistakes ever made when it came to live albums. It would, on the other hand, have made a truly historic and memorable recording had the unique rapport between artist and audience that was a John Martyn concert been captured at Lancaster University.

John, who sadly died in 2009, had a magical relationship with Lancaster. It had been built up over several years while John graduated from interesting support act to major star, at Lancaster. Latterly, his shows would sell 1500 tickets and it is simply impossible, in words, to describe the unique atmosphere he created. I don't really remember how it first happened but John, sat on his own, on a single chair, on the vast, empty stage, looked and felt lonely. Onto the stage came his audience, soon to become his friends. Joints were rolled and passed around from audience member to audience member, from audience member to John and from John to audience. The shows were remarkable as nobody, especially John, wanted them to end. And end they didn't. His shows would last two to three hours and beyond. John just enjoyed creating those incredible guitar sounds, a one-man Pink Floyd, and he loved sharing the experience with all his friends.

I was close friends with his manager, Robb Winn. Yep, the same provincial agent who had booked The Who for us all those years ago, small world isn't it? Robb now worked at Island Artists. I was staying with Robb for a few days at his place in Cookham whilst I was in London sorting out a few deals. We had been out for a meal at a beautiful restaurant on the Thames and had had a few – quite a few – vodka and fresh oranges. This was a music business tipple of the moment, as people fooled themselves into believing the fresh orange made it healthy; worked for me! Back at the house the phone rang. It was 2.00 am, who would be ringing at that hour? "Oh it'll be John," said Robb, "he always phones, no matter what time it is, when he has an idea." It was. "He's a bloody genius," said Robb, "but bloody hard work to manage."

I could imagine. I said to Robb that John's shows at Lancaster were brilliant and always did the business, but them going on so long was getting counter productive. You could almost see the audience, sat around at his feet, looking at their watches. They wanted to go home but would not dream of offending a friend. You all know the old music hall adage, leave them wanting more. Robb could see my point but …

At the next John Martyn show at Lancaster I was in the foyer, putting up posters, when I heard this booming Scottish voice: "Hey you!" Now John Martyn was a bit of a scary legend, a great drinker, a bit of a battler, a fiery Scot and unpredictable. Not a great combination. What the hell was wrong? "What the fuck have you been saying to my manager about my shows here?" Obviously Robb had helpfully passed on my thoughts and observations. Thanks Robb, my old pal, bet you're in your local Cookham hostelry right now.

"Well John, I just said that maybe you could cut the act a bit …" I just got it out when John said "What the fuck's it got to do with you? I'm who they are paying to hear."

No arguing with that so I demurely agreed. After all he was right, they loved him, he was the star and … he was scary.

Anyway it still should have been 'John Martyn Live at Lancaster' – big mistake, Island.

Barry Lucas

John Mayall

29 April 1972

Supports: Eggs Over Easy | Matching Mole

John Mayall OBE, is a blues singer, guitarist, organist and songwriter from Macclesfield, Cheshire, whose musical career spans over fifty years. In the 1960s, he was the founder of John Mayall & the Bluesbreakers, a band which has counted among its members some of the most famous blues and rock musicians. Past members of John's band include: Eric Clapton and Jack Bruce of Cream, Peter Green, John McVie, Mick Fleetwood and Mick Taylor (who went on to have a five-year stint with the Stones.) The studio album recorded with Clapton, entitled *John Mayall & The Bluesbreakers*, was recorded in 1966 and is widely considered on both sides of the Atlantic to be one of the great classic blues albums.

At the start of the 1970s Mayall relocated to the USA, where he spent most of the next fifteen years, recording with local musicians for various labels. Here he assembled a band and recorded a live album, *Jazz Blues Fusion*, which was released in early 1972, with Mayall on harmonica, guitar and piano, Blue Mitchell on trumpet, Clifford Solomon and Ernie Watts on saxophones, Larry Taylor on bass, Ron Selico on drums and Freddy Robinson on guitar. This was John's lineup for his visit to Lancaster.

John Mayall continues to record and tour in his eighties.

Eggs over Easy were an American country rock band of the early 1970s who, after visiting London, decided to stay, record an album and become the resident band in a North London public house called The Tally Ho, starting what was to become known as pub rock. The album that started it all for Eggs Over Easy was *Good 'N' Cheap*, released in 1972. The band existed from 1969 to 1981 and featured ex-Animals drummer John Steel.

Matching Mole were an English progressive rock band associated with the Canterbury scene, formed by Robert Wyatt in October 1971 following his departure from Soft Machine. With Wyatt providing vocals and drums he was joined by David Sinclair, of Caravan, on organ and piano, Phil Miller on guitar and Bill MacCormick, formerly of Quiet Sun, on bass. Matching Mole disbanded in late September 1972.

The Lancaster story contains many momentous events, but it also includes many missed opportunities. Moments when readers of this book will say, "Wow, really?!" or "Bloody hell I remember that, why didn't I go?" or, "OMG, I didn't realise that they had played there!" Or some such thing.

Well in 1972 John Mayall played his only college date in Europe, at Lancaster. Talk to any R&B, rock, or blues musician from the middle '60s to the late '70s about John Mayall and they will have either played with him (if they were good enough), or been massively influenced by him. Every British musician was in awe of John Mayall.

Not the Lancaster audience though. It is almost impossible to believe now but only about 600 people turned up. I could not believe it at the time and find it even more confusing today, that, even if they didn't have his records, more did not come just to say they had seen a legend. Bet there's many more today regretting the missed opportunity.

Barry Lucas

John Miles

10 March 1978 — Support: Johnny Cougar
30 April 1979 — Support: Bandit

John Miles, from Jarrow, Tyne and Wear, is an English rock music vocalist, songwriter, guitarist and keyboard player, best known for his 1976 Top 3 UK hit single 'Music'. John made two visits to Lancaster for headlining concerts having previously appeared in March 1976 as support to Procol Harum.

Throughout the late '80s and into the '90s John Miles was musical director to Tina Turner on her various tours, as well as playing on several of her albums. He also played Hammond organ on Joe Cocker's 1992 album *Night Calls*. Today he is still making music, which he famously refers to as his "first love".

2002 saw him issue the DVD *John Miles – Live In Concert*.

John Miles brought along **Johnny Cougar** to provide support for his 1978 Lancaster show. Johnny's first record was released under the stage name of "Johnny Cougar" at the behest of Tony DeFries, his first manager. A few years later in 1982, he made his breakthrough with the album *American Fool*, which included the hit singles 'Hurts So Good' and 'Jack and Diane' under the stage name John Cougar.

With 1983's *Uh-Huh* album, he added back his real last name to become known as John Cougar Mellencamp. By the time 1987's *The Lonesome Jubilee* album had appeared he had dropped the Cougar moniker altogether and has been known since as John Mellencamp.

Bandit were a British rock band that existed from 1976 to 1979. Bandit included future AC/DC bassist Cliff Williams, former founder and guitarist of Colosseum, James Litherland, and drummer Graham Broad, now of Roger Waters' band. The band released two albums on Arista records with two different lineups. Interestingly, the only member of Bandit to appear on both of these albums was Danny McIntosh who is now guitarist for, and husband of, Kate Bush. 1977 saw Bandit also provide support at Lancaster to The Sensational Alex Harvey Band.

Johnny Winter Band

12 February 1971 — Support: Mogul Thrash

John Dawson Winter III, known as Johnny Winter, was an American musician, singer, songwriter, multi-instrumentalist and producer. He was born cross-eyed and albino and disregarded Mother Nature's unkindness to fashion himself a career as one of the few great white blues-rockers.

Johnny Winter was something of a musical child prodigy, growing up in Beaumont, Texas, on a diet of blues and rock 'n' roll. His first instruments were the clarinet and the ukulele, eventually settling on the guitar by the age of eleven.

Over his career he released a total of nineteen studio albums and seventeen live albums, including the March 1971 release of his album *Live Johnny Winter And,* shortly following his Great Hall concert.

The album was recorded live during the autumn of 1970 at the Fillmore East in New York City and at Pirate's World in Dania, Florida, and as Barry describes was basically the Lancaster University set.

Lancaster band lineup:
Johnny Winter – vocals, guitar
Rick Derringer – vocals, guitar
Randy Jo Hobbs – vocals, bass
Bobby Caldwell – drums, percussion

Brother of rocker Edgar Winter, Johnny sadly passed away in 2014, aged seventy, whilst on tour in Switzerland.

Mogul Thrash were a UK progressive rock band active in the early 1970s. The band consisted of former Colosseum guitarist James Litherland, plus future Average White Band members Michael Rosen and the so-called "Dundee Horns", aka saxophonists Roger Ball and Malcolm Duncan. Mogul Thrash also included future King Crimson and Uriah Heep bass guitarist John Wetton.

Following the demise of Mogul Thrash in 1971, Wetton immediately joined Roger Chapman's Family for a year. The band released just the one album, the eponymous *Mogul Thrash* in 1971. It was produced by Hammond organ maestro, Brian Auger, who contributed piano on one of the tracks.

Johnny Winter on stage in the Great Hall

Over the last forty-seven years one question has been asked of me more than any other: "OK, so what was your favourite concert?" Probably impossible to answer, I hear you say – memorable, unique, momentous, exciting, innovative, unusual, history making – what definition to use?

But every time over those forty-seven years I have answered instinctively with this show. If you were not there and you want to know what I am talking about, listen to *Johnny Winter Live And*; it is the Lancaster set and captures, as well as any recording can, the feel of a live show.

It was an early booking of mine and made through the John and Tony Smith Agency. To me, Winter was a legendary figure; not many albino rock/blues guitarists around and I didn't need a hard sell. The agency had a young booker there at the time called Harvey Goldsmith (you'll hear more of him at other points in the book) who was a bit reluctant to put the date in as he had the band in Redcar the day before and he wanted to be assured there would be no audience clash. I suggested he consulted a map of the UK – the last bus to Lancaster from Redcar probably left in 1935, and not at twenty-five to eight!

If you were there it will have been a show you will never forget. It was so exciting people were stood on the balcony rails, dancing (health and safety, where were you when you were needed?), though nobody died! Two duelling guitarists, Johnny Winter and Rick Derringer (already a great in his own right, he was in The McCoys – 'Hang On Sloopy' – and then played with Steely Dan and Alice Cooper) trying to outdo each other. Then Johnny Winter split the audience down the middle and we had a panto-style singing competition, his half against Rick's, with "A Whole Lotta Shakin' Going On". Can't remember who won it, but WHAT A NIGHT!

Barry Lucas

Judas Priest

27 January 1978 — Support: English Assassin
4 November 1978 — **Killing Machine Tour** — Support: Lea Hart

Leathery and loud, Judas Priest were another band that tried to undermine the structure of the Great Hall. They enjoyed playing Lancaster so much that they came back for more, eleven months later in 1978.

Led by Rob Halford, decked out in leather and chains, the band fused the gothic doom of Black Sabbath with the riffs and speed of Led Zeppelin, as well as adding a vicious two-lead guitar attack; in doing so, they set the pace for much popular heavy metal from 1975 until 1985. Judas Priest have released seventeen studio albums, six live albums and thirty-three singles, their best known being 'Living After Midnight' which reached No. 12 in 1980.

English Assassin were a short-lived rock band that featured Nigel Benjamin, previously a singer and guitarist with Mott The Hoople from 1974–1976. They recorded an album for Arista but it was never released.

Lea Hart Band were a heavy metal band led by frontman Lea Hart. Hart featured on many top name rock albums as a backing vocalist or guitarist, including Joan Jett's *Bad Reputation* album.

Judy Tzuke

28 April 1982 — **The Shoot The Moon Tour** — Support: Danceclass

Judie Tzuke is an English singer-songwriter. She is best known for her 1979 hit 'Stay With Me Till Dawn', which reached No. 16 on the UK Singles Chart. In 2010, Tzuke released a thirty-year celebratory double album entitled *Moon On a Mirrorball* and continues to record and tour.

Danceclass were a UK power pop quartet from the North East of England, and the band featured Dave Taggart on vocals, Tony McAnaney on bass, Ali Reay on guitar and Trevor Brewis on drums. Danceclass were signed to A&M Records in 1981 and their self-titled album, produced by Mike Chapman, was recorded and released in 1982.

JUDAS PRIEST
ANGUS
PLUS
LEA HEART
UNIVERSITY OF LANCASTER
SAT. NOV. 4TH 7.30PM £1.75

John Angus

Juicy Lucy

20 February 1970 Support: California Purple

Juicy Lucy were a British blues/rock band formed in 1969, following the demise of a band called The Misunderstood. Vocalist Ray Owen, steel guitarist Glenn Ross Campbell and saxophone player Chris Mercer later recruited another guitarist in Neil Hubbard, along with bassist Keith Ellis and a drummer, Pete Dobson, to form Juicy Lucy. The band are best known for their UK Top 20 hit, a cover version of the Bo Diddley composition 'Who Do You Love?' which reached No. 14 in 1970.

In August 1971, Juicy Lucy appeared on the bill at the Weeley Festival near Clacton-on-Sea, Essex.

Information is scant regarding the support band **California Purple.**

I didn't book this as it was before my election but I did attend. It was an incredible show and if anybody reading this book has not listened to the album *Juicy Lucy* I suggest they do so as soon as possible. The slide guitar (which I must confess I am a sucker for) of Glenn Ross Campbell is fantastic. Listen to the album and then envisage 700 people sitting crosslegged on the Great Hall floor, shakin' their heads. Yes, that's what we were all doing back then – out of control head shakin'. Wild or what?

Barry Lucas

Kevin Coyne Band

9 May 1975 Support: Starry Eyed and Laughing

Kevin Coyne from Derby was a musician, singer, composer, film-maker and a writer of lyrics, stories and poems.

Coyne was notable for his unorthodox style of blues-influenced guitar composition and the intense quality of his vocal delivery.

Kevin worked from 1965 to 1968 as a social therapist and psychiatric nurse at Whittingham Hospital near Preston in Lancashire before going on to work for *The Soho Project* in London as a drugs counsellor. During this period of working with the mentally ill he performed regularly. His writing also reflected the injustice of the treatment of the mentally ill. Subsequently, his musical aspirations took precedence and he signed a record deal in 1969.

Notably, in Coyne's band was lead guitarist Andy Summers, before later joining The Police.

Championed by John Peel, Kevin Coyne released numerous albums and singles and was widely admired amongst his contemporaries, including Sting and John Lydon, but sadly Kevin did not achieve any real chart success in his career.

Kevin passed away in 2004.

Starry Eyed and Laughing were a British Rock band of the 1970s. Formed in London in1973, they released two albums on the CBS label, recorded three Peel Sessions and undertook a US tour, before dropping the 'Laughing' and evolving into Starry Eyed. The band finally dissolved in 1976.

Kid Creole and The Coconuts

9 October 1982 Support: Musical Youth

Kid Creole and the Coconuts are an American band created and led by August Darnell. Their music incorporates a number of styles, including big band jazz, disco and in particular Caribbean and Latin American salsa. The Coconuts are Kid Creole's glamorous trio of female backing vocalists.

The band achieved three UK Top 10 singles during 1982. 'I'm a Wonderful Thing, Baby' reached No. 4, 'Stool Pigeon' No. 7, and 'Annie, I'm Not Your Daddy' went to No. 2 in the UK Singles Chart. The band also has fourteen studio albums under their belt to date.

A tremendous live act, Kid Creole and The Coconuts continue to tour stateside. August Darnell currently has a home in Sweden and one in Hawaii, where he runs a Martini bar.

Musical Youth are a British reggae band from Handsworth, Birmingham, formed in 1979. They are best remembered for their successful 1982 single 'Pass the Dutchie', which became a No. 1 hit around the world and remained at No. 1 in the UK Singles Chart for three weeks, selling over five million copies worldwide.

The band recorded two studio albums and released a number of successful singles throughout 1982 and 1983, including a collaboration with Donna Summer.

Musical Youth earned a Grammy Award nomination before disbanding in 1985 after a series of personal problems. The band returned in 2001 as a duo and continues to tour and record, with an album due for release in 2017.

Like many bands, Kid Creole's crew had major difficulties with the physical structure of the Great Hall. While it was designed to be acoustically perfect for classical music concerts, it was not ideal, by any means, for rock'n'roll. The sound did have a tendency to bounce from the back wall. But Kid Creole, on being informed of the difficulties his crew was having doing the pre-sound check, just responded like a true pro. "No problem. I've played so many college sports halls in the States, same construction. Just stick some blankets or sheets up on the back wall. It'll be OK, man. Let's do it."

Barry Lucas

The Kid and his Coconuts in the Great Hall ©Geoff Campbell

King Crimson

8 October 1971

Supports: Ashton Gardner and Dyke | The Reason Why

British art rockers King Crimson were formed in early 1969, emerging out of an outfit called Giles, Giles and Fripp (aka drummer/singer Mike Giles, bassist/singer Peter Giles and guitarist Robert Fripp). Later the band added bassist Greg Lake and lyricist Peter Sinfield.

The lineup of King Crimson has varied drastically from album to album. Original lead singer and bassist Greg Lake left the group after a year – as did lyricist Peter Sinfield – and went on to fame with Emerson, Lake & Palmer in 1970, replaced by Gordon Haskell, Boz Burrell and, briefly, Jon Anderson of Yes. Also from Yes came drummer Bill Bruford, who joined King Crimson in 1972 and became one of the more enduring members. For the next three years, Bruford and Fripp were joined by future Asia frontman, John Wetton.

Robert Fripp has been the sole consistent member throughout the group's history and continues to front the current incarnation of King Crimson that are still active today.

King Crimson 1971 Lancaster band lineup:
Robert Fripp – guitars
Ian Wallace – drums
Boz Burrell – bass guitar
Mel Collins – sax, flutes
Peter Sinfield – keyboards, synthesizers

This was the first King Crimson tour since 1969, with the band performing tracks from the the album *Islands*, which was released in December 1971 and reached No. 30 in the UK and No. 76 in the US album charts.

Ashton, Gardner and Dyke were a rock trio, most popular in the early 1970s. They are best remembered for their 1971 hit 'Resurrection Shuffle' which got to No. 3 in the UK Singles Chart. The song was their only hit record, earning them the designation 'one-hit wonder'. The song has since been covered by a number of artists, including Tom Jones.

The Reason Why completed the night's triple bill but little is known about the band.

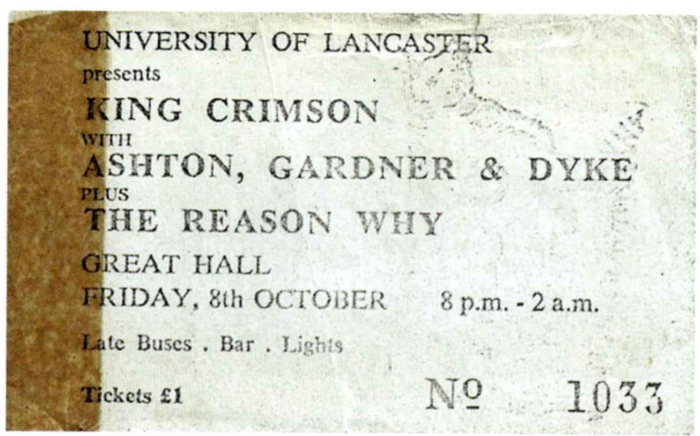

The Kinks

26 February 1971 **Rag Ball** Supports: Quintessence I Shakin' Stevens and The Sunsets
15 March 1974 Support: Snafu
12 March 1976 Support unknown

The Kinks were an English rock band formed in Muswell Hill, North London, in 1963 by brothers Dave and Ray Davies with bass player Pete Quaife, later joined by drummer Mick Avory. During the early to mid 1970s, The Kinks visited the university on three occassions. The band rose to fame during the mid 1960s with singles such as 'You Really Got Me', a No. 1 hit in the UK and reaching No. 7 in the US in 1964. 'All Day and All of the Night' in 1965 was followed up by the single 'Dedicated Follower of Fashion' in 1966. The Kinks were active for more than thirty years between 1963 and 1996, releasing twenty-eight regular albums in the UK (twenty-four studio and four live), along with seventeen Top 20 singles. Ray Davies was recognised in the 2016 New Year's honours list with a knighthood for services to the arts.

Support for this 1971 Rag Ball event was provided by the jazz/psychedelic outfit **Quintessence**, who appeared with The Who in their 1970 Great Hall concert.

Shakin' Stevens put the university's Bechstein grand piano through its paces!

Snafu's first Great Hall support slot prior to returning a year later with Status Quo.

> **The Kinks**: I have lots of affection for the chroniclers of 60s Britain and glorious songcraft. Ray Davies is in a white flared suit. The set ends and they leave the stage to a rapturous response. House lights stay down but the stage remains empty and there is no encore. A deflated audience wanders off into the night.
>
> Maurice Hubbard (Pink Custard Light Show)

The only thing I can remember about this show – a Rag Ball I think it was, I was booking them by then – was the fact that an artist of Shakin' Stevens' calibre was demanding a grand piano, tuned to concert pitch on the day. It was the day that convinced me – or rather the Director of the University's Music Department – that we should purchase one. I had persuaded him to let me borrow the department's Bechstein grand. It took a lot of doing; after all, would a pop star off *TOTPs* treat a concert grand with the respect it deserves? Of course he would, I assured the good doctor.

I sat in the balcony as Shakin' Stevens jumped up on the piano then sat and played the song by banging the keys with his heels – enough said!

Barry Lucas

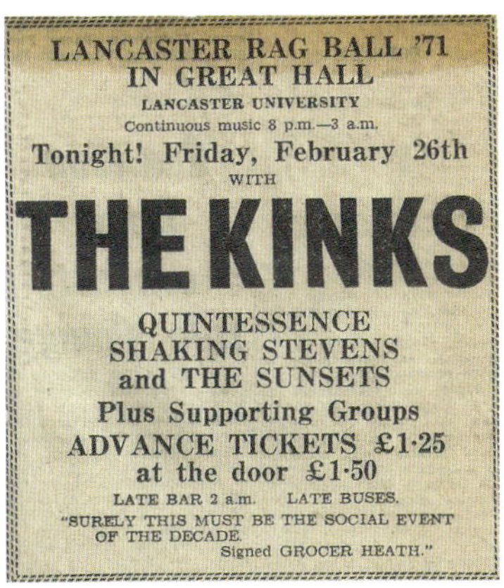

Kursaal Flyers

30 January 1976 Support: Eddie and The Hot Rods

The Kursaal Flyers were a British band formed in Southend-On-Sea, Essex, in 1973 and had a solid reputation on the London pub rock scene. They are most famous for their November 1976 single 'Little Does She Know', which reached No. 14 in the UK Singles Chart; their one and only hit.

Soon after the success of The Kursaal's single, the lead guitarist Graeme Douglas became concerned about the over-commercialisation and general direction of the group's music and left to join their support act on the night, Eddie and the Hot Rods.

Eddie and The Hot Rods' first visit to the Great Hall was as support to the Kursaal Flyers, soon after making a name for themselves on the London pub circuit.

Later in 1976, Eddie and The Hotrods headlined at The Marquee club in London.

Their opening act was a young band named the Sex Pistols, playing their first London gig, which descended into chaos with the Pistols smashing the Hot Rods' gear. October 1977 saw the Hot Rods back at the university as headliners.

This was THE concert poster, the one that began a long and very fruitful relationship between myself and John Angus. There is some disagreement between us as to how it all began. I think that John's wife, Mary, came to see me to say that she had got a teaching post at the University and her partner was coming up from Birmingham to join her. She explained that he was an artist/screen-printer and asked if I would be interested in giving him work producing my concert posters. They tell the story differently, that it was John and not Mary who came to see me. Well, it *was* over forty years ago!

Whatever the beginning, it was a very opportune moment to meet John. Most of my 'artistic' posters were produced in Yorkshire by an old friend of Gaz Taylor. He had been doing them since 1970 and had created some great ones, but the distance did have its problems. I frequently required a poster at a few days notice and BR's Red Star Service was in constant use. It was fairly efficient but it naturally added a couple of days to each turnaround. Having somebody based in Lancaster seemed a godsend so I gave John 'Kursaal Flyers' to see how things went. Now, John doesn't particularly like this poster, but to me it is so important. As soon as I saw it I knew that I had, fortuitously, stumbled on a winner.

About three shows in Mike Lloyd came up to see me to discuss that year's Graduation Ball's artists. I always booked the acts through Mike, who owned a couple of record shops, a small provincial booking agency and was also a promoter at Hanley Victoria Hall, Stoke-on-Trent. He was a good sounding board in the early days and taught me a great deal. He was also able to recommend the big bands, jazz groups, comics etc. that I had started to use on the, now formal, balls. Before we went to lunch I had to show him John's posters. I was so excited by my discovery of this new talent that I couldn't wait to show it off. I spread out three posters for different shows. "Aren't they great?" I enthused. Mike was not as excited, indeed he was most underwhelmed.

"They're OK, but can you see them at night, on a billboard, in the rain, on the top deck of a number seven bus in Stoke-on-Trent? Dayglo, that's your answer, black letters on orange background. That's a poster, that'll do the job for you."

Well, he had a point, but John's posters were works of art, real collectors' pieces. Many a time I had been sticking posters up on the Spine's noticeboards, only to find on the return journey to my office that they had been carefully peeled off and removed to some student's bedroom to dry out.

To me this book has four key, unique elements: Paul Tomlinson's meticulous research and collecting of memorabilia, memories and photos; Geoff Campbell's great photographs; my narrative and reminiscences of the period; and John Angus' iconic posters. No single element is more important than any other but without any one of these elements the book would be significantly diminished.

In total, John produced gig posters for around seventy-five concerts and everybody has their favourite – I personally loved the Stiff Little Fingers poster – but the John Angus style is instantly recognisable and memorable. John kindly agreed to allows us to reproduce over forty of them in this book.

Barry Lucas

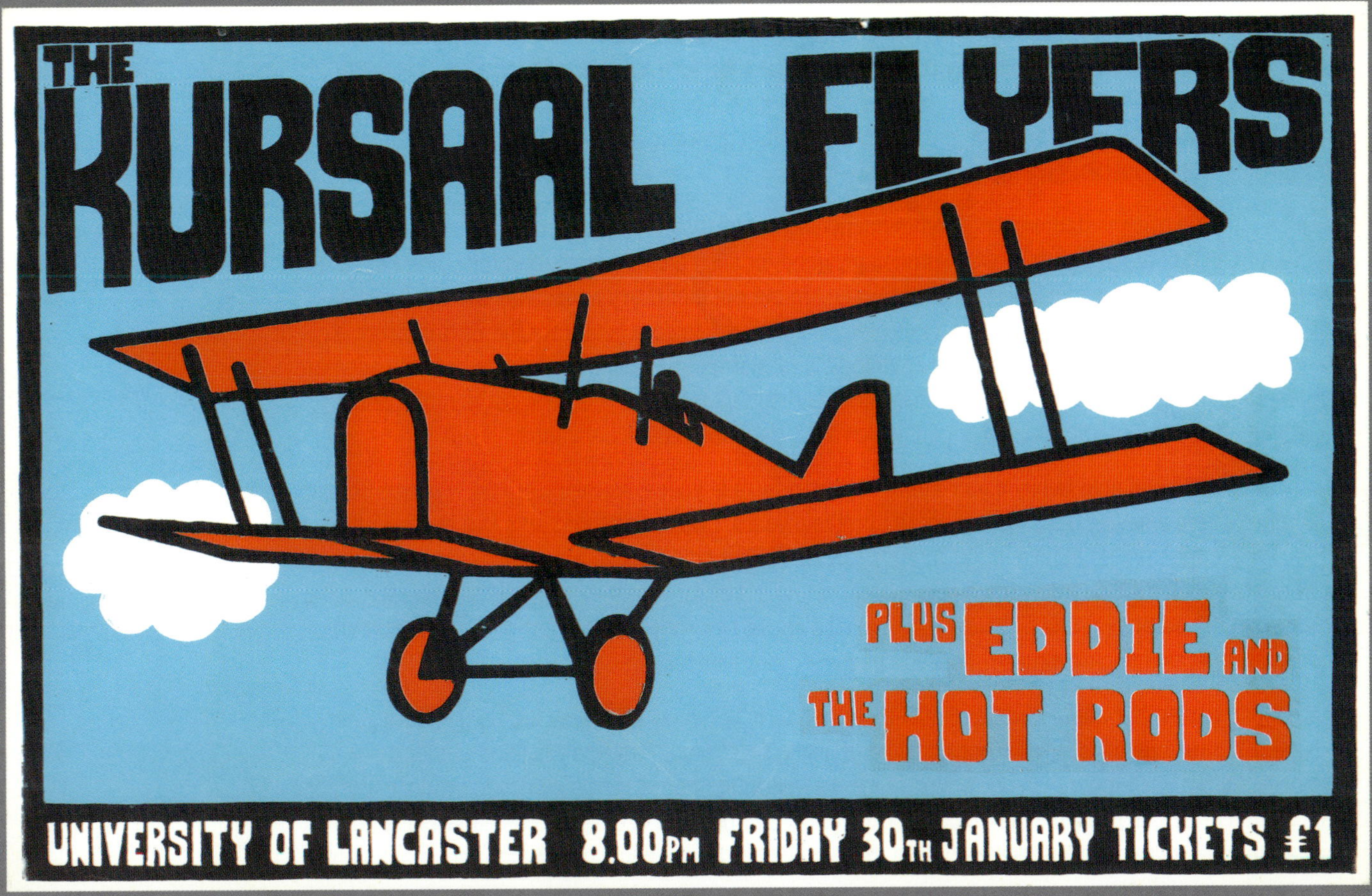
THE
KURSAAL FLYERS
PLUS EDDIE AND
THE HOT RODS
UNIVERSITY OF LANCASTER 8.00PM FRIDAY 30TH JANUARY TICKETS £1

John Angus

Lancaster University Gig Posters 1976–1981
by John Angus

In 1975, I was based at Birmingham Arts Lab, designing and screen-printing posters for various arts and music events and organising exhibitions. I had decided not to pursue an academic career in genetics and had learnt screen-printing from two friends. I had no plan and I hadn't been at the Arts Lab for long, but it was a great place to be. Then my partner, Mary, got a job as a lecturer at Lancaster University, so I had to decide whether to move too. My friends thought it was crazy: "It's a tiny place with nothing going on and there won't be any demand for posters". I had grown up in big cities, so I shared these misgivings, but decided to give it a go.

Looking around, the most interesting events happening in Lancaster were the rock concerts up at the university. In fact the programme was surprisingly good for such a small place, and they didn't seem to have any posters. This seemed like an opportunity! I found out that Barry Lucas was the man to speak to, so I took some of my work along to show him. He asked me to do a poster for the next concert, a band called Kursaal Flyers. I didn't know anything about them, but a bold drawing of a bi-plane seemed appropriate. Barry was presumably satisfied with the result as he asked me to do some more, and a fruitful regular working relationship began, which helped me to settle in Lancaster.

Mary and I had been able to buy a four-storey Victorian terrace house, as they were fairly cheap here at that time. There was lots of space and for the first few years, I was printing posters in a room on the top floor. I made the printing table and the screens myself. At first I didn't have a drying rack, but spread the wet prints out on the floor of the adjoining room. I set up a darkroom in the cellar and the screens were cleaned in the bathroom. Later, I found a huge space above two shops in the centre of town and that became my workshop, allowing our house to become more domesticated.

I produced posters for about seventy-five of these concerts between 1976 and 1981. For each poster, I screen-printed one hundred plus copies by hand, using two to four hand-painted and photographic stencils. I often used more than one colour of ink when printing from a single stencil to produce a graded or blended effect, so getting more colours for the effort and price. This effect is easy to achieve on a computer now, but it was a skilled technique then, especially to maintain consistency over many prints.

All these posters were produced quickly. I would get a phone call from Barry, with the name of the band, the gig date and ticket price. The finished posters were usually needed within a week, so there was not much time for thought. I would search around for appropriate images, in the library, the record shop and elsewhere, or would draw something. There was no internet.

I didn't know anything about most of the bands. For me, producing posters was about creating artworks which had a purpose. Barry was an ideal commissioner. As long as the name of the band was clear and all the other information legible, he didn't mind what was on the poster. He never asked to see a design and anyway, there was no time for that. So I had freedom to play, which was great. I was creating bold, brightly coloured images, with the intention that these images would attract attention to the information which the poster was intended to communicate.

Occasionally I used an image of the band, if I could find one, but that was rare – The Damned, Hazel O'Connor – and sometimes I did drawings based on photos of the performer, including Joan Armatrading, Graham Parker, John Cooper Clarke and AC/DC.

Sometimes I visually punned on the name. For a band called MAN, the letters of the name suggested to me the shape of a moulded jelly/blancmange. It seemed a bit contrary to any macho image, especially in pink, but no-one seemed to mind. I continued with Thin Lizzy as an elephant, Focus a pair of spectacles and Deaf School one of men with their fingers in their ears.

I used photographs I had taken, such as an old Citroen I saw somewhere in France (Jack Bruce), a billboard 100 yards from our house (Peter Gabriel), shop window mannequins (Wishbone Ash), a landscape (John Martyn), a closed cafe in Morecambe (Sad Cafe), the gasometer behind our house (Hot Chocolate), some gargoyles (Climax Blues Band).

I also used B&W photos I noticed in the newspapers which I used when cleaning the screens – The Undertones, Hawkwind, The Rezillos, and Judas Priest.

I made collages from these and other images – a band photo and other stuff (The Jam), eyes (The Adverts), various newspaper clippings (Third World). Sometimes it was a combination of my photos and found ones – a young woman in Birmingham and a newspaper clipping (Steel Pulse).

Producing these posters was a very satisfying activity. I was designing and making things by hand, delivering them and getting paid in cash. As posters, they had a function and were displayed in public. But they would not be around for long, so they were not precious and I felt I could experiment. This was my personal training ground and I tried to learn something about technique, colour or design with every poster.

An extra source of income was to print a few more than the 100 posters required and to sell these extras in the foyer at the concerts. We would get in early and set up stall. When the doors opened there was a rush and some kids would head straight for the posters. This sometimes seemed a bit scary as they were punks in black leather, torn T-shirts, chains and spiky dyed hair. They would even argue about the price (50p!). But when we got chatting, they were all perfectly friendly and harmless.

Bands didn't do much merchandising in those days, so they generally didn't care about me selling posters. On a few occasions the band or their staff would come for a look and to comment. The Jam complained that I'd made them look like a punk band, which I thought they were. Lindisfarne were the only ones who would not let me sell. Someone with Stiff Records asked me to work for them, but required me to move to London and to set up there.

The posters I was producing for these gigs at Lancaster University began to attract attention and other venues started asking me for posters. I went on to design posters for arts events across the North West and all around the UK, for the next twenty-five years.

I had exhibitions of posters, including at the Royal Northern College of Music in Manchester, which was reviewed in *The Guardian*, and an Arts Council tour of venues in North West. These exhibitions included some of the Lancaster gig posters. In 2012, the Peter Scott Gallery at Lancaster University hosted an exhibition entitled "Was I there?" which included about twenty of these posters and reflected on people's memories of these concerts.

These gig posters were only intended to last for a week, or two at most, so there was no thought of them being around over forty years later. Over the past few years, various collectors, including one living in Venice, have contacted me and purchased some of the posters I have kept. Some posters have appeared in books, such as *The Art of Punk* and someone sent me a photo of a framed Stiff Little Fingers poster which they had rescued from a nearby skip in Los Angeles, now on display by their swimming pool. You never know what will happen to things that you make, but I'm delighted that these ones still have a life.

John Angus 2016

Leo Sayer

15 January 1975 Support: Sundance

On the back of three UK Top 10 singles, Leo Sayer, real name Gerald Hugh Sayer, played the Great Hall to promote his 1975 album release *Another Year.*

There was a poor audience on the night according to accounts.

Leo Sayer first came to attention with his 1973 hit record 'The Show Must Go On', performing it dressed and made up as a Pierrot clown. His first seven hit singles in the United Kingdom all reached the Top 10; a feat previously achieved by his first manager, Adam Faith.

Shortly prior to this Lancaster appearance, October 1974 saw the release of his album *Just a Boy,* which reached No. 4 in the UK Albums Chart and featured hits such as 'One Man Band' and 'Long Tall Glasses'. The album also featured the single 'Giving It All Away' written by Sayer for Roger Daltrey's debut solo album *Daltrey.*

In October 1977 Leo Sayer released the album *Thunder in My Heart,* with the single of the same name reaching No. 22 in the UK Singles Chart that year. The track once again became a hit single in the UK when a remix by Meck (titled 'Thunder in My Heart Again') reached No. 1 in 2006 and stayed there for two weeks.

Sayer's career has spanned four decades and he now lives in Australia. He continues to record and tour, appearing in 2015 at The Grand Theatre, Lancaster.

A *SCAN* newspaper concert reviewer noted: "On the basis of Wednesday's performance he'll probably be around for a long time. If not at Lancaster then probably Las Vegas"

Not much is known about **Sundance** other than they were a Swedish jazz rock band that released one album in 1976.

Level 42

19 November 1982 Support unknown

Level 42 are an English pop rock and jazz-funk band, who had a number of worldwide and UK hits during the 1980s and 1990s.

Their most successful single in the UK was 'Lessons in Love', which reached No. 3 in the UK Singles Chart and No. 12 on the US Billboard Hot 100 Chart, upon its release in 1986. The earlier single, 'Something About You', was their most successful single in the United States, reaching No. 7 on the Billboard Hot 100 Chart.

After much success as a live and studio band in the 1980s, Level 42's commercial profile diminished during the early 1990s following a series of personnel changes and musical shifts. After disbanding in 1994, the band re-formed in 2001 and continue to tour and record.

Lindisfarne

11 November 1978	Supports: Chris Rea I Mike Elliot
7 October 1979	Support: Mike Elliot
11 October 1981	Support unknown

During the 1970s Lindisfarne were one of the hottest folk rock bands. Established in 1968 and originally called 'Brethren' they were led by singer/guitarist Alan Hull. The band also featured Simon Cowe on guitars, Ray Jackson on mandolin, bass player Rod Clements and drummer Ray Laidlaw. All were from the Newcastle upon Tyne area.

Lindisfarne were best known for their No. 1 single 'Fog on The Tyne', taken from their 1971 album of the same name which went on to become the UK best selling album of 1972. They also had major chart successes with songs such as 'Meet Me On The Corner', 'Lady Eleanor', 'Run For Home' and 'We Can Swing Together'.

Chris Rea is an English singer-songwriter and guitarist, recognisable for his distinctive, husky voice and slide guitar playing. Hailing from Middlesbrough his most well-known success was his 1989 UK No. 1 album *The Road to Hell*. With twenty-three studio albums and thirty-three UK hit singles under his belt, Rea is as busy as ever recording and touring.

Mike Elliot, also known as "Mike the Mouth", was a stand-up comedian, actor, television presenter and radio personality from Sunderland. Elliott had a number of acting roles, including George Watson in *Billy Elliot* and various roles in television drama series, including *Crocodile Shoes*, *Byker Grove*, *Spender*, *Harry* and *New Voices*.

This Lindisfarne story has nothing to do with their concert at Lancaster but everything to do with them as a band.

When I left Lancaster University, one of the ventures I became involved with was a company called Mayday. With fellow directors John Marsh and Steve Powell, we were involved in many fundraising activities for causes on the political left in the UK. These in included, among others, The African National Congress, Anti-Apartheid, and The Anti-Racist Alliance, and we were bi-annually committed to a fundraising event at The Labour Party Conference and the Trades Union Congress on behalf of *The Morning Star*.

The *Star* events had proved very successful as socials in raising much-needed funds for the newspaper. We had had bands such as Dr Feelgood, Climax Blues Band, Shane McGowan and Dick Gaughan etc., but for that year's Glasgow conference we were struggling. Obviously, *The Star* was the most left wing of the UK's national daily newspapers, with many past and current associations with the Communist Party, and this was a fundraising event, so a) the band couldn't mind the political connotations, and b) would play for a reduced fee. My two business partners and myself were scratching our heads. Steve suggested just sending a round robin letter to loads of bands. John and I shook our heads at such naïvety – we were worldly wise in the music business. "That will never work," we told him. A couple of days later, Steve rang to say that he had ignored our cynicism and sent the faxes anyway. By return, Lindisfarne had agreed to do it. That was brilliant but I was intrigued to know why. So, on the day, in Glasgow, I asked the band why they had so readily agreed to do it. One of the band pulled out a faded press cutting from his wallet. "When we were starting out *The Star* gave us our first national review. It raved about us. We always carry it around to remind us of the start and we like to repay a debt." Really says it all about this band.

Barry Lucas

Loudon Wainwright III

30 October 1980 Support: Beverley Martyn

Loudon Snowden Wainwright III is a Grammy Award-winning American songwriter, folk singer, humorist and actor who started his career in the late '60s, singing humorous and autobiographical songs.

He is the father of musicians Rufus Wainwright, Martha Wainwright and Lucy Wainwright Roche, and is the former husband of the late folk singer Kate McGarrigle. Loudon is probably best known for his song 'Dead Skunk' and continues to put out new albums and to tour.

To date, Wainwright has released twenty-six studio albums.

Beverley Martyn is an English folk rock singer, songwriter and guitarist. In 1969 she met John Martyn, whom she later married. As a duo they issued two albums, *Stormbringer!* and *The Road to Ruin,* both of which were released on the Island Records label. They couple were divorced in 1980. Beverley Martyn had previously appeared in the Great Hall as a support act to Sparks in 1974. Martyn released a new album in 2014 entitled *The Phoenix and The Turtle*.

Love

16 May 1974 Support: Casablanca

Love, founded by Arthur Lee in Los Angeles, are one of the seminal garage/folk/psychedelic bands of the1960s, recording three albums on the Elektra label including *Forever Changes*, an album that is regarded as one the greatest rock albums of all time.

Signed to Elektra records, along with the Doors (who were influenced by them in their early days), Love were the kings of the Los Angeles psychedelic rock scene during the late sixties.

Arthur Lee continued to make music under the name Love after the original lineup split in early 1968, as well as working on his solo material.

The original theme tune for the BBC's *Holiday* programme in the early 1970s was Love's 'The Castle'. Gordon Giltrap's 'Heartsong' was used as the theme tune from 1978 until the end of the 1985 series.

Written by Arthur Lee's fellow songwriter Bryan MacLean, the song 'Alone Again Or' was a single released by The Damned in 1987 on the MCA label. They recorded it as an acknowledgement to one of their influences, the band Love.

Arthur Lee spent his last years touring the *Forever Changes* album with a new backing band following his release from prison in 2001, and performed the entire *Forever Changes* album in a concert in the Royal Albert Hall in 2003.

Arthur Lee died in Memphis in 2006, aged sixty-one.

A version of the band called Love Revisited is still active, featuring original guitarist and co-founder Johnny Echols.

Support on the night came from an eight-piece band called **Casablanca** who were fronted by singer-songwriter Aliki Ashman, known for her previous role with Ginger Baker's Air Force around 1970. Also in the lineup was former Dada and Vinegar Joe bassist Steve York.

Lynyrd Skynyrd

12 February 1977 **The Street Survivors Tour** Support: Clover

The Street Survivors Tour was the sixth major concert tour by American Southern Rock band Lynyrd Skynyrd. It was one of their last ever UK concerts and was a fabulous gig at Lancaster University.

Band members:
Ronnie Van Zant – vocals
Allen Collins – guitars
Gary Rossington – guitars
Steve Gaines – guitars
Billy Powell – keyboards
Leon Wilkeson – bass
Artimus Pyle – drums

Setlist on the night: 'Workin' For MCA', 'I Ain't The One', 'Saturday Night Special', 'Whiskey Rock-A-Roller', 'That Smell', 'Travelin' Man', 'Ain't No Good Life', 'Gimme Three Steps', 'Call Me The Breeze', 'T For Texas', 'Sweet Home Alabama', 'Free Bird'.

The tour took place in North America, Europe, and for the first time Asia. It was also the final tour of the original band, as a number of the band members were tragically killed in a plane crash on 20 October 1977 following the final show of the tour. The hired plane carrying the band ran out of fuel and crashed in Gillsburg, Mississippi, near to the end of its flight from Greenville, South Carolina, to Baton Rouge, Louisiana. Lead singer Ronnie Van Zant, guitarist/vocalist Steve Gaines, backing vocalist Cassie Gaines (Steve's older sister), assistant road manager Dean Kilpatrick, pilot Walter McCreary and co-pilot William Gray all died as a result of the crash. Twenty others survived.

Lynyrd Skynyrd were the definitive Southern rock band with a hard rebellious Southern image, playing hard-driving Southern rock and roll. For those who don't know and for those who are curious, the band's name was a mocking tribute to a physical education teacher at Ronnie Van Zant's High School, Leonard Skinner. Mr Skinner was notorious for strictly enforcing the school's policy against boys having long hair.

Over Lynyrd Skynyrd's career they released a total of fouteen studio and six live albums.

Following the air tragedy, survivors Gary Rossington and Allen Collins teamed up to form The Rossington Collins Band in 1980 and were scheduled to appear at Lancaster University that same year, but cancelled due to the sudden death of Allen Collin's wife.

Clover were an American country rock band formed in San Francisco in 1967. They are best known as the backing band for Elvis Costello's 1977 debut album, *My Aim Is True.* Notable members of the band included lead singer Hugh Anthony Cregg, better known as Huey Lewis, who joined the band in 1972 and performed with them until their split in 1978. Providing pedal steel guitar was John McFee, who went on to join The Doobie Brothers in 1979. The band had previously appeared at the university as guests of Thin Lizzy in November 1976 and would return again to support Graham Parker in November 1977.

Ronnie Van Zant ©Gina Thistlethwaite

Gary Rossington ©Gina Thistlethwaite

Allen Collins ©Gina Thistlethwaite

Lynyrd Skynyrd

Huey Lewis and Clover providing support to Lynyrd Skynyrd ©Gina Thistlethwaite

I can't say a great deal about Lynyrd Skynyrd's performance except that it was monumentally important for all the wrong reasons. Put into Lancaster by Paul Loasby at Harvey Goldsmith's, the only university date in the UK. It was also one of their final dates in the UK. Sadly, later in October that same year three band members along with others would die in a plane crash in the United States.

Also on the bill that night were a support band called Clover. A superb band. I had them on three times as a support act. Graham Parker and the Rumour and Thin Lizzy were other headliners involved. *College Event* – a magazine for the college circuit in particular and the business in general – asked ten major figures on the music scene, one Christmas, for their predictions as to who would make it big in the coming year. I was one of those asked but I was very disappointed that every other contributor picked a band that had almost made it already, not an up and coming unknown. I picked Clover and had to endure months of ridicule from within the business. Later that year they changed their name … to become Huey Lewis and the News. I rest my case!

Barry Lucas

Magazine

30 November 1978 Support: Neo

Magazine were an English post-punk band formed in Manchester by Howard Devoto shortly after he left Buzzcocks in 1977. The band were active from 1977 to 1981, then again from 2009–2011. This Great Hall appearance was included in the band's UK tour to promote the release in June 1978 of the acclaimed album *Real Life*, which went on to reach No. 29 in the UK Albums Chart. In total they produced five studio and four live albums, along with ten singles.

Magazine's music continues to be an influence today. Radiohead in particular draw on the lyrical style of the group and have performed the single 'Shot By Both Sides' from *Real Life* in their live sets.

Neo were an early new wave band formed in London. The group were formed by the American-born singer/bassist Ian North, who was the frontman and the only continuous member from the band's formation in 1977 to their split in 1979. Neo guitarist Robert Simon left the band in late '78 to join Ultravox, only to leave them in 1980 and join up with Magazine.

Howard Devoto in the Great Hall ©Geoff Campbell

Manfred Mann's Earth Band

9 November 1973 Support: Steve Gibbons

Manfred Mann's Earth Band are an English rock band formed by South African musician Manfred Mann. The band's hits include covers of Bruce Springsteen's 'Blinded by the Light' in 1976 and 'Spirit In The Night'. After forming in 1971 and despite a short hiatus in the late 1980s/early 1990s, the Earth Band has continued to perform and tour through to the present.

Mann started in the 1960s with the self-titled British invasion band that had such hits as 'Do Wah Diddy Diddy' and 'The Mighty Quinn', and then moved on to jazz fusion-inspired Manfred Mann Chapter Three, before forming the Earth Band in 1971.

Manfred Mann's Earth Band have been releasing albums and singles since 1971 and to date have released seventeen studio albums, three live albums and seven compilation albums. The band are also well known for their 1978 single 'Davy's on the Road Again'.

Steve Gibbons from Harborne, Birmingham, is an English rock vocalist and guitarist.

1971 saw Steve Gibbons form his new band and begin to work the pub and club circuits until 1975 when they were spotted by Peter Meaden, the former manager of The Who. This led to The Steve Gibbons Band joining The Who's management stable and recording their first Polydor album *Any Road Up* in 1975 (with John Entwistle of The Who playing on a few tracks). This was followed in 1976 by a tour with The Who in the UK, Europe and the United States.

Playing large concert arenas, the band shared stages with Little Feat, Lynyrd Skynyrd, Electric Light Orchestra, The J. Geils Band and Nils Lofgren. Their next album, *Rollin' On*, included their biggest hit single 'Tulane', a covered Chuck Berry song. They eventually went on to make three more albums with Polydor.

January 1977 saw Steve Gibbons back in the Great Hall for a concert as guests of Bill Nelson's Be-Bop Deluxe.

Marc Almond

1 November 1985 Support unknown

Probably one of the worst attended concerts I came across during my research, former member of Soft Cell, Marc Almond, attracted an audience of just over 200 souls according to the concert review in *SCAN* newspaper.

A concert-goer remembered Marc Almond announcing to the audience: "At this point I normally introduce the band to you, but I think it would be quicker if you introduced yourselves to us."

Soft Cell are an English synth-pop duo who came to prominence in the early 1980s, consisting of vocalist Almond and instrumentalist David Ball. The pair are best known for their 1981 hit version of 'Tainted Love'.

'Tainted Love' is a song composed by Ed Cobb, formerly of American group The Four Preps, and was originally recorded by Marc Bolan's girlfriend, Gloria Jones, in 1964.

By 1983, fame and near-constant drug use were having a bad effect on Soft Cell and led to the duo splitting, with Almond pursuing a solo career. He achieved Top 10 UK single chart successes with 'Something's Gotten Hold of My Heart' (featuring Gene Pitney) in 1989 and 'The Days of Pearly Spencer' in 1992.

In 2011 Soft Cell re-formed and the band periodically still tour.

Marillion

9 May 1982	**Saliva Tears Tour**	Support unknown
12 February 1984	**The Fugazi Tour**	Support: Rage

Marillion were formed in 1979 as Silmarillion, after J.R.R. Tolkien's book *The Silmarillion*, by drummer Mick Pointer and guitarist Steve Rothery.

Derek William Dick, better known as "Fish", joined Marillion in 1981 and came to the public's attention as the band gained popularity over the next couple of years, leading to the release of their Top 10 debut album, *Script for a Jester's Tear,* in 1983. The band achieved further chart success in the UK, attaining Top 10 hit singles in 1985 with 'Kayleigh' and 'Lavender', and again in 1987 with 'Incommunicado'.

Fish has sometimes been compared to Peter Gabriel, lead singer of Genesis in the early 1970s, and his voice has even been described as "uncannily close" to Gabriel's.

Fish left Marillion in 1988 to pursue his solo career.

In 1999, DJ Simon Mayo commented on BBC Radio 1: "Marillion … where are they now? And who cares anyway?" Fans objecting to the comment brought the station's computer system to a standstill with thousands of emails of complaint.

Marillion continue to record and tour.

Formed in 1984 under the name Avenger, **Rage** are a German heavy metal band, founded by Peter "Peavy" Wagner, who are still active today.

I was asked to take a date on Marillion in about 1983 but unfortunately the period they wanted was in the Easter vacation. Now, I had promoted some acts when the students were on holiday but these were considerably bigger draws than Marillion: Clapton, Peter Gabriel, Hawkwind (with Ginger Baker), Steve Winwood and Souixie and the Banshees, for example. As the audience would all be locals, and as the Students' Union would get the bar take, I offered them The Sugar House. They, somewhat reluctantly, agreed and we did the date. The audience was about four hundred and fifty, so approximately what I had expected. However, Fish was not amused with the gig, the stage and the dressing room etc. In fact he wrote with indelible marker all across the dressing room walls, "This is the worst shit'ole I have ever played". You must remember he was a major star then! I wonder if that statement is still true today? The graffiti lasted considerably longer than their "stardom".

Barry Lucas

Motorhead

17 November 1979 **Bomber Tour** Support: Saxon

Motorhead were a British heavy metal band formed in London in 1975 by bassist, singer and songwriter Ian Fraser Kilmister, better known by his stage name of Lemmy.

Although Motorhead are typically classified as heavy metal their fusion of punk rock into the genre helped to pioneer speed and thrash metal. Lemmy disliked such labels, preferring to describe the band's music simply as "rock 'n' roll", and usually opening live their shows with the line "We are Motorhead. We play rock and roll".

Prior to forming Motorhead, Lemmy was bassist for Hawkwind, joining them in 1971. In 1975 Lemmy was arrested at the Canada/US border in Windsor, Ontario, on drug possession charges; he spent five days in jail, causing Hawkwind to cancel some of their North America tour dates, but was released without charge. Nonetheless he was fired from Hawkwind. He immediately set about forming a new band which he called Bastard. When his manager informed him that a band of that name would never get a slot on *Top of the Pops*, Lemmy changed the band's name to 'Motorhead' – the title of the last song he had written for Hawkwind. Motorhead's discography includes twenty-two studio albums and nine live albums.

Lemmy and Motorhead visited Lancaster to support the release of the album *Bomber* in October 1979. The album reached No. 12 in the UK Albums Chart. Lemmy died on 28 December 2015 from prostate cancer and heart failure. After his death, drummer Mikkey Dee and guitarist Phil Campbell both confirmed that Motörhead would not continue as a band.

Support on the evening came from South Yorkshire band **Saxon**, who were established in 1976 and one of the leaders of the so called new wave of British heavy metal. The band still tours regularly and has sold more than fifteen million albums worldwide to date.

This concert was memorable for two reasons. Firstly, the mind-blowing stage set, obviously inspired by the name of the album and tour, *Bomber*. The audience walked through those heavy, wooden Great Hall doors to be greeted by a replica of a Second World War bomber which dominated the whole stage. As the band took to the stage the hall was filled with the sound of engines firing up and then the propellers were created by several bright, sheer white spotlights. They slowly revolved, speeding up as the roar of the 'engines' got louder and louder, until, in a blur of spinning light and screaming, deafening engines, the band sprang onto the stage. Tremendous.

I understood that Motorhead had a biker following in those days but I must admit we were not prepared for the sight of three Hells Angels chapters arriving at the doors of the Great Hall. However, they all paid their entrance money without any complaint and we had no problems whatsoever. But these were proper Angels, not the local gang who couldn't afford a bike between them and used to arrive on the bus. Our lot frequently caused trouble, trying desperately to ape the Angels at Altamont, although they didn't quite live up to their scary name – Satan's Slaves – as they always had to leave a fight early to catch the last bus back to Lancaster! At about 8.00 pm another group of bikers approached. They were enormous, and one turned to speak to the others as they arrived at the main door. On his back it just stated 'Hells Angels – President', and on the next one, 'Hells Angels – Treasurer'. These were the real deal. I suggested to the door staff that they were on the band's guest list – I had no idea if that was true and I wasn't about to stop them to find out!

In 1985 I went to work with/for Paul Loasby, initially on The Return of the Knebworth Fayre with Deep Purple, Meatloaf, Scorpions, et al., and then out of Paul's offices in London. One of the tours we did that autumn was with Saxon, and at Hammersmith Odeon they broke the decibel record for that venue. Talk about bleeding ear drums!

Barry Lucas

Mott The Hoople

2 October 1970 — Support: Stonefeather
15 October 1971 — Supports: Graphite | Inner Sound
16 November 1973 — Support: Queen
30 November 1974 — Support: Sailor

Mott The Hoople were a glam rock group that was formed in 1968 in Herefordshire, led by lead vocalist Ian Hunter, until his departure in 1974. The band itself eventually broke up in 1976. The group are best known for their 1972 international hit single 'All the Young Dudes', written by David Bowie.

Mott The Hoople also found chart success with the hit singles 'Honaloochie Boogie' and 'All the Way from Memphis', both featuring Andy Mackay of Roxy Music on saxophone.

Lancaster saw the first appearance of Mott The Hoople in 1970 following the September release of their album *Mad Shadows,* with a lineup of Ian Hunter, Mick Ralphs, Verden Allen, Pete "Overend" Watts and Dale "Buffin" Griffin.

Almost exactly a year later the band returned with the same lineup, along with two support acts, to promote the upcoming release of the band's fourth album *Brain Capers.*

Two years on, in November 1973, with Aerial Bender replacing the departed guitarist Mick Ralphs (who left to join Bad Company), a legendary Great Hall concert takes place, remembered not for the performance of Mott The Hoople, but for the unknown support act: Queen.

Almost everybody who was there on the night will remember Queen blowing Mott The Hoople off the stage with a short but explosive set. Those who don't remember must have been in the bar area, waiting for the main event of the evening.

Eventually a visibly annoyed Ian Hunter took to the stage with his band to try to follow Queen, with shouts of "we want Queen!" ringing around the hall.

As the tour progressed it was suggested that Mott The Hoople cut down the duration of Queen's set, to minimise collateral damage as it were.

1974 and Mott The Hoople are back in Lancaster, this time featuring ex-David Bowie guitarist Mick Ronson. The tour promoted the release of the band's seventh album, *The Hoople*, and included charting singles such as 'The Golden Age Of Rock and Roll' and 'Roll Away The Stone', the latter a UK No. 8 single, and the album reaching No. 11 in the UK.

Stonefeather started life in 1967 as a band called Sweet Feelings. After releasing only three singles, Sweet Feelings then evolved into the psychedelic rock outfit, Rupert's People. Rupert's People continued playing live up until the late '60s, by which time they were being handled by future Police manager and music mogul, Miles Copeland III. At the beginning of the 1970s, they changed their name to Stonefeather, and featured Miles' brother, and future Police drummer Stewart Copeland on drums. Stewart Copeland was to return to the Great Hall in 1975 on drums, performing with Curved Air.

Graphite were a rock band from the early 1970s formed at Reading University. They gigged professionally on the rock circuit from 1970 to 1973, supporting many big names of that era, such as Pink Floyd, Arthur Brown's Kingdom Come, Mott The Hoople and T-Rex. Graphite returned a year later to Lancaster as back up for Roxy Music. Amazingly, Graphite got a billing above Queen at a festival in Truro, Cornwall, in 1971.

Inner Sound were a Scottish rock band from the Gourock area.

Nils Lofgren

I've had many of the world's greatest guitarists on the stage at Lancaster University but I don't think I've had any better than Nils Lofgren. However, as I own three of his solo albums, I would say that, wouldn't I?

After the first couple of years I rarely watched any whole performances, but I always tried to watch the intro, the first number, the last number and the encore. The feeling of anticipation and, at the end, the roar of appreciation, followed by that legendary Lancaster stomp, was what it was all about for me; the fan, not the businessman.

Well, Nils Lofgren produced the greatest final number ever. Across the front of the stage every week were the wedges, black boxes acting as sound monitors for the artists to hear themselves. Nils Lofgren had one monitor disguised – it was actually a mini trampoline. As he hit the final notes he raced across the stage, jumped into the 'monitor' and somersaulted backwards, still playing and just before he landed the lights cut out. There was no way he could follow that with another encore. We knew that was definitely the end – safely on with the house lights.

Barry Lucas

NILS LOFGREN
+ SPECIAL GUESTS:
TOM PETTY + THE HEARTBREAKERS
UNIVERSITY OF LANCASTER
7.30PM MONDAY MAY 9TH
TICKETS: £2

John Angus

Paul McCartney and Wings

14 February 1972 No Support

It was on 10 April 1970 that The Beatles announced their split to the world.

Following his second solo album *Ram* in 1971, ex-Beatle Paul McCartney and his wife Linda formed Wings, which was intended to be a fully-fledged recording and touring band. Denny Laine, a former guitarist for the Moody Blues, and drummer Denny Seiwell joined the lineup, with Wings releasing their first album, *Wild Life*, in December 1971.

McCartney and Wings, which now featured former Grease Band guitarist Henry McCullough, spent 1972 as a working band, releasing three singles: the protest tune 'Give Ireland Back to the Irish', the reggae-fied 'Mary Had a Little Lamb' and the hard-rocking 'Hi Hi Hi'.

February 1972 saw Paul, Linda, the band and their three daughters set off from London for an impromptu tour of ten universities. Following visits to Nottingham, York, Hull, and Newcastle the band arrived in Lancaster for a Valentine's Day gig in the Great Hall.

Setlist (this is from Nottingham University five days earlier on 9 February 1972, but it would have been similar for the Great Hall gig): 'Lucille', 'Blue Moon of Kentucky', 'Seaside Woman', 'Some People Never Know', 'The Mess', 'Bip Bop', 'Say, Darling', 'Smile Away', 'My Love', 'Henry's Blues', 'Wild Life', 'Give Ireland Back to the Irish', 'Long Tall Sally'.

©Sheryl Walmsley

©Sheryl Walmsley

Around Christmas 1971 I was reading a three week series of articles in the *NME* about The Beatles. One of the main parts of the third week was an account of the problems the band faced, later in their career, playing live. After Shea Stadium it soon became obvious that The Beatles were simply too big to play live in any venue, in any town in the world. New York, the biggest city in the world (I know, not in terms of population but arguably in terms of stature) had had to shut down when The Beatles landed at their airport. Imagine that today, London, New York, Paris, Rome etc. CLOSING because a pop group was arriving! It's unimaginable to people under fifty reading that today but The Fab Four were just that important, that big, that the authorities could not control the media attention and the fans. That is why today, when I hear people saying a band are "the new Beatles", I just shake my head and smile.

Well, the article talked about an idea, a suggestion, by Paul that the band should just arrive at a small village hall, with just a few posters advertising them – e.g. 'Bert and the Beers' for a Saturday night dance. 50p (ten shillings) to get in. But those that chanced it would find themselves facing The Beatles. Ringo was up for it but John and George weren't. I thought it was a brilliant idea.

I had formed a great relationship with June Whyton over the previous few months. She was an agent of the old school and we got on really well, chatting about the state of the music business and indeed the world. She had booked John Mayall into Lancaster, and she understood, and had contacts with, those legendary acts from the '60s. I asked her if she knew – or more importantly could 'get to' – Paul McCartney.
I had an idea ...

In a couple of months I had a Rag Week, culminating in a Rag Ball. What if Paul McCartney and the new band he had just put together, Wings, were to put in an unannounced appearance? I would make up a name, stick them third on the bill and the audience that turned up would see a Beatle and his new superstar band. June thought the idea was a runner and promised she would get it to Paul – that was great, you can never be certain in the music business that any idea or concept will ever find its way through the innumerable layers of management and representation that surround artists today. Here was a chance.

I heard nothing for several weeks, then on the Monday morning of Rag Week June phoned me just to say, "It's on!" This was almost impossible to grasp. I had started with The Who, and now The Beatles (well almost, you know what I mean).

I went to see Paula Richardson, who was in charge of Great Hall bookings. I'm not sure why, probably just to make certain nothing could stop Friday's Rag Ball happening. When I returned to my office Alan Murray was sitting with two strangers, long hair, jeans etc., you know the usual looking blokes in 1972. Alan announced, "Hey Barry, these guys say they're Paul McCartney's roadies and they're playing here tonight!"

Now, I had naturally assumed from June's message that 'the' date was, as I suggested, Friday's Rag Ball. But this was Monday. Wait a minute, this is Rag Week – jolly japes etc.

"Hang on, if you're the crew where are the band?"

"On some grass, near the hall," came the answer.

"Ok, let's see," I said, still unsure.

We all went over to the Great Hall. On the grass, by the Barbara Hepworth statue, was a group of people. A lady, cradling a baby, and some guys playing football. Suddenly, I could see Paul McCartney, Henry McCulloch and Denny Laine. Bloody hell, it's a Beatle! McCartney asked if it was OK to play tonight and of course I said yes but I would have to sort out the Great Hall porters. Sid and Mick were busy getting 900 chairs out of the cellar. Don't you just love architects? Employ ex-forces, fifty-plus year olds? Well let's put the chair store under the stage. Provide a Lift? No, just steps. Light plastic chairs? Nope, just big heavy wooden ones. Eventually after some ten years the University did put in some strange kind of Stannah stair lift contraption – in response to the half a dozen or so heart attacks I suppose.

Well Sid and Mick had put out around 300 chairs, complete with cast iron securing rods, when I burst in. "Stop! Sorry you two but there's a rock show on tonight." They were setting up for a classical music concert the next night so I received a very short response. "Piss off."

"No honestly, in a few minutes Paul McCartney will walk through those doors, he wants to play here tonight."

"Piss off, it's Rag Week," was the considered response.

"Look, honest ..." I was interrupted by the appearance of Mr Paul McCartney.

"Hi, are you two the guys I'm giving heart attacks to?"

They were like putty in his hands. "What kind of music do you usually have on here?" Paul asked.

"Proper music, we have classical on tomorrow. Not your pop rubbish," replied Sid. So after a short discussion we decided to leave the seats that were up out but the rest of the hall would be empty. Now all I had to do was get an audience – five hours. OK. The thing that really upset me was that my regular audience, the ones that attended religiously week-in week-out, some 1000 plus, were scattered from Blackburn to Barrow. How could I let them know so that they could have a share in the reward that they deserved?

I phoned all the nine ticket agencies I had in the NW and asked them to stick up notices in their windows. I then borrowed a megaphone and proceeded to walk round campus announcing that tonight, for 50p, you can see Paul McCartney and Wings in the Great Hall. I was told on numerous occasions to "Piss off." I ended up pleading with people to believe me – honestly, it really was harder than you would think!

Now I had to sort out Bill Taylor, the Students' Union Executive member who had an event booked that evening in Bowland Refectory. I am indebted to Bill, now Sir William, who takes up the story:

"We had organised a disco with a semi-pro band, the lads came from Preston, one took the day off work and hired a van etc. We were paying them £40. I was 'avin' me tea in the refec. When you came through with a loud hailer and said, "Are you all coming to see Wings tonight, only 50p?" I told you to eff off. What the hell was going to happen to our gig?"

The next problem was Gray Austerberry, the Secretary of the Students' Union. He was from Normanton, a Yorkshire mining community, and this was the height of the miners' strike. Gray and I were good friends; he persuaded me, a couple of years later, to come out of retirement and take up rugby league again for the university team. He had helped organise the show in Bowland refectory, to raise money for the Miners' Strike Fund. "Who the bloody hell is going to come to Bowland refectory tonight with the fucking Beatles 100 yards away?" he moaned at me and then demanded to go down to the Great Hall and meet Mr McCartney. "Leave it with me, you'll get a crowd," Paul assured a rather skeptical miner's son.

I was talking to the leader of the band who played in the refectory that night and he told me a story ...

Re-wind a few hours earlier. He had taken the afternoon off work to drive up to the university and set up the PA for the evening. In his words, "I arrived on the campus with no idea where I was going, where on earth Bowland refectory was. I parked up next to the Great Hall and saw some blokes playing football. I went to them and asked them if they knew where Bowland refectory was. They said that they weren't students and had no idea. I said that I needed to find the Social Secretary as I had a band and we were playing in Bowland that night. This Scouser said that they were also in a band, looking for a gig that night as well. So I said to him that if he wanted I would have a word with the Social Secretary and ask if they could support my band. Then the Scouser, in the big, baggy suit looked at me, smiled and said, "Thanks, that's really kind of you". I looked around at them. Suddenly I realized that Paul McCartney, Denny Laine and Henry McCullough etc. were grinning at me and Linda, with babe in arms, just winked. I felt about a foot high but they all thought it was hilarious."

Back to the main story now. Come the evening, my stewards had turned up; they didn't believe the rumours either and admired my attention to detail in bringing in a PA to complete the Rag stunt. "What do we do charge them, 50p to get in and £1 to get out?" they asked. "For fuck's sake it's Paul McCartney and Wings. Look at the PA."

"Struth, that's an elaborate stunt," they all agreed.

"Oh, bloody hell, never mind just man the doors!"

Well, 1100 not too hopeful people turned up, but unfortunately not, as I had planned, to see the first ever date on Wings because the band had played a couple of dates on the way up to us. It was a really memorable night, although the band didn't have a full set to play; they repeated 'Hippy Hippy Shake' and 'Roll Over Beethoven' three times I think.

At the end of the show, Paul McCartney explained to the audience that they had to finish as they had no more numbers to play. However, there was a great band, friends of theirs, playing in Bowland refectory after the show and he and the rest of the band would be going down. Well that meant Bill and Gray had to cope with approximately 1000 descending on them – serves 'em right for moaning!

Paul and the guys didn't go down as they were leaving in their minibus straight away. Rachel, Alan and I went to their bus with a brown paper bag full of £550, mostly coins, from the door. Except for some petrol money, Paul gave the rest back, telling us to put it in the miners' strike fund.

My outstanding memories of that crazy day? Just what a nice guy Paul McCartney was, and I also thought Linda was a terrific, a friendly person as well, totally unrecognisable from the picture painted at the time of a hard, driven business woman.

Band on the run indeed!

Barry Lucas

Paul Young and The Royal Family

14 October 1983 Support: The Passion Puppets

Paul Young, from Luton Bedfordshire, was a former member of the band Q-Tips who dissolved in early 1982, allowing Young to pursue a solo career.

Before joining Q-Tips, Paul Young was the vocalist in an outfit called Streetband, who had a hit with the quirky song 'Toast' which peaked in the UK Singles Chart at No. 18 in November 1978.

Young is famous for his solo hit singles such as 'Love of the Common People', the 1983 No. 1 'Wherever I Lay My Hat', 'Come Back and Stay' and 'Every Time You Go Away' which all reached the top 10 in the UK Singles Chart.

The band came to Lancaster promoting the July 1983 release of his debut album *No Parlez*, the UK number one album that turned him into a household name.

Paul's backing band on the right comprised Ian Kewley, Laurie Latham, Mark Pinder and Pino Palladino, known as The Royal Family, along with two female backing singers, Kim Lesley and Maz Roberts, otherwise known as The Fabulous Wealthy Tarts.

In July 1985, Young appeared at Live Aid held at Wembley Stadium, London, performing the Band Aid hit 'Do They Know It's Christmas?'

Paul Young presently fronts a touring Tex-Mex band called Los Pacominos.

Formed in 1983 in Camden, London, **Passion Puppets** were a British new wave band that caught radio listeners with one clever single, 'Like Dust', on the Stiff label, before abruptly vanishing. Seemingly an ode to Italian Western films, 'Like Dust' was a cult hit on Canadian radio in 1984 and is better remembered than the group that actually performed it.

Paul Young had first performed at Lancaster in The Nuffield Theatre as part of that year's Graduation Ball, which in those days utilised the Great Hall, the Nuffield Theatre and Cartmel Refectory. He was lead singer with a band called Q-Tips. I went to watch the first number to see if they were going down OK – remember, there were approximately twelve bands on at a Grad Ball so I was only intending to see one quick number. But oh no I wasn't, I couldn't leave. The band were all right but the singer was something special. I spoke later, at about 3.00 am, to their manager and offered my opinion: "You have something amazing there, ditch the band, concentrate on the singer". Well …

In the summer of 1983 Paul Loasby had left Harvey Goldsmith's and set up his own, very successful (at that stage) promotions company, but Harvey was still putting the occasional act into Lancaster. He had phoned, wanting to do Wham! for Freshers' Week. Did I want it? Wham! were massive at that time and were playing Wembley among other arena dates on this tour. Of course I wanted it. So, Freshers' sorted, off I went on holiday to Guernsey.

I was just laying out my suitcase on the hotel bed when the room phone rang. It was Paul Loasby. Don't ask me how he knew I was there, I have no idea to this day. He wanted to put Paul Young into Lancaster … For Freshers'. "Sorry Paul, no can do, Harvey has just put in Wham!." Paul pulled every trick in the book; best mates, favours done, in a hole, promised date, everything he could think of. I had to blow Harvey out and give him the date, his very company depended upon it! Well mates are mates. Eventually persuaded, I called Harvey to say I couldn't get the hall that night and I put Paul Young on instead, hoping that Harvey wouldn't notice the tour schedule. To this day I'm not sure I did the right thing – Paul Young is a better singer but to have had George Michael (so to speak) …

On the night Loasby couldn't make it up for the show but he rang me to say that he had a great idea. 'Wherever I Lay My Hat' was No. 1, would I get a top hat, fill it with ice and a bottle of champagne and take it into Mr Young's dressing room? Ok Paul, but you're paying.

Barry Lucas

Pentangle

13 November 1970 — Support: Amazing Blondel

1 December 1972 — Supports: Wizz | C.O.B.

Pentangle are an electric folk band, first active from 1967 to 1973 with a lineup of Jacqui McShee (vocals), John Renbourn (vocals and guitar), Bert Jansch (vocals and guitar), Danny Thompson (double bass), and Terry Cox on drums.

Pentangle rapidly established itself as one of the earliest exponents of the British folk rock movement and became very successful, touring North America in 1968, playing at Carnegie Hall and the Newport Folk Festival. However, in addition to attracting fans of traditional British folk, they also drew audiences from the rock, pop and psychedelic folk worlds.

On New Year's Day 1973, Bert Jansch decided to leave the band. "Pentangle Split" was the front page headline of the first issue of *Melody Maker* of that year.

In 1994, McShee formed a new band named Jacqui McShee's Pentangle which, with a few personnel changes, is still performing today.

Support on the evening were **Amazing Blondel**, making their second visit to Lancaster following their gig with The Who earlier in the year.

Pentangle's second Great Hall concert featured **Wizz** Jones the English acoustic guitarist, singer and songwriter still performing today.

C.O.B. or Clive's Original Band featured Clive Palmer, former founder member of The Incredible String Band. Clive was an old friend of Wizz Jones, the pair having busked in Paris together in the mid '60s. COB split up in early 1973.

Clive Palmer's death on 23 November 2014 in Penzance, after a long illness, was announced by Wizz Jones, who referred to him as …

> "One of the finest musicians I have ever known … an inspiration and a well loved friend."

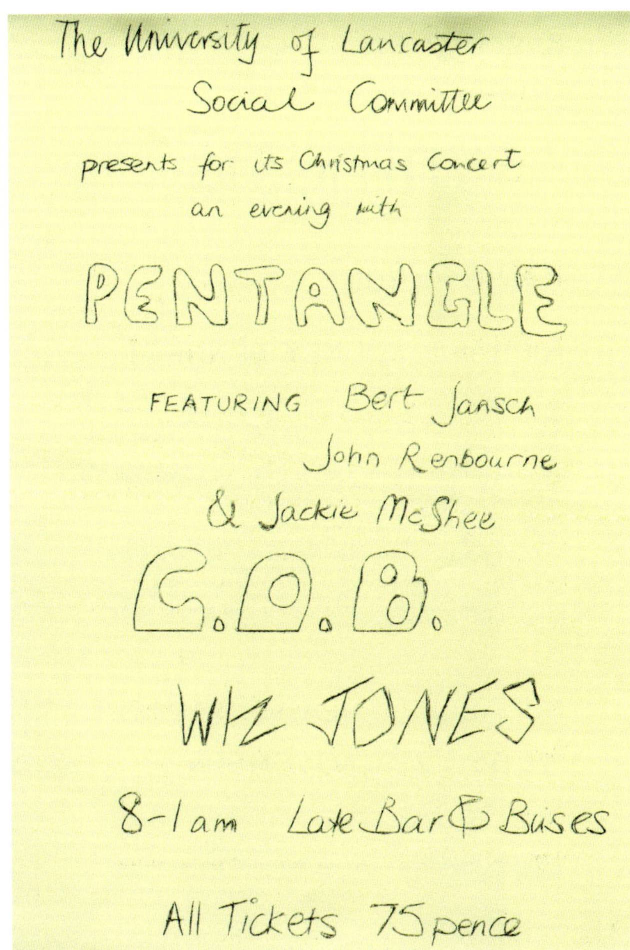

Peter Gabriel

25 August 1978 No support

Peter Brian Gabriel was the original lead singer and flautist of the progressive rock band Genesis. Following his departure in 1975 Gabriel went on to forge a successful solo career with the 1977 release of 'Solsbury Hill', his first single, which went to No. 13 in the UK Singles Chart.

Other notable singles from Gabriel included 'Games Without Frontiers' 'Sledgehammer' and the 1986 chart hit with Kate Bush 'Don't Give Up'.

His 1978 Great Hall concert promoted the release of his second eponymously titled solo album in June 1978, otherwise known as *Scratch*, which referred to the Hipgnosis album cover (Hipgnosis was an English art design group based in London that specialised in creating cover art for the albums of rock musicians and bands). The album was produced by Robert Fripp.

Lancaster setlist: 'On The Air', 'Moribund The Burgermeister', 'Modern Love', 'Flotsam And Jetsam', 'White Shadow', 'A Wonderful Day In A One-Way World', 'Humdrum', 'Waiting For The Big One', 'Band Intro/D.I.Y', 'Home Sweet Home', 'A Whiter Shade Of Pale', 'Here Comes The Flood', 'Slowburn', 'Mother Of Violence', 'I Don't Remember', 'Solsbury Hill', 'Perspective', 'The Lamb Lies Down On Broadway'.

Once again I was offered a world superstar at an inconvenient time – the summer vacation. Since leaving Genesis, he had built a very successful solo career and been instrumental in setting up the highly acclaimed Womad Festival. He had such stature in the music world that I simply could not turn the date down, despite the fact that there would be no Lancaster University students around. It was a no-guarantee, door-percentage, so no money was at risk, so there was a certain profit for the Students' Union coffers. Anyway, I rationalised, there were plenty of students about – local schools and colleges as well as students returning for their own summer vacation from colleges around the country.

I'm not a great fan of Peter Gabriel so I can't really comment about the show. It wasn't a massive audience but that was just as well because I do definitely remember the first number. Mr Gabriel, in full theatrical dress, decided to enter, singing, with a radio microphone, from the back of the Great Hall at the foyer doors. He had to make his way through the audience to the stage. It wasn't as easy as it sounds, as people were continually refusing to let this guy through because they assumed he was just a punter trying to get to the front to get a closer view of Peter Gabriel. I eventually had to send stewards in to protect him and clear the way. As a way of arriving on stage for an opening number it isn't really recommended – put it this way, I can think of better.

Barry Lucas

PETER
GABRIEL
in
con
rt
ANGUS
PRESENTED BY
UNIVERSITY OF
LANCASTER
+
HARVEY
GOLDSMITH
ENTERTAINMENTS
FRIDAY
AUGUST 25TH
7.30 PM
TICKETS: £3

John Angus

Pink Floyd

7 May 1971 Support: Ron Geesin

The Pink Floyd, as they were billed, were formed in 1965 by students Nick Mason, Syd Barrett, Roger Waters and Richard Wright. David Gilmour joined the band in 1967 as the fifth member. They went on to be one of the biggest bands on the planet and one of the most commercially successful and influential groups in the history of popular music. The early Pink Floyd were very much the creation of Syd Barrett, the band's frontman on lead guitar and vocals. Barrett departed the band in 1968 due to mental health problems from excessive drug taking and died in 2006. In October 1970 Pink Floyd released the album *Atom Heart Mother*, which was orchestrated by their guest support act on the evening, Ron Geesin (note the misspelling in the concert ad).

Ronald Frederick Geesin is a Scottish musician and composer, noted for his quirky creations and novel applications of sound. In 1970 Geesin released *Music from The Body,* the soundtrack album to Roy Battersby's 1970 documentary film *The Body*, about human biology and narrated by Vanessa Redgrave and Frank Finlay. The music was composed in collaboration between Ron and his friend and golfing partner, Roger Waters.

I received this email from Ron Geesin in reply to a request for his memories around the gig:

Hello Paul.

No, I don't recall much of any gigs! The point is that they were designed as sub-conscious eruptions, so I left that part of my brain to deal with the situation when out on the stage. Obviously I had a palette [store] of modules that could be organised in many different ways on the spot. I do remember that Lancaster University was a particular appreciator of my cavortings, so I must have visited several times. My diary has no mention of PF for that day, but I played golf with Roger Waters the day before.

Best waves,

Ron Geesin

It was Friday 7 May 1971 and I was wandering down the Spine to the Great Hall, early afternoon. I was going with some trepidation, not because my finals were starting in three days time and I should have been revising, but because I was going to meet one of the biggest names in rock music.

Pink Floyd – even then a legend (probably even more so today) – were going to play the Great Hall that night. I was paying the unprecedented sum of £1500, a fee I was not to exceed as a guarantee for about seven years. I had been summoned by Sid Cooper, the Great Hall porter, to come to the hall because they had arrived and there seemed to be a problem.

The perfectionist nature of the band was already well known and for some reason they had arrived at the venue early for those days. It was only later in the '80s that roadies and artics used to arrive at 8.00 am, or even occasionally 7.00 am. This doesn't look good. Damn, I should be revising Anglo Saxon – actually there was no point really, I was never going to pass that one!

But what was wrong? I walked in the back of the hall and the guys were on the stage, arguing. What the hell was the problem? The stage was too small? The sloping roof over the stage was going to cause difficulties? The acoustics in the hall? Yes, that must be it – Floyd were all about their sound, the attention to detail, after all.

It was a sell-out, obviously. Would it go ahead? Would they cancel? Who would be blamed? I walked, with dread, up to the stage. What on earth could I do about the acoustics – rebuild the back wall before 7.30 pm, fly some acoustic mushrooms from the roof, like they had put up in The Royal Albert Hall to sort out their sound problems – where am I going to get mushrooms from on a Friday afternoon, Stanley's Fruit and Veg. stall in Lancaster Market? Don't think so.

"What's the problem?" I asked nervously, not really wanting to hear the answer.

"Oh, are you the Social Sec? Sorry, but we are having a slight disagreement. Two of us want to go back to London tonight to watch the FA Cup Final at home, but two of us want to stay in The Royal King's Arms tonight, have a few beers and watch the match in the hotel tomorrow afternoon."

Remember, in those days the Great Hall concerts, for some reason beyond my recall, went on until 1.00 or 2.00 am.

Bloody hell, they're human after all, arguing about watching the Cup Final! Brilliant, I could cope with that!

The PA was set up in a way I had never seen before or since in the Great Hall, whereby speakers were placed all around the floor of the hall, encasing the audience in the sound.

A fantastic night – I've still got the drum stick Nick Mason broke on the gigantic gong at the back of the stage. Of course the whole concert was made by our own in-house Pink Custard Light Show – exploding blobs of coloured ink, projected onto a backcloth of Lonsdale College's white bed sheets, borrowed for the evening. By now, the previously mentioned Maurice Hubbard (ex-Lonsdale College President) was a convert to the concept of the Great Hall concerts and was running a light show with Duncan.

As I'm writing this I'm playing 'Piper at the Gates of Dawn', part of a fourteen disc set of Floyd's that Paul Loasby (who will appear in several parts of this book) gave me for my sixtieth birthday. Little did I know that my best mate from the business and Leeds University Social Secretary for two years, main man at Harvey Goldsmith's and the most imaginative, innovative promoter ever, was to become Dave Gilmour's manager and later Dave Gilmour's son was to become a student at Lancaster Uni. Jane Silvester, of the Alumni Department, was showing them around the university and asked Dave if he could remember his gig in '71. He replied that he couldn't remember anything from those years.

Barry Lucas

ANGUS
THE
PIRATES
+ LAZER BLAZER
UNIVERSITY OF LANCASTER 7.30PM FRIDAY 13 OCT. £1.50

John Angus

The Pirates

13 October 1978 Support: Lazer Blazer

Formed in 1959 and originally known as Johnny Kidd and The Pirates, the band scored numerous hit songs from the late 1950s to the early 1960s, including 'Shakin' All Over' and 'Please Don't Touch'.

Their stage act was theatrical and included full pirate costumes, complete with eye-patches and cutlasses.

'Shakin' All Over' reached No. 1 on the UK Singles Chart in August 1960 and has been covered by numerous bands, including Suzi Quattro, Cliff Richard and The Who, who would cover it on their 1970 album *Live at Leeds*.

Tragically Johnny Kidd died aged thirty in 1966, in a motor car accident on the A58 Bury New Road, Breightmet, Bolton, Lancashire.

Many years later in 1976, three former members of the band re-formed: drummer Frank Farley, bassist/singer Johnny Spence and guitarist Mick Green. Mick Green was famous for his unique "choppy-style" guitar playing (lead and rhythm at the same time) which influenced such great musicians as Wilko Johnson of Dr. Feelgood and Pete Townshend of The Who.

The band eventually split in 1983.

Little is known about support act **Lazer Blazer.**

©Geoff Campbell

Planxty

21 February 1975 Support: Steve Ashley

Formed in 1972, Irish folk rock band Planxty were one of the most influential bands in the history of Irish traditional music.

The original lineup consisted of Christy Moore (vocals, acoustic guitar, bodhrán) Andy Irvine (vocals, mandolin, mandola, bouzouki, hurdy-gurdy, harmonica), Dónal Lunny (bouzouki, guitars) and Liam O'Flynn (uilleann pipes, tin whistle). They quickly revolutionised and popularised Irish folk music, touring and recording to great acclaim.

Steve Ashley is a British singer-songwriter, recording artist, multi-instrumentalist, writer and graphic designer. Ashley is best known as a song writer and first gained public recognition for his work with his debut solo album *Stroll On.* He was a member of the short-lived Albion Country Band in the early 1970s. Steve Ashley the graphic designer was most probably responsible for the striking concert advert reproduced here. Steve Ashley still tours and performs, having released his tenth solo album in 2015.

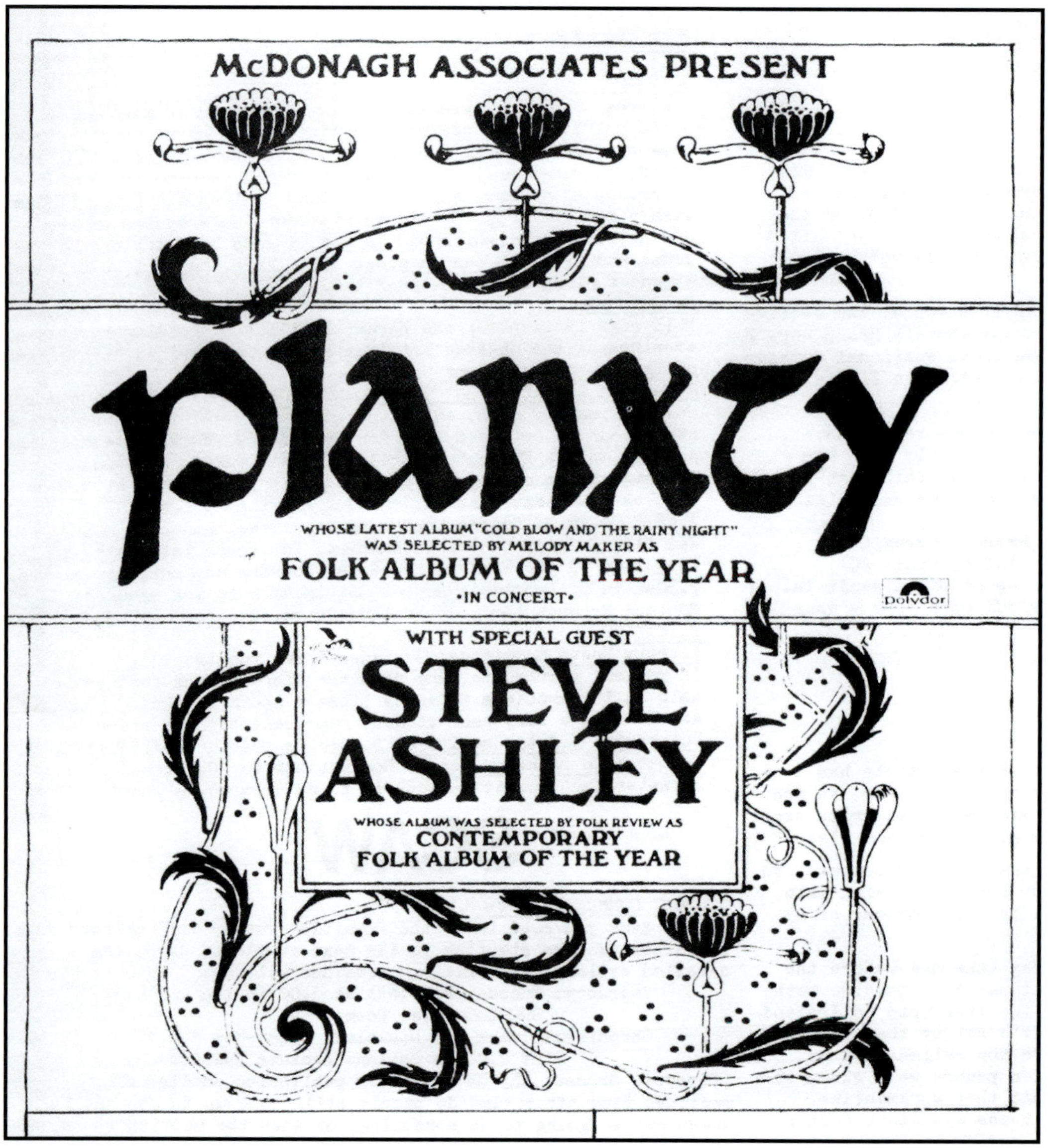

Prefab Sprout

4 May 1984 Support: Hurrah!

Prefab Sprout are an English pop band formed in 1976 in Witton Gilbert, County Durham, which rose to fame during the 1980s. Though critically acclaimed and considered by many to have released some of the best pop albums of the decade, the band never matched this acclaim with commercial success. Their biggest success came with the 1990 album *Jordan: The Comeback* (one of two albums produced by Thomas Dolby), which reached No. 7 in the UK album chart and was nominated for a BRIT award. The band also had a UK Top 10 hit with their 1988 song 'The King of Rock 'n' Roll'.

The band's best-known lineup comprised Paddy McAloon (vocals, guitar, keyboards), Wendy Smith (vocals, guitar, keyboard), Martin McAloon (bass) and Neil Conti (drums).

Hurrah! also hailing from the North East of England were a British jangle pop band, previously known as The Green Eyed Children. They were formed in the early 1980s and remained active until 1991.

They were a solid band from the '80s, without any major chart success, but they nevertheless attracted reasonable attention and audiences.

Paul Loasby, promoting on his own as PLP, had bought either the whole tour, or most of it, but he assured me that he wasn't too bothered about not getting the, usually most lucrative, London date because he had Newcastle, near to their home town, which he was obviously confident would do excellent business.

Well, Lancaster didn't, and when he arrived with the band he was unusually subdued.

"What's the matter, other than the fact you're losing money tonight?" I enquired.

"You bloody well wouldn't believe it," he explained, unwittingly doing his best Victor Meldrew impersonation, "I had the home town date but it wasn't selling tickets as well I had expected. I asked the local ticket agencies why not? They pointed out, rather pityingly, that the gig night was also Kevin Keegan's last appearance in a Newcastle United shirt. A god, saying farewell to his loyal followers … Who'd go to a rock 'n' roll gig on a night like that?"

The details you have to be aware of to be a music promoter.

Barry Lucas

The Pretenders

14 October 1980 Support: Moondogs

The Pretenders were formed in 1978 in Hereford and fronted by American singer songwriter, Chrissie Hynde. The band first came to prominence in 1979 with the release of their first single 'Stop Your Sobbing' during the punk and new wave movement of the late 1970s. Completing the lineup of the original band were Pete Farndon (bass), James Honeyman-Scott (guitars) and Martin Chambers (drums).

January 1980 saw the hit single 'Brass in Pocket' reach No. 1 in the UK Singles Chart. Tragically the band broke apart in 1983 as a result of the drug-related deaths of James Honeyman-Scott and Pete Farndon. Since then, numerous subsequent personnel changes have taken place over the years, with Hynde as the sole constant member.

In September 2012, as part of the entertainment lineup for the 2012 Singapore Grand Prix, The Pretenders re-grouped, with Hynde and Chambers from the original lineup, along with Nick Wilkinson, James Walbourne and Eric Heywood. Glastonbury 2017 saw the band appear on The Other Stage.

The Moondogs (alternatively known as just 'Moondogs') were a power pop trio from Derry in Northern Ireland that had some success in the late '70s and early '80s. They were made up of Gerry McCandless (guitar, vocals), Jackie Hamilton (bass) and Austin Barett (drums).

Chrissie Hynde and James Honeyman-Scott ©Geoff Campbell

I was very disappointed when I saw The Pretenders' tour schedule for the Autumn of 1980. They were to play Blackpool Opera House on 14 October, a day that would have opened that year's Lancaster concert season after the Freshers' Ball. Phil McIntyre was promoting the show and, as a Preston lad and ex-Preston Polytechnic Social Secretary, he knew the area well. I was doing several shows with Phil so I phoned him to ask him how the Blackpool date was doing. "Bloody crap, on the floor," was his answer.

Chrissie and the band, crap sales, I couldn't believe it. Well I had no students, it was the end of August I think, so I said pull it and put it into Lancaster. I guarantee it will fly. 14 October; no real selling time but, I believed, no real problem either. I told him I could sell it out in a week. I like Phil, no nonsense, quick decisions. He agreed, it was done and it certainly flew when I put it on sale, remembering to keep some tickets back for the returning students this time (n.b. Free).

The band's tour manager (he might actually have been the manager) was very insistent that Chrissie would not tolerate any photography. If she saw anybody taking shots she would walk off the stage, simple as that. So I had to double up on the security into the hall and confiscate any cameras. Of course in the days before mobile phones it was an easier, but by no means straightforward, procedure.

Some of you will remember that occasionally we put the front lighting truss' legs on the floor at the corner of the stage, in order to create a larger, freer stage area. When we did this we put three 6ft tables, inverted, around them and a steward in each to stop the audience rocking the rig. We had to do this for this show. Geoff Campbell was my head of humpers by this point. Geoff is an outstanding photographer, as can be seen throughout this book. He started working for me on the concerts as part of the humping team, soon graduating to running the get-in and get-out. He was always taking photos of the shows and they were much admired and sought after in the music business. He became a member of the Students' Union staff, as my assistant, in '81 when we were in the process of expanding the entertainments by opening The Sugar House, a 1200-capacity nightclub in Lancaster. We were both extremely upset that we wouldn't have any shots of Chrissie Hynde but then I had a thought. I suggested to Geoff that if he went down to the stage left exit, and got in via the steward, he could get into the area around the lighting truss' legs and take some shots before anybody saw him. A plan! Geoff did just that. Chrissie saw him. Bollocks! She'll walk off the stage! But no, she smiled and acted up to the camera, posing, pouting, licking the fret of her bass guitar, brilliant photos! But the manager also saw Geoff. He couldn't cross the stage with the show in full swing so he tried to get across the front of the audience. Some hope – it was as full as only the Great Hall could be. The legendary 10ft golden shoe horns had been used that night. Geoff left it as long as he could, getting as many shots as possible. It was like a slow motion Hollywood thriller but it probably needed the band to break into The Keystone Cops music. Geoff made his escape in the nick of time. I denied any knowledge of his existence when I was quizzed later by the manager.

After I left the University at the end of December 1984 Geoff continued to run the shows and The Sugar House. At least he did until July 1985, when he left to become the first professional Entertainments Manager at Exeter University, very much their gain and Lancaster's loss. He became a very successful promoter in that area and stayed until he retired in 2014. He had many years of success in Exeter, bringing major artists, using the experience he had accrued at Lancaster. Yet another Lancaster concerts success, taught him everything he knew, you know (!).

Barry Lucas

Ralph McTell

1 November 1974	Support: Jack The Lad
6 March 1976	Support: Prelude
25 February 1977	Support: Magna Carta
27 April 1979	Support: Bob Fox & Stu Luckley

Originally from Kent, folk singer Ralph McTell is best known for his 1974 Christmas hit song 'Streets of London'. First recorded in 1969 for McTell's album *Spiral Staircase*, McTell re-recorded 'Streets of London' with Lindisfarne bassist Rod Clements and backing vocalists Prelude.

The song was a million-seller, which gained him an Ivor Novello songwriting award in 1993.

With Ralph making his debut in 1968 he is now approaching fifty years as singer-songwriter and continues to record and perform.

Jack the Lad were a folk rock/electric folk group from north-east England, formed in 1973 and consisting of three former members of Lindisfarne.

Formed in 1970 from Gateshead, Tyne and Wear, **Prelude** are a vocal harmony folk band, with Brian Hume (vocals, guitar), his wife Irene Hume (vocals) and Ian Vardy (guitars, vocals). Prelude are best known for their a cappella version of the Neil Young song 'After the Gold Rush' which had a nine week stay in the UK Singles Chart of 1974, peaking at No. 21. The band returned to Lancaster in 1977 for a concert as guests of John Martyn. Prelude continues to tour today.

Magna Carta are a progressive rock group originally formed in London in April 1969 and still in existence today. The original lineup of the band was Chris Simpson (guitar, vocals), Lyell Tranter (guitar, vocals) and Glen Stuart (vocals). In the early '70s Tranter left the band, being replaced for a year by Davey Johnstone, Elton John's current long serving guitarist.

Bob Fox & Stu Luckley were a British folk duo. The pair recorded an album called *Nowt So Good'll Pass*. This album was enthusiastically greeted by the music press and won Folk Album of The Year in 1978. It still remains one of the most respected recordings in the genre. Bob, originally from Seaham in County Durham, has had a long solo career since 1982, specialising in traditional and contemporary songs of the North East.

Recently I met up with Tom Levitt, who had been Students' Union Secretary in 1973 and Labour MP for High Peak from 1997–2010. He told me of a rather unusual event at a Ralph McTell concert. He was employed as a steward in the Great Hall at the time and at one particular McTell show two 'Satan's Slaves', Lancaster's very own Hell's Angels chapter, decided to ensconce themselves on stage, either side of the mic stand. Not a pretty sight at any time, but at a folk concert?

Tom bravely decided that this was going to spoil the ambience of the evening somewhat and undertook to sort the situation on his own. He approached the two bikers, saying that Mr McTell would like them to vacate the stage before he came on. No response. So Tom decided to tell them that Barry Lucas wanted them to move. No response. Running out of options, Tom had to play his trump card, telling them that Edge (the Angels' leader) demanded that they move. They looked at each other and decided that discretion was indeed the better part of valour. To Tom's immense relief, they left the stage and went with him out of the hall. Who was the first person they met in the corridor? Edge, of course! Tom gulped. "Did you want us to get off the stage?" they asked Edge. Edge caught Tom's pleading look: "Yes, and stay off!" he said. Passing Tom, Edge whispered, "That's a pint you owe me".

Barry Lucas

Ravi Shankar with Allah Rakah

31 October 1972

Ravi Shankar was an Indian musician, composer and master of the sitar, an instrument with between eighteen and twenty-one strings used in Indian classical music.

Ravi was George Harrison's sitar teacher, and a big influence on the Beatles and countless other bands while performing at the great '60s festivals such as Woodstock and Monterey.

In August 1971 George Harrison organised The Concert for Bangladesh at Madison Square Garden in New York City, in which Ravi Shankar participated. After his musicians had tuned up on stage for over a minute the crowd broke into applause, to which the amused Shankar responded: "If you like our tuning so much, I hope you will enjoy the playing more."

This Lancaster concert was billed as the only European university appearance; it was also the only UK appearance outside London during that European tour.

Ravi as always, was accompanied on stage by Alla Rahkar, his trusty tabla player. Alla, an exponent of Hindustani Classical music was an electric showman with his frenzied displays of percussive wizardry.

Ravi Shankar is the father of both Grammy Award-winning singer Norah Jones, and Anoushka Shankar, also a noted sitarist. He passed away in 2012 at the age of ninety-two.

Refugee

3 February 1973

Support: Darien Spirit

The band Refugee was assembled by former The Nice members bassist Lee Jackson and drummer Brian "Blinky" Davison, with the addition of Swiss ace virtuoso keyboardist Patrick Moraz, who later went on to join Yes from 1974 to 1976 and The Moody Blues from 1978 to 1990. The band played epic classically based rock music.

Refugee released the one self titled album on Charisma Records in 1974.

Darien Spirit were a three-piece folk rock band that included former Bonzo Dog Doo-Dah Band bassist, Dennis Cowan. They released only one album, *Elegy for Marilyn*, in 1973.

Ravi Shankar

The only university date in the UK for Ravi, which I thought was a real coup. Ravi Shankar had become the darling of the popular music world by this time, thanks to The Beatles and the darling of the liberal middle classes, thanks to The Concert for Bangladesh with George Harrison and a vast collection of concerned superstars. That box set sold in phenomenal numbers around the world and featured the brilliant, never-to-be-forgotten, moment when the whole American audience gave Mr Shankar a standing ovation, only to be interrupted by the legendary sitar player explaining that he had only been tuning up! Well at least nothing quite so embarrassing happened at Lancaster.

I had to find him a good hotel in the area – not an inconsiderable feat in the 1970s. The only place around here at the time was The Midland Hotel in Morecambe. Although not as good a hotel as it is now after its restoration, it was at least a proper hotel with a history and an imposing architecture. Alan Murray and I picked Ravi Shankar up from Lancaster railway station and took him in Alan's old Ford Consul to Morecambe. In his room Ravi was impressed, looking out of the window he said that it was just like Cannes. Alan and I looked at each other, suppressed giggles and agreed. But I know we were both wondering what kind of "cans" he meant. We left and arranged to pick him up at 6.00 pm.

Driving down Morecambe promenade, Mr Shankar was waxing lyrical about the beauty of Morecambe Bay while periodically winding down the window to spit large amounts of phlegm out. I could see that Alan was nervously watching to make sure that the window was wound fully down each time. By now Ravi couldn't decide whether it was Cannes or St Tropez that Morecambe most reminded him of. I could see Alan looking in the car mirror. "Just come back in bleeding February mate and let's see," we were both thinking.

Now to the concert. I must confess that the sitar leaves me a bit cold. I can appreciate the musicianship and the technical brilliance but one 'tune' – you know about twenty-five minutes – is usually enough for me, although I would later promote Ali Akbar Khan (known as Ustad – master), who was allegedly a better sitar player, in The Nuffield Theatre. In those days, for that type of show, the audience sat cross-legged, or more often, given the nature of the tobacco smoked, laid full-length on the Great Hall floor. Not for Ravi Shankar you didn't. The first thing he did after walking onto the stage was to tell the audience to sit up straight. Next, he proceeded to lecture them on posture. He then demanded they put out their cigarettes, tobacco was bad for them he insisted. I remember wondering how well that had gone down with Messrs Lennon and Harrison.

Life lesson given, on with the show.

Now, given the world status of Ravi Shankar at that time, and the fact that it was the only university date in Europe, it was obviously a sell-out wasn't it? Well, no it wasn't, for we only sold about 600 tickets. Why? Answers on a postcard to me please because I haven't the faintest idea; perhaps the audience was in Morecambe Bay watching the millionaires' yachts pull in from St Tropez to visit the £1 shops.

Barry Lucas

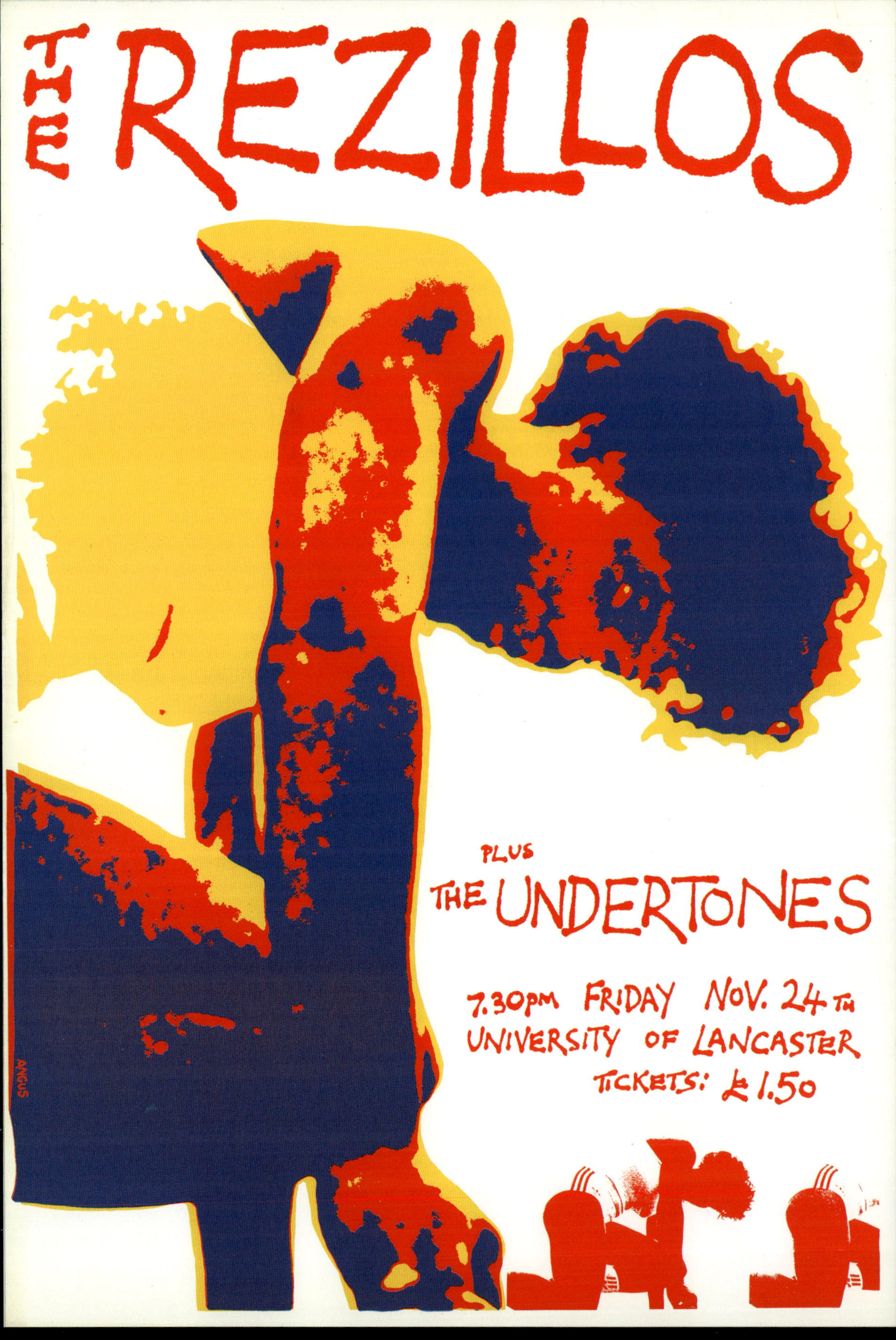
THE
REZILLOS
PLUS
THE UNDERTONES
7.30pm FRIDAY NOV. 24TH
UNIVERSITY OF LANCASTER
TICKETS: £1.50
ANGUS
John Angus

The Rezillos

24 November 1978 Support: The Undertones

The Rezillos are a punk/new wave band, formed in Edinburgh in 1976 and are best known for their 1978 UK Top 20 hit 'Top of the Pops'.

The Rezillos originally consisted of Eugene Reynolds (vocals), Fay Fife (vocals), Jo Callis (guitar), William Mysterious (saxophone), Angel Patterson (drums), Hi-Fi Harris (guitar) and Dr D. K. Smythe on bass guitar.

This visit to the university promoted their 1978 album *Can't Stand the Rezillos*, released in July and reaching No. 16 in the UK Albums Chart.

Following the split of The Rezillos in 1979, the band morphed into The Revillos until 1996, then back again to be re-formed as The Rezillos. They continue to play live and record to the present day.

Another tremendous Lancaster support act on the evening was the Northern Irish band **The Undertones,** fresh from the release of their debut single 'Teenage Kicks' in June '78.

The Undertones returned to play the Great Hall in December 1980 as headliners.

The Rich Kids

3 February 1978 Support: Circus

Formed in 1977 by Glen Matlock, following his departure from the Sex Pistols, The Rich Kids also featured Midge Ure and Rusty Egan. Rusty later founded the band Visage, along with Mick Jones of The Clash, who featured as a live session player. The Rich Kids released the one album, *Ghosts of Princes in Towers*, and three singles during their short existence from March 1977 to December 1978.

Support on the night was provided by **Circus**, an American power pop band active in the early and mid '70s.

Robin Trower

7 February 1975 Support: Mandalaband

From 1967 to 1971 Robin Trower was the lead guitarist with Gary Brooker's Procol Harum.

Before launching his own eponymous band, he joined singer Frankie Miller, ex-Stone the Crows bassist/singer James Dewar, and former Jethro Tull drummer Clive Bunker to form the short-lived combo Jude. This outfit did not record and soon split up.

However, for his solo project Trower retained Dewar as his bassist, who took on lead vocals as well, and Trower then recruited drummer Reg Isidore (later replaced by Bill Lordan) to form the Robin Trower Band in 1973. Robin Trower's most famous album is *Bridge of Sighs* (1974).

Mandalaband were the 1970s creation of composer and producer David Rohl. The original band (Mandalaband I) was short-lived and produced only the one eponymous album.

The theme of the album was centered around the Tibetan resistance movement against Chinese occupation; however, Rohl, while chief engineer at Strawberry Recording Studios in Manchester, went on to record a second album, *The Eye of Wendor* (Mandalaband II), using the talents of many well-known musicians and vocalists, including Justin Hayward, Maddy Prior, Paul Young, all of 10cc and Barclay James Harvest.

Following a thirty-year break from music composition and production, Rohl reformed a new incarnation of Mandalaband and released the first album of a two-part progressive rock concept work, *BC – Ancestors*, in 2009, followed by its partner album, *AD – Sangreal*, in 2011.

For this visit to Lancaster Mandalaband consisted of David Rohl (piano), Vic Emerson (Hammond, Moog and Claviolines), Ashley Mulford (guitar), John Stimpson (bass), Tony Cresswell (drums) and Dave Durant (lead vocals).

I used to love Robin Trower – my kind of rock – but it was the threat of cancellation that made this gig stand out. Roadies are a peculiar breed; in the '70s they were mainly young guys on the road, different town every night, plenty of booze, drugs and girls. The associated glamour of rock 'n' roll meant that they basked in the reflected glory of the stars they were working for. When they hit the hall they were the show, at least for the five or six hours before the actual stars turned up, and then they, like Cinders, disappeared, no longer belles of the ball, just humpers and bumpers! But for those few hours, how they loved it and how they lorded it – perhaps not all of them, but in my experience the vast majority.

The day I had Robin Trower in the Great Hall (he had played the Lower Ashton Hall, with Nazareth, some years before) I knew we were going to lose money, a rare event for the Students' Union in those years. I think we were paying £750 but I had only sold about £500 worth of tickets, so add on the promotion costs and you can see I was about to lose a great deal; the 'walk-up' would never cover it. There I was in the porters' lodge of the Great Hall, trying to guesstimate how much that loss would be, so I was not in a good mood. In walked the band's head roadie, "Where's our beer?" he demanded. Now, there was nothing in the band's rider about beer for the road crew, just teas, coffees and sarnies. I pointed this out to him but to no avail. "We want two cases of lager and a case of beer or the show doesn't go on!"

Oh music to my ears on that particular day! I got up, reached down half a dozen Trower gig posters, turned them over and with my big, red marker pen started to write "Gig Cancelled". "What are you doing?" the now confused roadie asked.

"Well, you said no beers, no show, so, as I'm not providing any beers, I take it you're calling off the show. No problem. I'm just going to put these up around the hall's doors".

I reckoned that I would lose less with a cancelled show, especially if they cancelled it (no artist's fee), than if the show went ahead – so quids in! I wouldn't have wanted to cancel, too many people had travelled long distances for me to let that happen if I could possibly avoid it. But …

I could just see the realisation beginning to spread across the roadie's face. How was he going to tell Robin Trower when he arrived that a roadie had cancelled the show and the band wouldn't be paid that night – all because he didn't get any beer!

After a couple of minutes he slunk out of the office and the crew began unloading the van – sober!

Barry Lucas

ROCKPILE
+ SUPPORT
UNIVERSITY OF LANCASTER
FRIDAY OCTOBER 17TH 7.30 PM
TKTS: £3.00
ANGUS
John Angus

Rockpile

8 February 1980 — Support: The Fabulous Thunderbirds
17 October 1980 — Support: Gary Myrick and The Figures

Making two visits in the same year, Rockpile were a short-lived yet influential British rock group that were founded in 1976. Rockpile were Dave Edmunds (vocals, guitar), Nick Lowe (vocals, bass guitar), Billy Bremner (vocals, guitar) and Terry Williams (drums).

Formed around the partnership of Lowe and Edmunds, the band took its name from the title of a 1972 album by Edmunds. Whilst Rockpile were primarily known as a backup group to those two artists' solo projects, Rockpile did release one official album titled *Seconds of Pleasure* in 1980, spawning the minor hit 'Teacher Teacher'. Rockpile broke up in 1981.

The Fabulous Thunderbirds are an American blues rock outfit from Austin Texas who are still performing today. Best known for their 1986 hit single 'Tuff Enuff' the band featured guitarist Jimmie Vaughan, the older brother of the late Texas blues guitar legend Stevie Ray Vaughan. The Fabulous Thunderbirds are still fronted by their original lead singer and harmonica player, Kim Wilson.

Texan blues rocker Gary Myrick formed his band **Gary Myrick and The Figures** in Los Angeles in 1980 and they are still touring and playing Texas blues at its best.

UNIVERSITY OF LANCASTER *presents*

Rockpile

featuring Dave Edmunds & Nick Lowe

\+

THE FABULOUS THUNDERBIRDS

on FRIDAY, FEBRUARY 8th, 1980 at 7.30 pm.

£3.00 — Nº 333

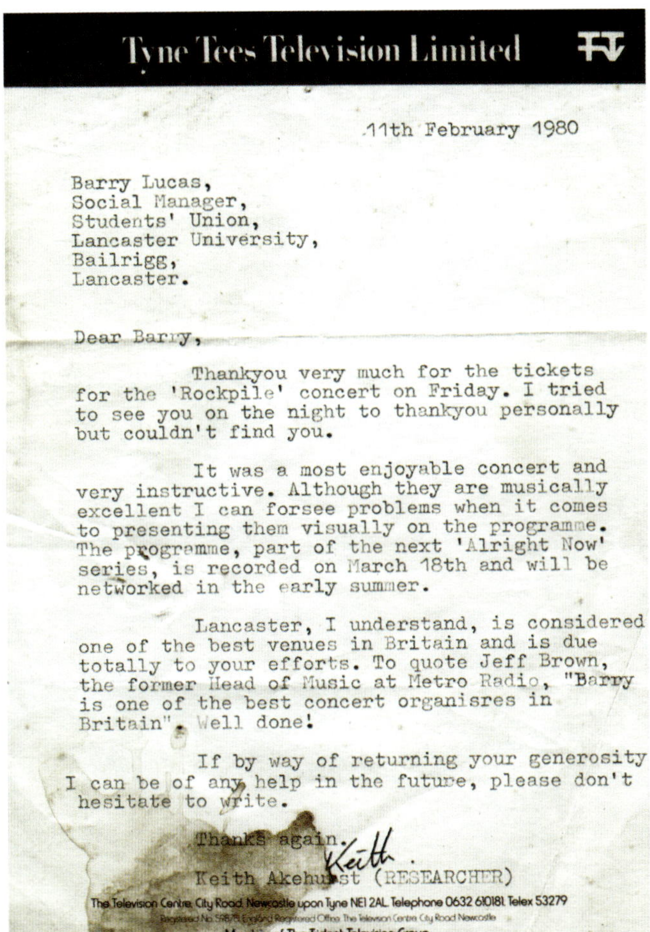
Tyne Tees Television Limited

11th February 1980

Barry Lucas,
Social Manager,
Students' Union,
Lancaster University,
Bailrigg,
Lancaster.

Dear Barry,

Thankyou very much for the tickets for the 'Rockpile' concert on Friday. I tried to see you on the night to thankyou personally but couldn't find you.

It was a most enjoyable concert and very instructive. Although they are musically excellent I can forsee problems when it comes to presenting them visually on the programme. The programme, part of the next 'Alright Now' series, is recorded on March 18th and will be networked in the early summer.

Lancaster, I understand, is considered one of the best venues in Britain and is due totally to your efforts. To quote Jeff Brown, the former Head of Music at Metro Radio, "Barry is one of the best concert organisres in Britain". Well done!

If by way of returning your generosity I can be of any help in the future, please don't hesitate to write.

Thanks again,
Keith
Keith Akehurst (RESEARCHER)

The Television Centre City Road Newcastle upon Tyne NE1 2AL Telephone 0632 610181 Telex 53279
Member of The Trident Television Group

Rory Gallagher

3 December 1971 — Support: Mick Abrahams Band
24 April 1975 — Support: Jackie Lynton Band
28 January 1977 — Support: Joe O'Donnell Band
29 November 1981 — Support: Rage

Rory Gallagher graced the Great Hall stage with his famous battered sunburst-finish Fender Stratocaster for four classic Lancaster University concerts.

Born in Ballyshannon, County Donegal, Rory originally featured centre stage, with his blues band Taste, from 1966 to 1970, the band releasing a total of four albums (two studio and two live).

One classic performance from Taste came in 1970 as part of the Isle of Wight Festival, alongside Jimi Hendrix and The Who.

Taste were hailed as one of the best power rock blues bands of the day and supported Cream at their 1968 farewell concert in The Royal Albert Hall.

1971 saw Rory Gallagher start a band under his own name and assemble the musicians, with Wilgar Campbell on drums and his long-serving bassist Gerry McAvoy.

This was the lineup for Rory's first Lancaster gig in 1971, as ever dressed in his check shirt and blue jeans performing tracks from the recently released album *Deuce*.

Subsequently Campbell was replaced by Rod d'Ath on drums, and keyboardist Lou Martin was added to the outfit, forming the lineup for the next two concerts.

Prior to the 1981 concert, drummer d'Ath had been replaced by Brendan O'Neill and the keyboards had been dispensed with, effectively trimming the band back down to the original Taste three-piece power trio.

The 1970s were Gallagher's most prolific period. He produced ten albums in that decade, including two of them live: *Live in Europe* and *Irish Tour '74*.

Many modern guitarists such as The Edge, Johnny Marr of The Smiths and Joe Bonamassa have cited Rory Gallagher as an influence on their careers.

Tragically, Rory Gallagher died in June 1995 from complications following a liver transplant. In 2010 a bronze statue of Rory was unveiled in his birthplace of Ballyshannon.

Mick Abrahams is an English guitarist and was the original guitarist in Jethro Tull, performing on their 1968 album *This Was* before leaving the band. He went on to found the bands Blodwyn Pig and the Mick Abrahams Band.

The **Jackie Lynton Band** provided support for the 1975 concert. Jackie has been in the rock and blues business since the 1950s and continues to tour today.

The **Joe O'Donnell Band** is a Celtic rock outfit from Limerick, Eire. Joe is a classically trained violinist. He is still active with his current project, Joe O'Donnell's Shkayla.

Rage were a British heavy metal band active in the early eighties that emerged from the ashes of a band called Nutz. They recorded three studio albums before disbanding in 1984. Not to be confused with the German heavy metal band Rage who appeared as support to Marillion in 1984.

Simply the nicest guy I have ever met in rock 'n' roll. With his brother, Donal, who was his manager, head roadie and personal assistant all rolled into one, they made a great team and were so grounded. Donal would set the PA up and then take a chair into the middle of the hall and listen to Tchaikovsky full blast through it.

One of the greatest blues guitarists in UK history, in his two-hour sets he would send his band off for a well-earned rest while he did a half hour solo, acoustic numbers. He simply had no idea how to act out the superstar role.

Barry Lucas

SAD CAFÉ
& CHINA STREET
UNIVERSITY OF LANCASTER
7.30PM FRIDAY JANUARY 20TH £1.25

John Angus

Sad Café

20 January 1978 — Support: China Street
24 January 1982 — Support: Rocking Horse

Manchester band Sad Café visited Lancaster on two occasions, the first being prior to the September 1979 release of the bands best known single 'Every Day Hurts' which reached No. 3 in the UK Singles Chart.

The original lineup of Sad Café included Wythenshawe vocalist Paul Young, guitarists Ian Wilson and Ashley Mulford, bassist John Stimpson, Vic Emerson (keyboards), Tony Creswell (drums) and Lenni (saxophone).

Frontman Paul Young went on to achieve greater chart success as the co-lead singer (with Paul Carrack) of Mike + The Mechanics.

Lancaster band **China Street** provided support for their 1978 gig.

Little is known about the 1982 support act **Rocking Horse**.

Sammy Hagar

6 February 1982 — Support: Grand Prix

Rock vocalist and guitarist Samuel Roy "Sammy" Hagar, also known as "The Red Rocker", hails from California and first came to prominence as the lead singer and guitarist of the 1970s band Montrose. He subsequently went on to pursue a solo career, scoring a hit in 1984 with the single 'I Can't Drive 55', a reference to the US road speed limit.

He also went on to enjoy huge commercial success when he replaced David Lee Roth as the lead singer of Van Halen in 1985, but left the band in 1996.

His present musical project is as lead singer of a band called Chickenfoot.

Grand Prix were a new wave of british heavy metal band that released three albums during the 1980s, the best being the 1983 album *Samurai,* on the Chrysalis label. Their softer approach to heavy metal earned them comparisons to the American band Journey.

This was in the early days of the fitness 'fads' – there were certainly very few rock 'n' roll icons pumping iron in the gym, or rather there were none who admitted to it! Sammy Hagar was different; his stage show was so dynamic, his lycra-clad body thrown around the stage so enthusiastically, that he had to be extremely fit. And he was. I had heard the rumours of his five-mile dawn runs every day but I didn't really believe it. I should have done because that is what he did. However, not many of the band joined him running in the morning after the show the night before.

Barry Lucas

Siouxsie and The Banshees

Punk was at its height when I was offered Siouxsie and The Banshees, and at the time she was arguably the hottest punk act. The only problem was that it was in August when there were no students on campus, but by then the concerts were seen as an income-generating business for the SU so I had no difficulty justifying the event.

I'd had some problems with violence at the smaller punk shows, where you could still swing a punch or a boot, but I felt quite confident that a gig this big would go off without any such incidents.

On that August day, however, I saw 1800 or so punks queued up outside and I had a feeling of slight disquiet. Just then the heavens opened – I told the porters I was going to hold the doors for about half an hour and they were to put on the hall's heating at full blast.

"But it's August, about sixty degrees, what do you want the heating on for?"

"Trust me, just do it."

The audience streamed in, punks wringing out their Mohicans like paint brushes. Once inside the heat did its work – it was like a sauna, steam filling the hall. Ever tried fighting in a sauna? No? No one tried it on this occasion either, and it was a great show and a quiet night.

PS. A further little story about Siouxsie happened in the late '80s when I was running, for three months, a large 6000-capacity tent in Finsbury Park. One of the shows in there that summer was Siouxsie and The Banshees. The promoter rang me the week before the show to say that Siouxsie was very anxious that she had a clean, upmarket toilet near her dressing room, for her exclusive use. Not an unreasonable request for the headline act, I thought. So I duly ordered one. It came on the Tuesday for the Saturday show – big mistake.

The site crew had been using the designated staff Portaloos for about six weeks and by then there was evidence of life forms unknown to the scientific world appearing out of various cracks and orifices in those strange, plastic sentry boxes. Worried about the possible effects of these alien organisms on the more delicate areas of the human body, the crew managed to discover a way of entering the executive loo and using it for five days. I was unaware of this, but on Saturday afternoon I was to discover the horrendous truth.

Siouxsie's manager came running up to me: "What the bloody hell are you doing? We had to have a toilet for Siouxsie's exclusive use. A top of the range facility!" he screamed.

"But you have, it's there," I, rather smugly, pointed out. However he then opened the toilet door. "She can't use this, she's going ballistic, and she says it's a shit house!"

I tried to keep a straight face as I replied, "Well actually that's …"

"I know, I know, that's what it is," he said breaking into a grin, even he could see the joke, although I did have to bring in, at considerable expense, an emergency cleaning company.

Barry Lucas

The Sisters of Mercy

7 October 1984 **First and Last and Always Tour** Support: Skeletal Family

Formed in Leeds in 1980 by Andrew Eldritch (vocals, drums) and Gary Marx (guitar), The Sisters of Mercy are one of England's leading Goth bands of the 1980s and took their name from a Leonard Cohen song.

The band soon released their debut single, 'The Damage Done' in 1980 on their own independent record label, Merciful Release, going on to release three studio albums and sixteen singles; the best known being 'The Temple of Love' reaching No.3 in the UK singles chart of 1992.

The band visited Lancaster in March 1985 in support of the release of their debut studio album, *First and Last and Always*.

The Sisters of Mercy continue to perform live.

Skeletal Family were an English gothic rock band formed in Keighley, West Yorkshire, in December 1982. The group signed with Chrysalis Records and released two 1986 singles, 'Restless' and 'Just a Minute'.

Slade

6 March 1981 Support: Raid The North
15 December 1983 Support: Export

Originally known as Ambrose Slade, Slade are an English glam rock band from the Black Country in the West Midlands. They rose to prominence during the early 1970s with seventeen consecutive Top 20 hits and six No. 1s. *British Hit Singles & Albums* names them as the most successful British group of the 1970s based on sales of singles. They were the first act to have three singles entering at No. 1. All six of the band's chart-toppers were penned by Noddy Holder and Jim Lea. Total UK sales stand at 6,520,171 and their bestselling single, 'Merry Xmas Everybody', has sold in excess of one million copies.

Slade have released over thirty albums, three of which reached No. 1 in the UK Albums Chart. Their releases have spent 315 weeks in the UK charts and they had earned twenty-four Top 30 UK hits as of 2016.

Their 1983 Great Hall appearance was a fabulous Christmas concert.

Raid The North were a Middlesbrough rock band, originally known as Taurus.

The band **Export** were formed in 1980 by erstwhile Hard Stuff vocalist Harry Shaw. Following a self-financed album *Export*, the band achieved a major American deal with Epic Records, releasing an album in 1984, *Contraband*, and in 1986 the critically acclaimed Lance Quinn produced *Living In Fear Of The Private Eye*.

Christmas concert 1983 photo courtesy of Ian Edmundson @ www.slayed.com

Dave Hill of Slade photo courtesy of Ian Edmundson @ www.slayed.com

After their initial explosion onto the UK's music charts, Slade suffered a downturn in their recording fortunes. They were always a popular and exciting live act but their records mysteriously ceased to sell for a period. It was during this time that I went to drop off some more concert tickets at 'Ear 'Ere Records because they had sold out of that week's show. I went upstairs to see Nigel, only to find him entertaining Noddy Holder from Slade. He was being taken around the chart returns shops (a handful of record shops whose sales figures were collected nationally to determine that week's record charts) to enthuse them and their customers about Slade's latest single. Something worked, although I'm not sure it can all be attributed to 'Ear 'Ere's influence, and Slade's record sales recovered over the next few years. Having said that I still found it surrealistically absurd to hear 'Merry Christmas Everybody!' ringing out in March!

While Noddy was a really funny and engaging guy, it was nothing compared to another occasion when I went upstairs at 'Ear 'Ere to find Nigel and the gorgeous Kim Wilde eating fish and chips out of newspaper. She was making a tour of chart shops to push her new single. However, the sight of Kim with Lancaster chip fat slowly running from her lips down her chin was a northern lad's fantasy and a memory which will live with me forever …

'Ear 'Ere Records was a quite remarkable record shop. This had little to do with me (except it was my idea and my suggestion to drag Nigel back from the wilds of Lowestoft) but everything to do with the staff, especially Nigel and his carefully hand-picked lieutenants: Eric, Roger and Malcolm in particular. Everybody employed in that enterprise was intelligent and musically motivated, and they each knew and cared about specific music genres. Somebody in that shop could answer any query and generally obtain any recording, even some illegal bootlegs!

'Ear 'Ere is the only record shop in music history to be awarded a platinum disc when we sold the one millionth copy of Boney M's 'Rivers of Babylon'. I went down to WEA Records headquarters in London with Nigel and Malcolm from the shop. We were ferried around the capitol in a chauffeur driven Rolls Royce, and wine and dined, before being awarded the disc at a press conference. A platinum disc had never been awarded before, or since, to a record shop.

A couple of years ago Roger sent me a link to website devoted to great record shops of the world – the 'Ear 'Ere entry was sandwiched between a record shop in New York and one in San Francisco. A small market stall in Lancaster indeed!

'Ear 'Ere Records – the greatest record shop ever.

19 April 2014.
Courtesy of:
Michael Taylor
www.themarpleleaf.co.uk

Today is Record Store Day. It's brought back a flood of nostalgia for the greatest record store that ever existed.

Anyone who remembers 'Ear 'Ere in Lancaster knows what I mean. It was a cosier and friendlier version of the record shop in Nick Hornby's High Fidelity. It was also where you could get tickets for gigs at all kinds of places around the North of England. But from my early forays in there after school, to look meaningfully at prog album covers from the likes of Genesis and King Crimson, to the more serious record buyer I became, it was the centre of my world.

I remember going in as a young teen one Saturday and looking through the racks. Some lad approached me and asked me what music I liked. He was probably just being friendly, but it seemed at the time to be the equivalent of the "got the time, mate?" question at a concert or football match. So I bolted and caught up with my mum on Lancaster market. Back then there was a ferocious mob called the Marsh Mods who had lined up outside punk gigs and battered anyone in sight. Then there were the Morecambe Punks, who would use belts and chains to mash anyone who crossed them. We developed myths and scare stories about the violence these gangs would inflict on you, most of it wildly exaggerated, but it hung over you and was a caution not to stray too far from safety.

But in reality 'Ear 'Ere was safe neutral ground. As I became more confident (cocky?) I became a regular in there. You could listen on the headphones by the counter, get recommendations from the staff, especially one character who worked there called Malcolm. The manager was Roger, or to most of us "Beardie". A nostalgic Facebook post elicited the comment from an old mate that these guys had as big a stamp on his musical DNA as John Peel.

You could put your name down to pre-order records and it was the first time I'd used a nickname rather than my surname with adults. I remember a few of us sneaking out at lunch break from school to buy 'Going Underground' by The Jam in 1980, then swaggering back in possession of the fastest-selling single of that era.

I used to be in awe of people who would ask for rare records that they didn't have in stock, but would get the staff working hard looking through books and old stock lists and seeing if they could try to order it for you. They'd also sell fanzines, a few t-shirts and badges, some they'd even give away, but mostly it was shifting units in the golden age of pop music.

And their plastic bags were such a status symbol around school. You'd cart your school books to lessons in an 'Ear 'Ere bag, the height of cool, but woefully impractical for such a purpose.

I don't buy much music these days, but I fervently stick to the principle that the local record store is a totem of a civilised culturally advanced society. So when I want a new album by a band I still follow slightly slavishly – Elbow, Manics, etc. – then Piccadilly Records in Oldham Street, Manchester, get my custom. I also love their devotion to new music and always sample something from their Top 100 of the year. It's hit and miss, but those moments of serendipity are what makes life interesting. It's what has always made life interesting – so on this day of all days, I raise a glass to the greatest record shop ever: 'Ear 'Ere in Lancaster. May perpetual light shine upon your memory.

But its real claim to fame came with another celeb. superstar visit. This time we knew in advance and could publicise it in plenty of time, so that on the day vast crowds gathered to welcome David Bellamy to promote his legendary single 'Brontosaurus Will You Wait For Me', with the unforgettable flip side, 'Oh Stegasaurus'. And don't snigger – in 1983 it made No. 88 in the UK Singles Chart.

Barry Lucas

The Smiths

9 March 1984 Support: Red Guitars

Formed in Manchester in 1982 The Smiths consisted of vocalist Morrissey, guitarist Johnny Marr, bassist Andy Rourke and drummer Mike Joyce. The Smiths were the definitive British indie rock band of the '80s, marking the end of synth-driven new wave and the beginning of the guitar rock that dominated English rock into the '90s.

The Smiths released four studio albums, one live album, ten compilation albums, twenty singles, one video album, plus fourteen music videos on the Rough Trade, Sire and WEA record labels. Following emerging tensions and the exhaustion of Johnny Marr, the band dissolved in 1987 around the time of the release of the album *Strangeways, Here We Come*, which reached No. 2 in the UK Albums Chart.

The **Red Guitars** were an English indie rock band active from 1982 to 1986. Based in Hull, the Red Guitars' first single, 'Good Technology', was a minor hit, selling 60,000 copies. Their singles 'Marimba Jive' and 'Be With Me' both reached No. 1 on the UK Indie Singles Chart.

The tour was promoted by a relatively new kid on the block, Phil McIntyre from Preston, who by then had already become a major player. He was also refreshingly innovative compared to the big-name promoting dinosaurs. His younger brother, Nigel, had his finger on the pulse of the North West music revolution and had secured The Smith's major UK tour.

We had a massive sell-out on our hands but it was 7.30 pm and no sign of the band. I was worried. I asked Phil if there was a problem. No, he reassured me, they won't be here until about 8.50! Why, I wanted to know, what about sound checks etc.? He told me that all the guys in the band wanted to watch *Coronation Street* with their various mums, with Nigel having to drive to each one and pick them up after it was finished. Annie and Jack Walker would have been proud of them.

Barry Lucas

Status Quo

I had Status Quo on a couple of times, but one date, possibly around October 1978, isn't featured in this official history. One Monday morning Mike Lloyd from Hanley, Stoke, phoned me. I have mentioned him several times in this book; he helped me in the early days and taught me a great deal about commercial promoting. Mike was friendly with Status Quo and put them on numerous times at Hanley's Victoria Hall and other venues in the area. The band had just returned from an Australian tour and had asked Mike if he could find them a cash gig that weekend. Apparently they had met and befriended a few fans in Sydney and wanted to fly them over to see one of their shows in the UK. Mike wanted to know if I could do a date at Lancaster, leaving me only five days to organise, promote it and sell tickets. I have said elsewhere in this book that I love sorting promotion problems out and here was a beaut!

No Internet, no Twitter, no Facebook. Five days; book the hall, print the posters, flyers, tickets etc. Get them out and get the word out, sort some staff out and sell two thousand tickets, no problem …

Well the gig happened and I even got one of my security staff, an ex-student who was renting a bungalow in Westgate, to put the Aussie friends up for a night or two. Mind you, I did have several volunteers offering spare beds for four Bondi Beach beauties.

Status Quo's 1975 Lancaster concert was alas memorable for something other than the music. You might remember the Birmingham pub bombings of 1974, the six suspects of which had been arrested at Heysham Port and initially interrogated at Morecambe Police Station. In 1975 they were to stand trial at Lancaster Castle in one of the most famous court cases in the world at that time. There was a very tense atmosphere in the surrounding area. Before the show, I received a phone call from Lancaster Police. Apparently they had received a bomb threat/warning for an explosion at that night's Great Hall concert. The Police said that they would normally be fairly relaxed about this kind of call but a) the Birmingham six were on trial in Lancaster, and b) the caller had used a certain IRA code word, so they had to take it very seriously. They asked me if I could begin a check with my staff whilst they sent up some officers. Bloody hell, this was 6.30 pm and I was due to open the doors for a sell-out in an hour – how bloody inconvenient and annoying!

Well, I asked some staff to begin looking around the venue. I went down the side corridor and into the glass store/washing room. "Bloody annoying nuisance," I thought as I began to look around the area. I started kicking empty cardboard boxes. "No bomb here," I declared to myself. Suddenly I stopped, what the hell was I doing, kicking boxes to see if there was a bomb hidden inside? Hey, intelligent or what? You could tell I had a degree! Nothing went bang. Except the concert was a banging success. Phew!

Barry Lucas

Steel Pulse

4 February 1978 — Supports: China Street | The Venus Boys
27 October 1978 — **Handsworth Revolution Tour** — Support: China Street
9 May 1982 — Support: Handsworth Reggae Sound System

From the Handsworth area of Birmingham, Steel Pulse are one of the UK's most highly regarded roots reggae outfits being rivalled only by Aswad in terms of creative and commercial success. The band were formed in 1975 by rhythm guitarist and lead vocalist David "Dread" Hinds and guitarist Basil Gabbidon. In early 1978, following a successful tour as a supporting act to the Jamaican musician Burning Spear (aka Winston Rodney), Steel Pulse were quickly signed up to the Island Records label. In July 1978, their first highly acclaimed studio album, *Handsworth Revolution* went straight to number nine in the UK album charts, just ten days after its release.

Steel Pulse arrived in Lancaster for their October 78 Great Hall concert straight after returning from a twelve date European tour supporting Bob Marley and The Wailers.

Allying themselves closely with the Rock Against Racism movement, Steel Pulse chose to tour with sympathetic elements of the punk movement, including The Stranglers, The Clash, XTC etc.

The band once stated that: "Punks had a way of enjoying themselves – throw hordes at you, beer, spit at you, that kind of thing".

Steel Pulse were the first non-Jamaican act to win the Grammy Award for Best Reggae Album in 1987 for their sixth studio album *Babylon the Bandit.*

Over forty years after their formation, Steel Pulse are still busy touring and recording with founder member David Hinds and his long serving keyboard player Selwyn Brown.

Rock Against Racism was a campaign set up in the United Kingdom in 1976 as a response to an increase in racial conflict and the growth of white nationalist groups such as the National Front. The campaign involved pop, rock, punk and reggae musicians staging concerts with an anti-racist theme, in order to discourage young people from embracing racism. The campaign was founded, in part, as a response to statements and activities by well-known rock musicians that were widely regarded as racist.

October 1978 ©Geoff Campbell

FRIDAY
OCT. 27TH
STEEL PULSE
+
LANCASTER UNIVERSITY £1.75
ANGUS

John Angus

ROCK
AGAINST
RACISM
CONCERT
STEEL
PULSE
THE LOU'S
CHINA STREET
THE VENUS BOYS
+
7.30PM SAT
4TH FEBRUARY
GREAT HALL
UNIVERSITY
OF
LANCASTER
ALL
THIS
FOR
ONLY £1.00
UNITE
AGAINST
RACISM

John Angus

Steel Pulse were an excellent reggae band and the mainstay of the Rock Against Racism movement, but with this show it is the support band I wish to remember. China Street were a local Lancaster band – as you can probably guess from their name – and were as good as it gets.

With a little bit of luck, good management and record company support money – any one of those, or a combination of the above – they could have been superstars. Over the years I have been asked many times to manage local bands and I can say that I have never really been tempted. I was never hungry enough to sit outside office doors in London awaiting an answer and making a nuisance of myself until I was heard and noticed. But with China Street … maybe I might have made a difference, rolled the dice in their favour … we'll never know.

Go back to this time and you'll find a band that was truly innovative, unique and special. They blended rock and reggae, something common now but unheard of in the early months of 1978. They had attracted record company interest and were in a southern studio, putting down some tracks for a promo EP (older readers please translate). The studio next door had a newly formed band rehearsing and recording: the singer Sting, the band The Police. They came in to listen to the new arrangements being played by China Street in the adjoining studio. Something different, something new, something unique. Well, the band with millions behind them were impressed with this new sound and the rest, as they say, is history.

Barry Lucas

John Angus

Lancaster band **China Street** made four guest appearances in the Great Hall over the space of a year.

Formed in 1976 the band consisted of Martin Pilkington (guitars and vocals), Dusty Hall (saxophones and vocals), Adam Williams (bass guitar) and David Willan (drums), later adding Chris Sugden on keyboards, more specifically a Fender Rhodes piano.

China Street took their name from the Lancaster Street where some of the band members shared a flat in the mid '70s. Their first university gig was as guests of The Jam in December 1977, which resulted in an invitation to support the band for the whole of their first major UK tour. Their next appearance was as support band to Sad Café a month later in January 1978, before two dates in quick succession supporting Steel Pulse. China Street's first UK tour proper was to support Steel Pulse on the whole of their Handsworth Revolution Tour.

Rock Against Racism single cover

The band are remembered as pioneers of the independent record label Criminal Records, one of the very first and established in 1977. Their first 7" single – A side 'You're A Ruin'/ B side '(I Wanna Be) Your MP' – was released on their new label and soon attracted music press attention, with a special feature about the new independent label and a "how to do it yourself" article appearing in *Melody Maker*.

The subsequent press exposure eventually led to interest from the major record companies and in January 1978 China Street entered Surrey Sound Studios, after signing a deal with EMI, and recorded the single 'Rock Against Racism'.

China Street disbanded in early 1979 with Adam Williams going on to form local band The Pharaohs with James Mackie and Dusty Hall. Following Adam's spell with The Selecter he progressed on to production work with Annie Lennox and Dave Stewart of The Eurythmics and Bronski Beat. Moving into the 1990s he then became a producer and director, working on assorted video projects with artists such as Norman Cook, Adamski and Seal and produced the video for their 1990 hit single 'Killer'. Adam currently works in London and is involved in the development of 3D augmented reality and Telepresence systems in sound and vision.

More local entertainment came in the shape of former members of Lancaster punk band The Kassels. Jeff Hurst along with Ian and Andy Holmes teamed up with Kenny Matthews on vocals, to form **The Venus Boys**, later known as The Venus Mob.

Information is scant regarding the two other billed support acts, **The Lou's** and **Handsworth Reggae Sound System**.

October 1978 supporting Steel Pulse
©Geoff Campbell

Be Stiff

17 October 1978
Wreckless Eric
Jona Lewie
Rachel Sweet
Lene Lovich
Mickey Jupp

Route 78 Tour

The second Stiff Records UK package tour 'Be Stiff '78' kicked off its two-week run on 10 October 1978 and was undertaken by a specially chartered train that arrived at Lancaster Railway Station on the 17 October.

The troupe then continued on to the USA, with Mickey Jupp being left behind for the US leg, due to his fear of flying.

This '78 Stiff event was designed to build on the excitement of the 1977 Stiff promotional tour that had featured Nick Lowe and Ian Dury etc.

Although the lineup wasn't as strong as 1977, it was still a great night's entertainment and tremendous value for money.

The bands lined up as follows:
Lene Lovich & The Musicians Union
Mickey Jupp & The Cable Layers
Wreckless Eric & The Four Rough Men
Rachel Sweet & The Records
Jona Lewie & Two's Company

As in the 1977 Live Stiffs concert, all band members were on stage together for a finale, performing a rendition of the Devo single 'Be Stiff'.

Stomu Yamash'ta

27 November 1972

Stomu Yamash'ta is a Japanese percussionist, keyboardist, composer and experimental artist. He is probably best known for his work leading the jazz-rock fusion group Go, which released three albums from 1976–77. The band featured Steve Winwood, guitarist Al Di Mieola, and drummer Michael Shrieve.

Beginning in 1972 Yamash'ta started recording jazz rock fusion albums blended with traditional Japanese influences.

He released *Floating Music* in 1972 and visited Lancaster to promote the album, with his short-lived band called Come To The Edge featuring drummer Morris Pert, bass guitarist Phil Plant and keyboards and saxophonist Robin Thompson.

In 1973 he then formed Stomu Yamash'ta's East Wind, a band which included keyboardist Brian Gascoigne, guitarist Gary Boyle and bassist Hugh Hopper. This group released two albums, *Freedom Is Frightening* (1973) and the soundtrack *One By One* (1974). Gascoigne and Boyle also played on his next album, *Raindog* (1975), with vocals by Murray Head and Maxine Nightingale.

In the latter part of the 1970s, he then formed and led his super group Go, featuring Steve Winwood, Al Di Meola, Klaus Schulze and Michael Shrieve. Leaving Europe in 1980, Stomu Yamash'ta retired to a Buddhist temple in Kyoto. His retirement was brief and he later went on to release a number of recordings employing synthesizers, pre-recorded taped sounds, orchestral instruments and percussion. Of these recordings his so-called 'space music' of the 1983 album *Sea and Sky* is still available on CD. Stomu continues to occasionally release albums in his electronica/ambient genre. His 'Space Theme' was used by the BBC on *The Hitchhiker's Guide to the Galaxy* (the radio series).

Stomu was a genius and when he appeared in the Great Hall a unique concert occurred. However, he was also one of those favours to Island that I had to honour, to repay them for all the great Island superstars that appeared at Lancaster.

Robb Winn phoned me to ask if I would promote Stomu Yamash'ta on a Wednesday in the Great Hall. "Stomu who?" was my immediate reply.

"Don't worry, straight percentage to you so you can't lose money but I need to put a tour together for him – it's a bit political here (with a small p)."

"OK, we can't lose, but who is he? What does he do?"

Well, he bangs lots of drums; there must have been about forty on stage that night. He is also quite an important musical figure who wrote the score for Ken Russell's *The Devils* and several Kurosawa films, including the legendary *Seven Samurai*.

Anyway the date happened, the three men turned up but not the dog! I think the 90% of the ticket receipts that Stomu took, as payment, were £48.10p. Didn't even pay his train fare.

Barry Lucas

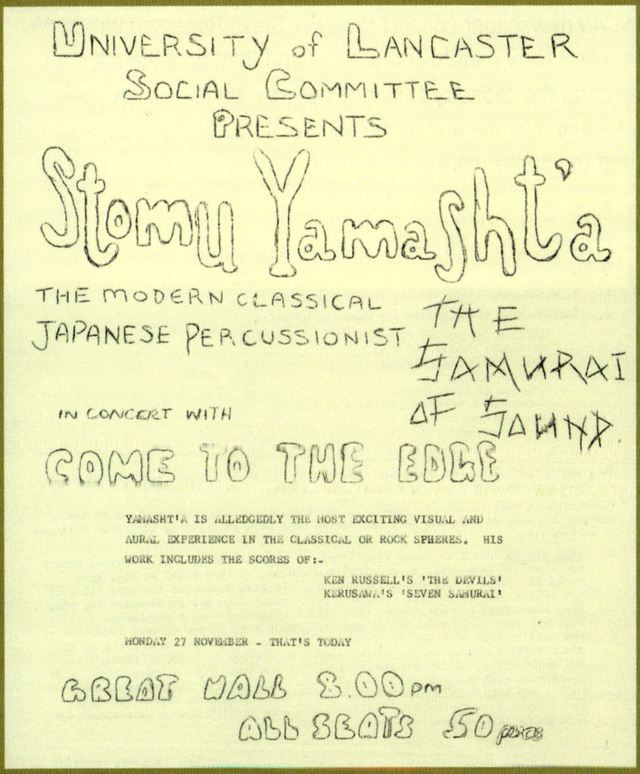

The Teardrop Explodes

31 January 1982 — Support: The Ravishing Beauties
10 October 1982 — Support: Screen 3

The Teardrop Explodes were a British post-punk/neo-psychedelic band formed in Liverpool in 1978. The band were formed by Julian Cope who had previously been in the short-lived yet locally renowned band Crucial Three along with Pete Wylie (who went on to form Wah!) and Ian McCulloch, later of Echo and the Bunnymen.

In 1981, the group were at the height of their popularity, achieving the No. 6 slot in the UK Singles Chart with the single 'Reward', and in April a Top 20 hit with 'Treason'.

The Teardrop Explodes released a total of three studio albums, promoting the release of the album *Wilder* on their first visit to Lancaster in January.

Following the band's dissolution in December 1982, Julian Cope began a career as a solo artist, appearing at The Sugarhouse in Lancaster in March 1984. He later went on to pursue a career as a writer and cultural commentator which continues to this day.

Screen 3 were a British post-punk new wave band from Norwich, active from 1980–1984 and again from 1990–1992. Heavily influenced by The Cure's first album, *Three Imaginary Boys*, the original Screen 3 lineup formed in 1980 and consisted of Neil Dyer, Richard Kett and Brett Cooper. Trumpet players Peter Jay and Jason Votier were added in late 1981.

The Ravishing Beauties were a three piece all girl punk pop band, comprising Virginia Astley, Kate St John and Nicky Holland. Virginia's father was Edwin Astley, a composer responsible for the theme music to TV shows such as *The Saint*, *Randall and Hopkirk (Deceased)* and *Dangerman*.

You might get an inkling of the Teardrop show from the photo but you really cannot understand the sheer size of the stage set and the problems it generated.

My mate, Paul Darwin, was tour managing the show and I think we were the second date. Obviously the band had sat in the pub over the summer with some theatre set designer luvvie and dreamed up this stage set. As the drink flowed they took to designing a rock show on the back of numerous beer mats.

Paul was at his wits end that morning as he phoned me at 8.00 am and asked me to get to the Great Hall. When I got there he explained that the previous night they had taken the hall's side doors off and then the windows in the roof. But still they couldn't get the whole structure, with the solid stage risers, into the venue. Well, we tried every which way, even taking off the Great Hall doors in the foyer but neither could we. So what you see is a fraction of that ridiculous stage set. As far as I know the vast majority of the set stayed on the artics for a scenic tour of the UK and never saw the light of day.

Barry Lucas

January 1982

Both images on this page October 1982 ©Geoff Campbell

Thin Lizzy

The legend that is Phil Lynott. I can still see him today, centre stage, using the follow spotlight on him and reflecting it off the scratch plate on his guitar to pick out the pretty girls on the balcony.

By this time Thin Lizzy had hit super stardom and their contract and rider reflected this. One demand was that the mixer desk had to be centre stage, a specified distance back – remember, by now the band were usually only playing festivals or stadiums. I signed the contract but explained, in writing, that this particular clause would mean that the mixer desk would be situated in the next building. Apparently this so amused the band's management that they carried it around with them to show others in the music business for months.

I must mention an interesting anecdote which occurred many years later. I was going to see Limehouse Lizzy, a Thin Lizzy tribute, at The Platform in Morecambe (at the time a very successful local authority venue managed by my wife, Mary). They are an excellent band and well worth checking out. I was going with a couple of friends and asked my son, Simon, if he wanted to come along. He did. He is a Professional Golf Association coach and his first job as an eighteen year old was at Malahide, just outside Dublin (the relevance of this will soon be revealed). About three numbers into the show I saw him texting. I absolutely hate the obsession with mobiles so I asked him to leave it alone for just ninety minutes. He said, "But I'm just texting Steve."

"Why? Who the hell is Steve?"

"I was telling him I was watching a tribute to his dad."

"Who's his dad?"

"Phil Lynott. I met Steve when I was in Ireland and we became good mates."

"Let you off."

A few minutes later he was holding up his phone. "What are you doing now?" I wanted to know.

"He wanted to watch some of the show."

Now, how cool is that from your son?

Barry Lucas

The unmistakable figure of Phil Lynott on the Great Hall Stage ©David Bradbury

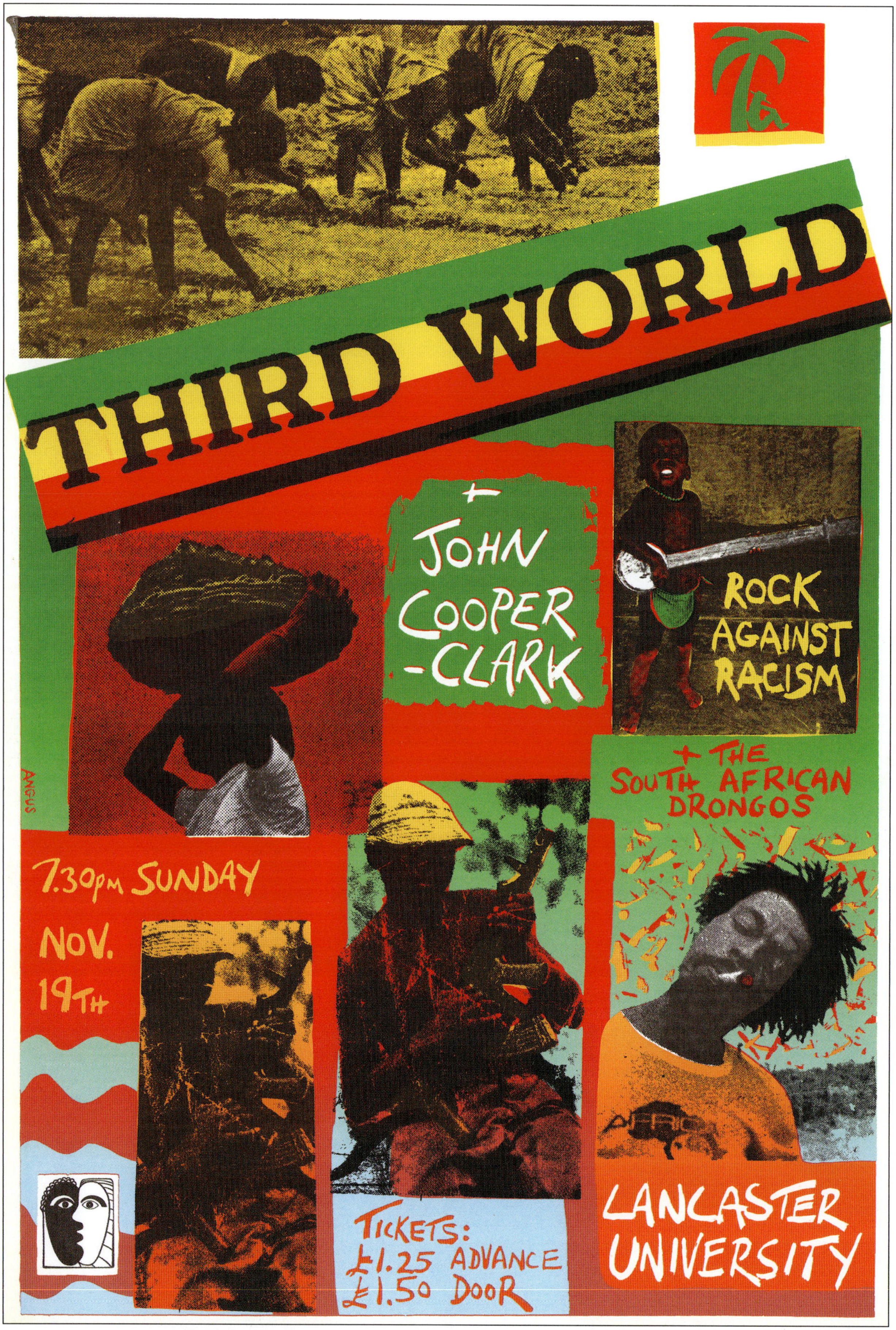
THIRD WORLD
+ JOHN COOPER-CLARK
ROCK AGAINST RACISM
+ THE SOUTH AFRICAN DRONGOS
ANGUS
7.30pm SUNDAY
NOV. 19TH
TICKETS:
£1.25 ADVANCE
£1.50 DOOR
LANCASTER UNIVERSITY

John Angus

Third World

19 November 1978 Supports: John Cooper Clarke | The South African Drongoes

Third World are a Jamaican reggae band formed in 1973 by keyboardist Michael "Ibo" Cooper and guitarist and cellist Steven "Cat" Coore. They are best known for the single 'Now That We've Found Love' released in 1978 and reaching No. 10 in the UK Singles Chart.

To date, the prolific Third World have recorded twenty-one studio albums, five live albums and over thirty singles.

This was another Great Hall concert in support of the Rock Against Racism movement.

The band continues to perform with six members, including three of the original core members at the forefront.

The "Bard of Salford" **Dr John Cooper Clarke,** as he is now known, was the tremendous supporting act on the night.

First up on stage that night was a band billed as **The South African Drongoes** of which little is known, although a special mention must be made here of a local Lancaster outfit who existed around the early 1980s similarly called, The Drongos.

The Drongos were part of a Lancaster Musicians Collective with three saxophonists in the lineup along with former China Street guitarist Martin Pilkington, Pharaoh drummer Bernie Kelly and Lancaster bass guitarist Geoff Dade.

I opened the book by describing the journey back to Lancaster with Tina Turner's promoter, Barry Marshall. Of all the acts to appear at Lancaster, Tina, in some ways, was the most remarkable and summed up what had happened to that small, new university in a mad fourteen years.

At the beginning of 1984 Geoff Campbell and I were getting worried. By now the audiences at Lancaster were spoilt and used to a steady procession of the world's superstars. But, as of January, we had no major star in place for the rest of the academic year. So, Geoff and I went to London to chat up a few agents and promoters as we simply had to find something outstanding. We ended up in Liverpool Street, Islington, at Paul Loasby's offices, in a bit of a desperate state – still no major act. We retired to Paul's favourite pub for lunch – favourite because it was fifteen yards outside his office door – and lunch was to be several pints followed by bottles of Chardonnay back at the office. Paul has dramatically changed since those days, as back then he was one of rock 'n' roll's legendary party animals. After about thirty minutes of listening to us bemoaning our/Lancaster's fate Paul left the table and borrowed the pub's phone (no mobiles then). He returned to the table: "Do you want Tina Turner?" he enquired matter of factly.

Do we want Tina Turner? To me she was a true music business legend who, from the early days of the '60s with Ike, had bestrode rock like an Amazonian colossus. Nobody who saw her perform in Monterrey will ever forget it. Do we want Tina Turner? Are you 'aving a laff?

The journey back to Lancaster was a joyous one for Geoff and I.

The tour was a massive success and re-established Tina, giving her a status she would never relinquish. The tour posters were those massive ones for building bill boards which were hopeless for our small, agency shop windows. It didn't matter though, the show sold out in a few hours. A couple of days later I was walking down the Spine when a mature student stopped me and went ballistic. He didn't know Tina Turner was playing the University and now it was sold out. Why hadn't I advertised it, he wanted to know. "Look, mate, of course I didn't advertise it, or rather I didn't come round to your room to tell you, but 2000 people did know it was on … somehow."

The interest and demand generated was immense. Mick Byron of Byron's Hair in Lancaster had six hair industry bigwigs (sorry) driving up from London. Could I do ANYTHING? He would pay ANYTHING. A senior police officer rang me: "I know it's a sell out, but could you get a couple of CID in the projection box at the back of the hall?"

"Oh, OK I suppose so, anything for the Old Bill."

"Great. There's fourteen of us coming up. Thanks!"

The show was brilliant, but, dear reader, do you remember my musings on Eric Clapton? Well Tina needed several changes of costume so we built a small changing area at the back of the stage. However, we found we couldn't use it because the balcony was packed and overlooked it, so she would have to dash back to the dressing room. It would all be a bit frantic. I was sitting in the porters' lodge with Barry Marshall when the tour manager came in, going berserk. Apparently my stewards (yes, the same ones I foolishly didn't sack over Mr Clapton's Southern Comfort incident) had burst into Tina Turner's dressing room as she was changing. Can it get any more embarrassing, or any worse? We went down to the backstage. I demanded to know what they were playing at. Would you believe the answer? No, you wouldn't. In front of the tour manager, tour promoter and me, they said, with totally straight faces, that they thought they heard her call out for some stewards to help her out of her dress!!

Only now, thirty odd years later can I see the funny side – I think.

Barry Lucas

Tom Paxton

14 May 1971 — Support unknown
2 February 1973 — Support: Bridgit St John
28 February 1975 — Support: Bryn Haworth

Tom Paxton is an American folk singer-songwriter who has had a music career spanning more than fifty years.

Paxton's songs have been widely covered over the years by musicians such as Bob Dylan, Joan Baez, John Denver and Dolly Parton.

He has performed thousands of concerts around the world.

His biggest successes as a songwriter were the songs that became hits for others. These were covered many times over and turned out to be Tom's most valuable copyrights. 'The Last Thing on My Mind', 'Bottle of Wine' and 'The Marvelous Toy' were his most popular works. But other artists were also attracted to such socially conscious compositions as 'What Did You Learn in School Today?' and 'Whose Garden Was This?', as well as his reflective, melancholy songs such as 'Ramblin' Boy' and 'I Can't Help But Wonder Where I'm Bound'.

In March 2015, Paxton released his new studio album, *Redemption Road*, his sixty-first album to date. Tom continues to perform yearly tours of the United States and UK.

Bridgit St John was back once more in the Great Hall, having previously provided support to Roy Harper in November 1969.

From Blackburn, Lancashire, acclaimed slide guitarist **Bryn Haworth** is a singer-songwriter who has been performing his own unique brand of rock, country and gospel blues for over thirty years. Over his career he has recorded, as a session guitar player, with top musicians including Chris de Burgh, Joan Armatrading, Cliff Richard and Gerry Rafferty. Bryn also writes his own songs and has had several of his compositions recorded by other artists, including Lulu, Sandy Denny and Mary Black.

What a lovely bloke – a true gentleman. A great folk legend who gave three fantastic concerts at Lancaster. But it was the first one that was really memorable for me, for the wrong reasons. In those days I still played sport in The Roses weekend, football for the Students' Union and cricket for the University First X1. So I was required for combat in York that year, the weekend Tom was due to play in the Great Hall. I was in an unprecedented run of twenty-eight consecutive profit-making shows, something of legendary proportions. I was leaving the show in my staff's hands, even my trusty right-hand man, Alan Murray, was over in York on football duty. But it was hardly an onerous deal, an international folk superstar, solo artist and one of the nicest people in music to deal with. I phoned on Sunday morning, before taking the field of battle, to ask how it went. To my dismay we had fallen seventeen people short of break even, eighteen short of another profit – we had lost £16.75, but a loss is a loss, the first for twenty-nine shows. I was devastated, so it was to the bar to revive my spirits for the footie match.

Barry Lucas

The Tremeloes

19 February 1971 Supports: Money | Ashley

The Tremeloes are an English beat group founded in 1958 in Dagenham, East London. They were formed as Brian Poole and the Tremoloes (*sic*), being influenced by Buddy Holly and the Crickets.

The original quintet consisted of lead vocalist Brian Poole, lead guitarist Rick West (born Richard Westwood), rhythm guitarist/keyboardist Alan Blakley, bassist Alan Howard and drummer Dave Munden.

On New Year's Day, 1962, Decca Records auditioned two bands at its London studios: Brian Poole and The Tremeloes, a veteran group from Essex and a relatively unknown Liverpool quartet known as The Beatles. Decca chose the Tremeloes over the newcomers because, as a London based outfit, they would be more easily accessible. To say it was a bad decision is more than an understatement, but the Tremeloes did produce some hits for Decca, ultimately placing thirteen songs in the British Top 40.

With Poole leaving to attempt a solo career (which proved unsuccessful) in 1966, the Tremeloes continued as a four-piece band with a revised lineup (Howard left the band in 1966). Len "Chip" Hawkes, father of 1990s hitmaker Chesney Hawkes, replaced Howard.

The band is best known for their 1967 UK No. 1 hit 'Silence Is Golden'.

A version of The Tremeloes is still together today.

Little is known about **Ashley**.

Also on the bill that night were a covers band called **Money** from Manchester. Later the same year Money had stepped into the breach for Barry Lucas to provide entertainment at very short notice when The Moody Blues pulled out of a concert at the last minute (see Blue Jays entry).

This was a Rag Ball featuring one of those legendary bands of the mid '60s. It really is amazing when you go to see one of the acts from that era, it's sixty to ninety minutes of non-stop hits. Your youth comes flooding back, well, it does if you're of a certain age. Of course the Singles Chart dominated music from that period and the top bands regularly released four, five or even six records a year. Most hit the Top 10 and so were played constantly on the radio and television, embedding themselves into your subconscious. It's embarrassing how many numbers you can sing along to!

This show is remarkable for one thing. The band were obviously very '60s in style, that is what the audience wanted after all, but were also dated in their show presentation. A few small PA column stacks, fitting into a transit van, proper '60s pop, was all the equipment on stage. This was, in some ways, very fortunate indeed. Many of the audience probably had a more impressive speaker set-up for their record players in their bedrooms at home. It was at this show, early in 1971, that the University administration started its determined attack on the Great Hall popular music concerts. So by 1985, when I resigned, no wonder I was tired of fighting this continual battle. They began it here by calling in the Audio Visual Aids Department to do an investigation (exposé) into sound levels. They hoped to use this to get the Great Hall shows stopped, curtailed or emasculated. Given the nature of this particular show, the very small PA and what was to follow in later years, their report makes for very amusing reading today.

Interpretation:

1) The above results are measurement of sound level and are not necessarily the same as noise, since noise can be generally defined as unwanted sound .

4) At no location other than within the building was the activity in the Great Hall measurable or even detectable.

5) Table 2 comprises measurements made while the dance was being held in the Great Hall. The figures for locations 1, 2 and 3 (Great Hall balcony, and foyer and Nuffield corridor) illustrate the very high level of sound generated by the equipment used by present day groups. It is comparable with the sound levels in the vicinity of a large jet airliner taking off. Close to the stage, levels must be approaching the Threshold of Pain and performers working constantly under these conditions (and possibly some members of the audience who regularly attend) are in some danger of suffering permanent auditory damage.

Conclusion:

There appears to be a majority opinion in favour of limiting in some way the level of sound produced by groups in the Great Hall.

The above results relate, I am told, to a "quiet" night in as much as the dance was not well attended and the groups appearing were "quieter" than many who have performed here in the past.

Good old Mr Glover, if only he'd have known what was to come. But how's that for a paternal attitude to 'young people enjoying themselves'? If he had turned up at The Scorpions he'd have prophesied Armageddon.

Barry Lucas

Ultravox

7 December 1980 Support: Fatal Charm

Ultravox are a British new wave band, formed in London in 1974 and originally called Tiger Lily. Between 1980 and 1986, they scored seven Top 10 albums and seventeen Top 40 singles in the UK, the most successful of which was their 1981 hit 'Vienna', notable for spending four consecutive weeks at No. 2 in the UK Singles Chart without ever getting to No. 1. It was kept off the UK No. 1 slot by John Lennon's 'Woman' for a week and then by Joe Dolce's novelty hit 'Shaddap You Face' for a further 3 weeks.

Other successful singles for Ultravox included, 'Dancing with Tears in My Eyes' and 'All Stood Still'.

The band has been led by two different front men who never played together in the band at the same time. From 1974 until 1979, singer John Foxx was the frontman and main driving force behind Ultravox. Foxx left the band in 1980 to embark on a solo career and following his departure, with the three remaining members in hiatus, Midge Ure took over as lead singer, guitarist and frontman.

The band came to Lancaster following the release of their fourth studio album *Vienna* in July 1980. The album had a slow start, but the release in January 1981 of the title track as the third single from the album heralded the band's commercial breakthrough.

Ultravox's eleventh studio album, *Brilliant*, was released on 28 May 2012. Following the album's release, the band, featuring the '80s lineup of Midge Ure, Billy Currie, Chris Cross and Warren Cann, embarked on the Brilliant Tour, performing shows across the UK and Europe in late 2012.

In November 2013 Ultravox performed as special guests on a four date UK arena tour with Simple Minds.

Fatal Charm were a female fronted, new wave/synthpop band from Nottingham.

Remember, I had a special relationship with Island. Island Artists wanted me to join them for several years and 'Ear 'Ere Records had a direct account with Island Records, one of only 120 in the whole of the UK, so we got to hear things …

Island had been at the forefront of the underground/ progressive music scene from the mid '60s through the '70s. They had arguably the most innovative and exciting stable of artists. They introduced the public to many new acts and styles of music and they had turned many local bands into superstars.

But Punk had happened and Island were suddenly becalmed, washed up on the beach. A flopping, gasping dinosaur. They needed a new act, a 'punk' band, an act that would once again enable them to speak to the kids. I remember the day when the Island Records rep. came into 'Ear 'Ere to announce that they had found the answer. The new, revolutionary saviour of Island was a band called Ultravox. Today that seems farcical but then they really believed it. Island thought they had their answer to The Pistols, The Stranglers and The Clash!

Obviously it wasn't and they weren't. But they were good and had fairly immediate success. I had a date on their sell-out tour. On the morning of the gig I had a call from their tour manager, Paul Darwin, an old friend from Manchester who had toured many bands into Lancaster over the years. He was enquiring whether we had any flying points at the Great Hall. I said that we hadn't but to wait as I was on my way up to the venue.

When I got there Paul told me that it was vital that they flew the front of stage monitors from the ceiling. I said once again that there were no flying points so it was the end of the conversation as far as I was concerned. Paul explained that there were so many comments going around referring to Midge Ure's height that they didn't want monitors on the stage as they gave the impression that he was even smaller than he actually was. The Great Hall's ceiling was wood and slightly lower than the actual roof so Paul wanted to know if they could just cut out some flying points. I nearly had a heart attack. I had had enough stick from University House about the shows and had spent years trying to out manoeuvre them as they tried to stop the concerts and the nasty riff-raff locals coming and despoiling their academic Camelot on the hill. "No, it can't happen," I told him categorically.

"OK, do they still serve Boddies in County Bar?" Paul asked, changing the subject. Paul was from Manchester, and Boddies was then still a very special local brew, with a distinctive, unique taste, not the anaemic rubbish sold all over the UK that it is now. "Fancy a couple?"

I was always a sucker for a good pint – still am. We went to County Bar. Four or five pints and several games of pool later we returned to the Great Hall. I walked in and nearly shit myself. Above the stage were several rock 'n' roll monitors, hanging from our lovely, wooden ceiling. "Paul …"

"Well, just think of it this way, we've improved your venue, at no extra cost, now you can offer flying points to touring bands."

The porters were sworn to secrecy and I got away with it. At least I thought I had, until that summer's Graduation Ceremony when the VC, slightly bored and dozing, looked around his lovely hall and his eyes scanned the ceiling above his throne only to see a series of black holes, staring like skeletal eye sockets at him. I was summoned to his office, yet again, on the Monday morning to explain …

Fast forward to September 2014, I was speaking at the University 50th Celebrations and I was a guest at the evening dinner in the Great Hall. I couldn't resist it. After the meal and speeches, as final drinks were being drained, I had to sneak up to the stage. Sure enough there were the eyes, still staring down at me … I'm sure one winked!

Barry Lucas

The Undertones

8 December 1980 **The See No More Tour** Support: Orange Juice

The Undertones were formed in Londonderry, Northern Ireland, in 1974 and from 1975 to 1983 and consisted of Feargal Sharkey (vocals), John O'Neill (rhythm guitar, vocals), Damian O'Neill (lead guitar, vocals), Michael Bradley (bass, vocals) and Billy Doherty (drums).

In November 1978 The Undertones played the university, appearing as a support to The Rezillos at the time of the release of their debut four-song EP *Teenage Kicks* on the Good Vibrations label. It became a hit with support from DJ John Peel, who considered the EP's title song ('Teenage Kicks') his all-time favourite single.

The Undertones released a total of thirteen singles, including 'Jimmy Jimmy' and 'My Perfect Cousin', along with four studio albums between 1978 and 1983 before Sharkey announced his intention to leave the band in May 1983, citing musical differences as the reason for the break up.

The Undertones re-formed in November 1999, initially to play concerts in Derry. For their re-formation, the Undertones replaced Sharkey (who declined to rejoin the Undertones) with singer Paul McLoone.

Since 1999, the Undertones have performed several tours across the UK, Ireland, Continental Europe, Japan, Turkey and North America and continue to perform live.

Orange Juice were a Scottish post-punk band founded in the Glasgow suburb of Bearsden. The band was formed by Edwyn Collins and existed from 1979 to 1985.

They were best known for the band's only UK Top 40 hit 'Rip It Up', which reached No. 8 on the UK Singles Chart in February 1983.

Edwyn Collins went on to pursue a solo career, having a chart hit with his 1994 No. 4 single 'A Girl Like You'.

Edwyn Collins of Orange Juice ©Geoff Campbell

the UNDERTONES
plus SUPPORT
LANCASTER
university
7.30PM MON. 8 DEC. £3.50
John Angus

Van Morrison

Paul Loasby was effectively running the Harvey Goldsmith office at this time, and when Harvey announced that he was to tour the legendary Van Morrison Paul had to set up the dates. Van had not played live for many years so this was an eagerly awaited tour. Paul rang to tell me he would try to secure me a date – I couldn't believe it, Van the Man, Van the legend, adding to the now growing Lancaster legend. But there were just a couple of little problems: Van insisted on no college dates, no stand-up venues … only minor problems then for Lancaster University's Great Hall!

Paul flew to LA to talk to Van Morrison with the sole aim of persuading him to play Lancaster. It wasn't really a college gig as such, it was a professionally run venue and was now established as part of the city hall circuit. The stand-up bit created its own quite unique atmosphere, Paul told him, and it was the best live venue in the UK where he would have an experience he would never forget. Van agreed and he did!

After announcing the date it soon became apparent we would have a monstrous sell-out on our hands. But what a sell-out! Quite simply the biggest, most spectacular one in the history of Lancaster University. In those days before phone and online sales, web sites etc. you had to write off or physically go to a ticket office to buy a ticket. Such was the demand that I had to get the Students' Union receptionists, Betty and Hazel, to come in early and open up at 8.00 am – not exactly an easy task I can assure you (if you remember them, then you know what I am talking about). Students were sleeping out on the two-floor staircase and into Alexandra Square. It was the same at all the ticket outlets and by 9.00 am we were totally sold out – an hour before tickets officially went on sale!

Show day. Van didn't do sound checks, his road crew did them for him. It had led to a tricky problem the night before in Glasgow. There they had an old fashioned orchestra pit and apparently Van, like many of us, doesn't like heights. The set was in place, he walked onto stage, saw the drop and did the whole show next to the grand piano, whilst at the front of the stage stood a lonely mic stand, still lit up by the spots, trying to dramatically emphasise the legendary singer. No such problems at Lancaster. He arrived backstage from his Lake District hotel, walked past the dressing rooms, throwing his jacket in, onto the stage and into his first song. End of set, walked past the dressing room, was handed his jacket, into car and back to hotel. Gig done.

But the man had a great night – I'll prove it later in this book.

A couple of years on and I once again had the opportunity to book Van Morrison, but this time I had to buy the date and pay a fee, as opposed to Harvey Goldsmith's pecentage hall hire. Well, ticket sales last time had been amazing so no problem, I thought. But this time – and as I sit here typing this thirty plus years on I still don't understand how – he died a death. The day before the show I was personally handing out show flyers around Bowland and Lonsdale coffee bars when a student said, "Oh dear, it must be really poor ticket sales!" Too right, we lost a bomb. Why? Answers on a postcard please – who in their right mind would be a promoter?

Barry Lucas

Velvet Underground

29 October 1971 **Loaded Tour** Support: Gravy Train

The Velvet Underground were an American rock band, active between 1964 and 1973, formed in New York City.

The group was briefly managed by Andy Warhol and served as the house band at The Factory in New York City and for Warhol's Exploding Plastic Inevitable events from 1966 to 1967.

The group's music and attitude shaped the work of David Bowie, Patti Smith, Mott the Hoople, Roxy Music, the Sex Pistols, R.E.M. and literally thousands of other bands.

Brian Eno, co-founder of Roxy Music and producer of U2 and others, famously said that "although the Velvet Underground didn't sell many albums, everyone who bought one went on to form a band".

The group's vocalist/guitarist Lou Reed, keyboardist and Welsh-born viola player John Cale, guitarist Sterling Morrison and drummer Maureen "Moe" Tucker played their first show together in 1965.

Their debut album, *The Velvet Underground and Nico*, featured a classic Warhol-designed popart jacket that depicted a big yellow banana. The album consisted of eleven songs that radically revised the rock and roll sensibility – especially two songs about drug addiction, one despondent and sobering ('Heroin') and another a ribald slice of Harlem street life ('I'm Waiting for the Man'). Several songs, notably 'Femme Fatale' and 'All Tomorrow's Parties', featured the heavily accented vocals of cool German chanteuse Nico.

Following the departure of Lou Reed in August 1970 and the release of their fourth album *Loaded,* Doug Yule (guitars and vocals) became the new frontman of The Velvet Underground and was joined by Willie Alexander (keyboard), Walter Powers (bass guitar) and Maureen Tucker (drums). This was the lineup for this Lancaster appearance.

Gravy Train were a progressive rock band from Lancashire, formed by vocalist and guitarist Norman Barratt in 1970. Together with J.D. Hughes (keyboards, vocals and wind instruments), Lester Williams (bass and vocals) and Barry Davenport (drums), they made four studio albums. Gravy Train disbanded in 1975. Later in Norman Barratt's career he performed with Robin Trower's uni support band Mandalaband on their second and final album in 1978.

Vinegar Joe

23 March 1973 **Rag Ball** Supports: The Roy Young Band **I** Blackfoot Sue **I** Yakety Yak

A great value for money Rag Ball triple bill with headliners Vinegar Joe, the British R&B band. Formed in 1971, Vinegar Joe issued three albums on the Island Records label and were renowned for their exciting live shows and also launching the solo careers of Elkie Brooks and Robert Palmer.

Vinegar Joe evolved out of a band called Dada, a twelve-piece jazz rock fusion band that previously provided support to Iron Butterfly and Yes for a Great Hall concert two years earlier in 1971. Elkie Brooks was known as the "Wild Woman of Rock" and comparisons were made to Tina Turner and Janis Joplin. Other band members were bassist Steve York, keyboard player Tim Hinkley and Elkie's husband, guitarist Pete Gage who also played piano, with Conrad Isidore on drums.

Vinegar Joe disbanded in the spring of 1974.

The Roy Young Band were back again following their support slot for Chuck Berry's Great Hall concert in March 1972.

Blackfoot Sue were a British glam rock band, formed in 1970 by the twin brothers Tom and David Farmer and Eddie Golga. A single released in August 1972, 'Standing in the Road', reached No. 4 in the UK Singles Chart. The band dissolved in 1977. Not to be confused with Blackfoot, who supported The Scorpions in 1980.

Yakety Yak, the fifties style rock 'n' roll band, completed the evening's entertainment with their unique brand of doo wap, and later returned to Lancaster in October 1973 to provide support for Ten Years After.

Wire

9 November 1978 — Support unknown

Wire are an English rock band, formed in London in October 1976 by Colin Newman (vocals and guitar), Graham Lewis (bass and vocals), Bruce Gilbert (guitar) and Robert Gotobed (drums).

Wire are arguably a definitive art punk or post-punk ensemble, mostly due to their richly detailed atmospheric sound and often obscure lyrical themes. The group exhibited a steady development from an early raucous punk style with 1977's *Pink Flag*, to the more complex, structured sound involving the increased use of guitar effects and synthesizers on 1978's *Chairs Missing* and 1979's *154*.

The band gained a reputation for experimenting with song arrangements throughout its career.

Wire appeared at the university in support of the album *Chairs Missing,* their second studio album. It was released in August 1978 and peaked at No. 48 in the UK Albums Chart

March 2017 saw the release of the band's sixteenth studio album entitled *Silver/Lead.* Colin Newman and Graham continue to tour with their band Wire.

Wishbone Ash

9 November 1976	**New England Tour**	Support: Supercharge
8 October 1978	**No Smoke Without Fire Tour**	No Support
21 May 1981	**Number The Brave Tour**	Support: Nicky Moore

Originating in Torquay, Devon, Wishbone Ash are a British rock band who achieved success in the early and mid '70s. Their best known albums included *Wishbone Ash* (1970), *Pilgrimage* (1971), *Argus* (1972), *There's the Rub* (1974) and *New England* (1976). They were one of the first bands to use twin lead guitars.

Wishbone Ash were formed in October 1969 by bass guitarist Martin Turner and drummer Steve Upton, eventually adding two more guitarists in Ted Turner (no relation) and Andy Powell, and being managed by music mogul and brother of The Police's Stewart Copeland, Miles Copeland III.

This was to be the first "classic" lineup of Wishbone Ash and on 8 October 1970 they made their first of four visits to Lancaster as the opening act for Free.

A year later in 1971 Wishbone Ash were again billed to appear headlining a concert, with Heads Hands & Feet as support. For reasons unknown, Wishbone Ash failed to turn up. The concert went ahead regardless, with Heads Hands & Feet providing the main entertainment of the evening.

Thanks to Lynne Owen for the *Lancaster Guardian* cutting of the concert and her confirmation of Wishbone's 'no show'. Lynne was there!

Following the release of four studio albums including *Argus* and *Wishbone Four,* 1974 saw the departure of Ted Turner, who was replaced by Laurie Wisefield on guitars. This was the Mk II "classic" Wishbone Ash formation that definitely played the Great Hall on two further occasions, in 1976 and 1978.

1976 saw the band arrive in Lancaster in support of their seventh album, *New England*, released in October of that year.

Lancaster setlist based on typical 1976 concerts:

'Jail Bait', from the album *Pilgrimage,* 'Time Was', 'Blowin' Free', 'Warrior', 'The King Will Come', all from the album *Argus,* 'Rest in Peace' from *Locked In,* 'Runaway', '(In all my dreams) You Rescue Me', 'Lorelei', 'Outward Bound', all from *New England,* 'Bad Weather Blues', 'Mother of Pearl', 'Persephone' and 'It Started in Heaven' from *Locked In.*

LANCASTER UNIVERSITY
AND JOHN SHERRY PRESENT:
WISHBONE ASH
IN CONCERT
7.30PM SUNDAY
OCTOBER 8TH
TICKETS: £2
THERE WILL BE NO SUPPORT BAND,
WISHBONE ASH WILL BE ON STAGE AT 8PM

John Angus

Wishful Thinking

14 February 1970 Support: The Committee

An early concert by Wishful Thinking who were a British progressive rock band, formed in the '60s and successful in the '70s with an album called *Hiroshima.* They were formed from a band called The Emeralds, with a lineup of John Franklin (lead guitar and vocals), Tony Collier (bass and vocals), Kevin Scott (guitar and vocals) and Brian Allen (drums and vocals). Wishful Thinking is a band prized by obscurantist pop collectors.

Little is known about support act **The Committee.**

The Pink Custard Lightshow

Pushing the Boundaries

FIVE

This chapter contains the artists and events of which I am probably most proud. I have been asked many times over the years to recount stories about all the world famous people that have graced the Great Hall stage. And I have recounted willingly! But it is the shows/concert/lectures in this chapter for which I would really liked to be remembered.

A fundamental change in Students' Union entertainments occurred at Lancaster when it professionalised the social secretary position. At Lancaster, as at every college in the UK, entertainments was run by an elected student given one year to put on his/her favourite bands. The usual scenario was that they lost money – one million pounds a year claimed *The Daily Express* in the early '70s – and Lancaster was no different. By the end of the yearly term of office, having gained experience and learnt how "the Business" ran, the social secretary often got a job with the other side, as a booker in a London agency. Brilliant idea; the students' unions trained up 'apprentices', then released them into the commercial world to rip off the newly elected soc. secs and their students' unions. Great business model!

Lancaster changed all that in 1971 by making the post of social secretary/entertainments officer full time, a member of the Students' Union staff. After all, the Students' Union shops, coffee bars, travel agencies and bars etc. were all run by staff employed by the student body to look after their interests. Frequently the entertainments budget was bigger than those other commercial areas and yet it was run, almost dictatorially, by an elected student. It was lunacy really and it didn't make any commercial sense, but the idea that entertainments be run by professional managers was anathema to students and Students' Union staff. A further complication was that entertainments was treated like the university clubs and societies – it was given a grant, a budget, to spend, to lose, each year. I don't care who you are, if you are told to budget to lose money over a year I can guarantee that you will lose more. It's almost impossible not to. If a show is a disaster you will lose far more than you could ever make on a success – especially as more and more shows were put in with percentage deals attached, a safety net for artists and agents. It was belt and braces for their judgement. Now they could never make a mistake, for if the show bombed the college lost money, paying artists fees and promotion costs; if it succeeded the artists would generally break the percentage and therefore get extra money on top of their negotiated fee. But social life was a massive part of the student experience in the '60s and '70s and the general belief was that only a student could organise that.

Gaz Taylor and I ran the shows at Lancaster from May 1970 until June 1971 – a lot of Great Hall shows and many smaller nights in Bowland and Lonsdale refectories. There were some great nights among the discarded chips and beans, with bands like Pretty Things, Groundhogs and Edgar Broughton belting out blues/rock until the early hours. Gaz was the frontman, he got up on stage and promised the Earth,

Moon and stars – especially the stars – for the next term. I was the backstage organiser. But my role must have been more appreciated than I thought at the time because the Students' Union President, Tim Hamlett, approached me and asked if they made the post a staff position, would I be interested in taking it. I told Tim, who later became a journalist with *The Visitor* in Morecambe and ended up editing the main English language newspaper in Hong Kong, that I didn't believe a Union General Meeting would pass that (see above). Tim said that I should leave the politics up to them, would I do it was all he needed to know. Well, my lady at the time, Rachel Totton, had another year to do, so, although I had a job lined up as a copywriter in Manchester, I said yes. It was passed – I've no idea how – and I was offered the post on the wage of a postgraduate grant (some of you will remember those, grants!). It was the princely sum of six hundred and fifty pounds per year, not enough to get my first Ferrari but I was more interested in delaying joining the real world for at least another year. One really unfortunate, and very sad, by-product of this was the destruction of my friendship with Gaz. Obviously, he thought that he should have had the job as he was the instigator of the whole project, and he certainly knew more about music and the music business than me at the beginning. He went to London and we have never seen each other since, although I did get a quite remarkable letter from him a year or so later, but that is story for another chapter of this book.

It was made explicit that entertainments had to make money and it was no longer to have a grant. That was fine with me. A grant meant you were to lose money on shows and losing money on shows meant that not enough people had bought tickets, which meant that not enough people wanted to see what you were putting on, and why would you book acts that people didn't want to see? To me that was not the job of a promoter; I have always believed your job is to entertain, not to educate. At the very least I had to make enough to cover the costs of employing me and if I wanted to turn what was effectively a sabbatical post into a real job, then I had to make it a commercial success for the Students' Union.

It was then, even in those early days, that I started to think about what "entertainment" actually means. From the '50s, through the '60s, student music was basically jazz, blues, folk and then latterly, mainly rock. But even at a small university like Lancaster, where two, three or four thousand students lived, I realised that they couldn't all count those genres of music as their main form of entertainment. Or, horror of horrors, perhaps they didn't care about music at all! I started to think laterally from quite early on, thanks mainly to guidance from Mike Lloyd from Hanley. What about other forms of entertainment or areas that would interest the student population? So over the next few years, I promoted a wide range of events, some more successful than others, and some with rather hilarious stories.

But initially I wasn't that brave when I decided to venture into other forms of music. One of the first concerts, out of the student norm, was with The Spinners. This legendary Liverpool folk group would have been a staple of the university scene in the '50s and early '60s. But by the '70s their success on mainstream TV family shows with mum and dad appeal meant that they were a not cool for colleges. Many of their songs were still popular in the rugby, football and cricket clubs so I decided that maybe there were enough people in the student body, the staff, the assistant staff and local population who enjoyed their music. It sold out, of course it did – 950 seated in the Great Hall, remember. The band wanted a meal before the show so I booked Cartmel College private dining room. The Spinners insisted I ate with them and the Cartmel refectory staff were ecstatic, not about me being there but about meeting some TV stars in the flesh. They all brought autograph books and wanted signatures – even mine! I tried to explain that I wasn't in the band, but to no avail. I was at the table, that was enough, sign the book. I still watch *Antiques Roadshow* hoping that an autograph book appears and the expert has to explain who this B.A. Lucas was with The Spinners. Other folk artists I promoted in the Great Hall complex who were outside the normal student folk of the time included The Five Penny Piece, The Chieftains, Planxty, Steffan Grossman and the legendary Al Stewart. Some of these were in the main hall, others in the Nuffield Theatre. Of course many other mainstream folk legends featured on the Great Hall stage and they are listed elsewhere in the book.

JOHN PEEL
ROAD SHOW
RAG '80
PLUS LOCAL BANDS: BLAST
AND THE NEW PHAROAHS
LANCASTER UNIVERSITY
FRI. FEB. 22 8.30-12PM
BAR-11.45
£1.25
ANGUS

John Angus

“Regrets, I’ve had a few but …”

SIX

Actually the regrets I've had I AM going to mention, sorry Frank. Maybe not all, but many of the significant ones.

I suppose most are in that first year or so. I was an elected officer doing the job in my final year and a half at university. I am sorry to confess here for the first time in public that I fully intended to 'break the bank' if I needed to, in order to bring Jimi Hendrix to Lancaster on what I thought would be my final glorious year as social secretary. Unfortunately as negotiations were beginning, Jimi died in September of 1970. In some ways I was relieved that I didn't have to betray my avowed principal of running the university's entertainments as a commercial undertaking.

I was employed from July 1971 for a year's contract, almost as a glorified sabbatical officer, and I was once again negotiating to bring one of my all-time favourite heroes to the Great Hall irrespective of cost (and I hate to admit it, irrespective of loss), The Doors. Here I have to remind you what happened that year when the dreaded rock 'n' roll curse, twenty-seven years, intervened and Jim Morrison died in his bath in Paris in July 1971. I was never again tempted to put my own favourites on, irrespective of commercial considerations.

In 1971, I suddenly received a letter, out of the blue, from Gaz Taylor. We had parted on rather bad terms, as I have said, and this was the first I had heard from or of him since we graduated in the June of that year. Apparently he had moved to London and was working in a bar. He had written to say that in the next flat was a musician who was looking for new management. Gaz had, for some unknown reason, mentioned me and the singer was very interested in talking to me about a management deal. I had heard of him but I thought of him as essentially a folk artist with a penchant for mime and poetry. I could not see that working – a lot of hassle for a few folk clubs and pub gigs. It didn't excite me at all so I politely refused, telling Gaz it would be a waste of my time. Oh, I forgot to mention the folk singer's name: David Jones, but he had changed it a couple of years earlier to David Bowie. Oops …

Elsewhere I have mentioned how not paying an atrocious support band £40, cost me a date for the Tom Robinson Band, who were monstrous in the mid '70s. I also talked of the terrible mistake of throwing away Mark Bolan's PRS form, which would now be priceless. Probably the biggest single – or multiple really – regret I have is throwing away, or not keeping, all the posters, programmes, contacts, signatures etc. I have had over the years. In the early '70s the banks also returned all your cashed cheques so I would have had all those payments to The Who, Floyd, Sabbath, Johnny Winter etc. etc. etc. Now that would have been something. *Antiques Roadshow*, eat your heart out.

The Off Campus Social Centre AKA The Sugar House

SIX

Actually the regrets I've had I AM going to mention, sorry Frank. Maybe not all, but many of the significant ones.

I suppose most are in that first year or so. I was an elected officer doing the job in my final year and a half at university. I am sorry to confess here for the first time in public that I fully intended to 'break the bank' if I needed to, in order to bring Jimi Hendrix to Lancaster on what I thought would be my final glorious year as social secretary. Unfortunately as negotiations were beginning, Jimi died in September of 1970. In some ways I was relieved that I didn't have to betray my avowed principal of running the university's entertainments as a commercial undertaking.

I was employed from July 1971 for a year's contract, almost as a glorified sabbatical officer, and I was once again negotiating to bring one of my all-time favourite heroes to the Great Hall irrespective of cost (and I hate to admit it, irrespective of loss), The Doors. Here I have to remind you what happened that year when the dreaded rock 'n' roll curse, twenty-seven years, intervened and Jim Morrison died in his bath in Paris in July 1971. I was never again tempted to put my own favourites on, irrespective of commercial considerations.

In 1971, I suddenly received a letter, out of the blue, from Gaz Taylor. We had parted on rather bad terms, as I have said, and this was the first I had heard from or of him since we graduated in the June of that year. Apparently he had moved to London and was working in a bar. He had written to say that in the next flat was a musician who was looking for new management. Gaz had, for some unknown reason, mentioned me and the singer was very interested in talking to me about a management deal. I had heard of him but I thought of him as essentially a folk artist with a penchant for mime and poetry. I could not see that working – a lot of hassle for a few folk clubs and pub gigs. It didn't excite me at all so I politely refused, telling Gaz it would be a waste of my time. Oh, I forgot to mention the folk singer's name: David Jones, but he had changed it a couple of years earlier to David Bowie. Oops …

Elsewhere I have mentioned how not paying an atrocious support band £40, cost me a date for the Tom Robinson Band, who were monstrous in the mid '70s. I also talked of the terrible mistake of throwing away Mark Bolan's PRS form, which would now be priceless. Probably the biggest single – or multiple really – regret I have is throwing away, or not keeping, all the posters, programmes, contacts, signatures etc. I have had over the years. In the early '70s the banks also returned all your cashed cheques so I would have had all those payments to The Who, Floyd, Sabbath, Johnny Winter etc. etc. etc. Now that would have been something. *Antiques Roadshow*, eat your heart out.

The Off Campus Social Centre AKA

The Sugar House

SEVEN

I was going to include a paragraph on The Sugar House as part of my *Regrets* chapter. However, on reflection, I believe that it warrants a whole chapter to itself. The history of the Off Campus Social Centre has never been told in its entirety and its significance to the story of popular entertainment in the area is vitally important. The repercussions of The Sugar House story had a fundamental effect on the Great Hall concerts. I am still, after thirty odd years, consumed with feelings of sadness, disappointment and anger. I sometimes feel that twelve years of my life were wasted on a project that could have been so important to the soul of Lancaster University Students' Union, and indeed to the University and its standing in the local community.

It all began with "The Craig Affair" in the early '70s, when the English Department lecturer, David Craig, and some of his colleagues were accused of left-wing bias in their teaching, and more importantly, in their marking of essays and exam papers. From the outset most could recognise it as a blatantly political manoeuvre, an attempt by a right-wing departmental management to purge its staff. A massive furore developed, students and staff alike were outraged. Strikes were organised, national demonstrations centred on Lancaster, and finally, alternative, parallel university courses were created. Lancaster suddenly had two universities. BBC's *Panorama* did a full one-hour special on the situation. The University administration ground to a halt. University House was occupied by the new student administration. What idealism, what fun!

But eventually, of course, it collapsed. However, the wounds were so deep that an independent commission was set up in order to "cure" the perceived ills. Under Lord Taylor (not the same as the ex SU Secretary who is only a "Sir" today) it produced a long and complex report. One aspect of it was that it stated that students, "up on the hill", were cut off from the town and from young people in the local community. In order to correct this he recommended that there should be a social centre created in the town where young like-minded, people could mix in a relaxed, recreational setting. Lord Taylor's report should be displayed on a blue plaque in The Sugar House today.

It took eight long, often frustrating, years to achieve. At times I was the only person keeping the project going but I suppose the nature of students' unions, lacking senior management for several of those years, led only by one-year student officers, meant that this was inevitable. While I found it very hard going at times, it was something I really believed in. Finally, we found an ideal property, the old City Council Architects Department offices in Sugar House Alley. The department was moving into new offices in Dalton Square and putting the building up for sale. At the end of the "tender" period we were the only ones to make an offer – job done, we thought. But no! Mysteriously, several days after the closing date for offers, the local brewing family, Mitchell's, made a bid to buy the building. Despite our

But it could all be summed up by a conversation I had with the Students' Union Treasurer one Christmas vacation, a Friday night, in the club. Now, I must ask you to remember that we employed people for fifty-two weeks a year, all our heating, lighting, rates etc. costs were for fifty-two weeks a year, students were at the university for thirty-one weeks a year – doesn't take a brain surgeon does it? We needed our local supporters to keep using the venue when the students weren't there. As readers of this book, you will all be aware of my passionate belief in the concerts etc. being available to all of the local community in the North West. This applied equally to The Sugar House. I should not have had to argue this point to students but I did to these two executives in 1983 and 1984. The Treasurer turned to me that night and said, "I can't wait for next week when the students are back and we don't have to put up with this lot any more." He looked around at three hundred and fifty local young people, drinking and dancing, having paid the Students' Union to come in, and he could not join up the dots, morally or commercially. He's probably securely salaried in British management today – say no more. But I was totally sickened.

It was on the overall musical management that we also fell out, probably fatally. The Executive just could not see the way Geoff and I wanted to take the venue forward. They could not see the long game – discos made money, bands are risky. I argued we should be doing both but they insisted live music should go. It was shortsighted and a major factor in my resignation in December 1984.

I need only to list SOME of the acts that graced that tiny stage in The Sugar House to justify my argument. If we had been allowed to continue it would now be a place of legend, a holy grail for young bands desperate to go on that stage where artists such as these had appeared:

Sisters of Mercy	The Mission
Hanoi Rocks	Grandmaster Flash
Bhundu Boys	Lenny Henry
Stone Roses	Alexie Sayle
Happy Mondays	Roy Harper
John Cooper Clarke	Orange Juice
Pop Will Eat Itself	Marillion
Travis	Roger McGough
John Peel	Eurythmics
Balamm & The Angel	Go West
Howard Jones	The Young Ones
Julian Cope	Ben Elton
Simply Red	Alien Sex Fiend
Rik Mayall	Wedding Present
Eric Bristow	Hull Truck Theatre Company
Maureen Flowers	Aswad

Now that's a pretty impressive list for the team of people booking acts into The Sugar House in those first six years. Myself, Geoff Campbell and Mark Harris (yes the very same Mark Harris the Executive were asking me to sack and whom they gave a job to after driving Geoff and myself out).

Sugar House alumni

There are a few stories around about those acts. Firstly, though, to explain Eric and Maureen. Anybody who knows anything about darts knows of Eric Bristow, the Alex Higgins, the George Best of darts. Multiple world champion, character, showman, TV personality, he was a minority sportsman who became a household name. Maureen Flowers was a feisty lady who was a many times world ladies darts champion and also his partner. They gave an amazing night of exhibition darts and a few darts lessons to budding student players!

Phil Mc Intrye, the ex-Preston Poly. Soc. Sec. and now BIG-time promoter, who is mentioned elsewhere in this book, was touring Rik Mayall. I had had The Young Ones show on at The Sugar House and was disappointed to see Phil had put Rik into Southport Floral Hall. I gave him a call asking if he remembered the old days when acts would sometimes do two venues per evening. He said that he sort of remembered it but it was a bit before his time and why was I asking anyway? Well, I said, I have a 2.00 am student venue, only forty minutes from Southport, did he fancy doubling up Rik, twice the money at no extra overheads? Phil's a no-nonsense Northern lad, "That'll do for me. I'll sort Rik," was his immediate reply. On the night they turned up at midnight with a very bemused, and I must confess very nervous, warm-up comic. His name was Ben Elton, a Londoner up North for the first time and not sure how he would go down. No worries, he was brilliant, even the northern lads loved him. Phil must have been impressed because soon after he became his manager; the rest, as they say, is history. Shrewd move, Phil.

Marillion and Fish's love affair with The Sugar House I have mentioned elsewhere in this book!

Alec Leslie was a Director of Island Artists during the period when I was working closely with them and they were constantly trying to persuade me to become a part of their company. He had now set up on his own as a management company and one of the first acts he had in his rota was Go West. He was touring them to gain some live experience and asked me if I would take a date. I knew the problems with the Great Hall and new acts so I said I could take a date in the club but I could only pay expenses. He said that this was not a problem as it was experience he was after for them. I said that I would put them on after a disco as that would guarantee them a crowd. OK by Alec. So those people turning up that night paid for a disco and got Go West thrown in for free!

Lancaster? Where's Lancaster?

EIGHT

"Is it anywhere near Redcar?" Harvey Goldsmith.

It's the end of a journey. Thankfully a lot of my distant memories have not eluded me so far. When I decided to look through Paul's carefully, painstakingly compiled lists of the acts that had played the Great Hall, I was not sure how many stories I was going to remember. 1970 was, after all, forty-seven years ago, but I sat with the list and several blank sheets of paper. Amazingly enough I have stories for over seventy acts; but perhaps it isn't that amazing. From 1985, when I left, until this year I have done many things: Deep Purple at Knebworth, UB40 at Finsbury Park, Paul Weller at Isle of Wight; Terry Marsh's World Championship winning fight, the amazing Nigel Benn vs Michael Watson fight, Walt Disney on ice, Ringland Brothers' Circus; Madness in the Isle of Wight, a series of concerts in Finsbury Park with New Order, Pogues, Hawkwind, Siouxsie and The Banshees, several concerts for the African National Congress, anti-racist festivals in London, Manchester and Cardiff, Jamiroquai in Highbury Fields, Viva South Africa, a celebration of Nelson Mandela's release from prison, among many others. Then the sixteen years as a primary school teacher – I know, the staff room couldn't believe it either that I had swapped rock concerts for numeracy lessons, but actually I really enjoyed that bit. However, the concerts at the University were so significant, so unforgettable, that, quite simply, I didn't forget.

Over the intervening years the local populace hasn't let me forget. They have wanted to talk about, reminisce about, ask about, those years and those shows. They were so important for so many people. There are certain questions which are always asked: "What was your favourite concert?" "Who were the nicest?" "Who were the nastiest?" "What was the most outrageous rider request?" But there are two questions they all end with: "Why Lancaster?" and "Why did they end?" The one I can answer accurately is the first.

It's funny that the music business has gone full circle from the '50s to the present day. In the early days bands toured to make money, gigs gave them an income and if, as a by product, they sold records, all the better. But by the mid to late '60s, the music business was all about record sales. You measured album and singles sales in the millions, not the tens of thousands of today. Record companies would sign bands for hundreds of thousands of pounds in advances, everybody was making money. In order to generate those sales, bands toured and toured extensively; twenty-, thirty-, even forty-date tours were not unusual, rather they were the norm. I once asked Alec Leslie, a director of Island Artists, why Free, at their commercial height, were playing so many twelve to fifteen hundred capacity venues. He told me that of course they all sold out and financially they could have maximised their tour income by playing fewer, larger halls. However, if they sold out a venue, fifteen hundred people would see and hear them, the local newspapers and maybe TV and radio, would preview and review the date, their record

Bad Company
RORY gallagher 1977 tour
I SAW UFO
Motörhead
Judas Priest on tour
Hawkwind
Thin Lizzy